Communication in High Risk Environments

Linguistische Berichte
Sonderheft 12

Edited by
Rainer Dietrich

in cooperation with
Tilman von Meltzer

BUSKE

Die Beiträge sind hervorgegangen aus dem Ladenburger Kolleg
„Group Interaction in High Risk Environments",
einem Förderschwerpunkt der Gottlieb Daimler-
und Karl Benz-Stiftung

Im Digitaldruck »on demand« hergestelltes, inhaltlich mit der 1. Auflage von 2003 identisches Exemplar. Wir bitten um Verständnis für unvermeidliche Abweichungen in der Ausstattung, die der Einzelfertigung geschuldet sind.

Weitere Informationen unter: www.buske.de/bod.

Bibliografische Information der Deutschen Nationalbibliothek

Die Deutsche Nationalbibliothek verzeichnet diese Publikation in der Deutschen Nationalbibliografie; detaillierte bibliografische Daten sind im Internet über ‹http://portal.dnb.de› abrufbar.

ISBN 978-3-87548-342-0

eBook ISBN 978-3-87548-952-1

LB-Sonderheft ISSN 0935-9249

© Helmut Buske Verlag GmbH, Hamburg 2003. Alle Rechte vorbehalten. Dies gilt auch für Vervielfältigungen, Übertragungen, Mikroverfilmungen und die Einspeicherung und Verarbeitung in elektronischen Systemen, soweit es nicht §§ 53 und 54 URG ausdrücklich gestatten. Gesamtherstellung: BoD, Norderstedt. Gedruckt auf alterungsbeständigem Werkdruckpapier, hergestellt aus 100 % chlorfrei gebleichtem Zellstoff. Printed in Germany. *www.buske.de*

Contents

Rainer Dietrich
Introduction... 5

Dagmar Silberstein and Rainer Dietrich
Cockpit Communication under High Cognitive Workload 9

J. Bryan Sexton and Robert L. Helmreich
Using Language in the Cockpit: Relationships with Workload and
Performance 57

Manfred Krifka, Silka Martens, and Florian Schwarz
Group Interaction in the Cockpit: Some Linguistic Factors 75

Rainer Dietrich and Patrick Grommes
The Organisation of Coherence in Oral Communication 103

Gudela Grote, Enikö Zala-Mezö, and Patrick Grommes
Effects of Standardization on Coordination and Communication in
High Workload Situations 127

Oliver Sträter
Investigation of Communication Errors in Nuclear Power Plants 155

Introduction

Rainer Dietrich

The complexity and the generally low chances of successful verbal communication under beneficial conditions would lead one to expect that when people are engaged with additional and difficult problems they would automatically forgo verbal communication. An excursive examination taken from everyday life strengthens this bottleneck-assumption quite well. Driving a car in bad traffic in an unfamiliar city is considered a complex cognitive and psycho-motorical activity in which verbal communication with passengers is automatically restricted; see Salvucci (2002). Listening to a live concert on the radio and reading a newspaper, solving a chess problem and discussing near east politics, preparing a complicated sauce and, at the same time, discussing with the children a fight with neighbours – all of these are examples of double or multiple tasks. Task related information from different cognitive fields arrive in tight chronological succession via separate cognitive channels in central cognitive information processing. The shorter the time gap, the more strongly decelerated the processing of the second task. The so-called PRP-Effect (psychological refractory period) appears (see Pashler (1998: 5–6 and Chapter 4 and 5)).

There are few dual task experiments that have been done in which language processing is a task (see Neumann, Sangals & Sommer 2002) and none have been done with complex language tasks in natural settings. Because of the complexity and the hard to control factors that are involved in such experiments they are not done as PRP-Studies, but are more often done as an exploration led by PRP-Heuristics.

The general presumption is that the higher the mental demand made by a primary problem solving task (for example as a consequence of complexity, time pressure, or fear of danger) the less communication there will be. This sounds and is plausible. And it is worthy of analysis because theoretical arguments can also be made for the opposite.

The central event of communication is language processing – the cognitive processes in the language processing system of the participants. There is some evidence to support the idea that this system works automatically, autonomously, and at the same time reflexively. In faculty psychology, this mode of processing is explained by the fact that the procedures involved in language processing are structurally and modularly organised.

According to Fodor (1983), a cognitive module is informationally encapsulated and is domain specific (in this case language specific). The operation of input is mandatory; there is only limited central access to the processing. A module functions fast, and it's location is neurally fixed. It is acquired in a specific manner and can break down independently. The acquisition of language ability can be disturbed separately; i.e. there is no other impairment of any cognitive ability. This is called Specific Language Impairment (SLI). Conversely, under the influence of alcohol the control of motor skills is strongly reduced, while language comprehension and production remains undisturbed – with the exception of the articulatory muscles. The language ability of Alzheimer patients can remain undisturbed at the same time that the performance of the memory processes is extremely limited.

Apart from being motivated by general interest in the cognitive foundations of psycholinguistics, systematic research of communication under changing task load due to primary cognitive tasks, is also motivated by observations and investigations into professional work environments. The results of an ASRS Study (NASA's Aviation Safety Reporting System) found that about a third of the accidents in air traffic were connected to complications in communication. (See Etem & Patten (1998)). The effect of linguistic misunderstandings on plane crashes is documented in the linguistic investigations of cockpit-voice-recorder data such as used by MacPherson (1998) and Cushing (1994). Ungerer (in press) describes the effects of time pressure and emotions on the verbal communication of members of rescue teams.

All of the work represented in this special edition considers the quality of linguistic communication under conditions of high task load due to non-verbal tasks. The authors are members of a research project that has been funded for the last five years by the Gottlieb-Daimler and Karl Benz Foundation. With the co-operation of the individual projects, the research and investigations were carried out in three different work environments: the cockpit of a commercial airliner, the hospital operation room (OR), and the control room of a nuclear power plant (NPP). By choosing these three work places, the goal was to find results from each in which members of a team worked, at times, under high task load due to the performance of the primary task and which differed in the factors that structure communication. The setting perimeters are as follows:

level of the risk; (measured on the size or level of damage in the worst possible case)	Cockpit: middle; OR: relatively low; NPP: high
size of the teams	Cockpit: small; OR: medium; NPP: large
frame of discourse	Cockpit: face-to-face and (with ground control) only aural contact; OR: face-to-face; NPP: face-to-face and (with dislocated locations/spots) only aural contact.
social hierarchy in team	Cockpit: middle (dependant on culture); OR: strong; NPP: weak

scriptedness of the discourse	Cockpit: strong; OR: none; NPP: little
the threat to the team in danger	Cockpit: yes; OR: no; NPP: yes
the overlapping of the area of attention during the processing of the primary task	Cockpit: middle; OR: wide/extensive; NPP: low

The articles in this edition are organised according to the type of work place examined in the research. At the beginning, the work focuses on cockpit communication, followed by the investigations into the operating room. Lastly, the work addresses communication in the nuclear power plant control room. All of the investigations were carried out with empirical methods, most of them were based on a broad range of data. The data has been collected under variously controlled conditions. Authentic data was used in the work done by Silberstein & Dietrich; Dietrich & Grommes; Grote, Zala-Mezö & Grommes; and Sträter. The simulator data used in the work from Sexton & Helmreich and from Krifka, Martens & Schwarz was carried out under more formal conditions. All projects that present findings here have the ambitious aim to conduct fundamental research and, at the same time, to attain results from which they can create guidelines for the improvement of communication in the work place.

References

Cushing, S. (1994): Fatal Words: Communication Clashes and Aircraft Crashes. Chicago, IL: University of Chicago Press.

Etem, K. & Patten, M. (1998): Communications-related Incidents in General Aviation Dual Flight Training. ASRS Directline 10. December.

Fodor, J. A. (1983): The Modularity of Mind. Cambridge, MA: The MIT-Press.

MacPherson, M. (1998): The Black Box. All-New Cockpit Voice Recorder Accounts of In-flight Accidents. New York: William Morrow & Co.

Neumann A., Sangals, J. & Sommer, W. (2002): "Language perception under concurrent task load". Meeting of the Society for Psycholophysiological Research, Washington, D.C.: Psychophysiology.

Pashler, H. (Ed.) (1998): Attention. Hove: Psychology Press.

Salvucci, D. D. (2002): "Modeling Driver Distraction from Cognitive Tasks". To appear in: Proceedings of the 24th Annual Conference of the Cognitive Science Society.

Ungerer, D. (in press): "Communication in Missions of Rescue Teams". In: Dietrich, R. & Jochum, K. (Eds.): Teaming up. London: Ashgate.

Cockpit Communication under High Cognitive Workload

Dagmar Silberstein and Rainer Dietrich

1 Background[1]

This article investigates the effects of high cognitive workload on communicative interaction in the cockpit. We report our findings from a study that served to identify stress-sensitive aspects of communication. The article is organised as follows: First, we give some background information on communication research in aviation – how it evolved and how it approaches its topic. Then, we argue for a different perspective and describe the methodology we used to analyze the data. We go on to introduce the different situation types relevant to our investigation, the linguistic categories found to be affected by high workload, and the quantitative results. Finally, we describe some methodological problems, summarise the results and briefly relate them to a model of language production.

When asked about the effects of time pressure on his communicative behaviour an air traffic controller, whose exposure to high workload conditions is similar to that of pilots, spontaneously told us: "I talk faster, a lot faster – I talk so fast that they have to slow me down because they don't understand me any more." In addition to the accelerated rate of speech, another obvious effect of high workload is the shortening of utterances. Just a superficial look at cockpit-voice-recorder transcripts reveals that under conditions of stress the utterances become shorter and that more reduced linguistic structures are used than under normal conditions.

In addition to this anecdotal evidence, experimental work has shown that language processing can be seriously impaired under conditions of high cognitive workload: Blackwell & Bates (1995), for example, show that normal subjects display ungrammatical profiles under a dual task condition, which is a very disturbing finding, in particular with regard to the importance of communication when dealing with dangerous situations in high-risk environments like the cockpit of an airplane – compare Sexton & Helmreich (1999) who show that the more the crew members communicate the better they perform.[2]

---

[1] The study presented in this paper was conducted within the framework of the international research project *Group Interaction in High Risk Environments* which is sponsored by the Gottlieb Daimler- and Karl Benz-Foundation.

[2] The existence of a correlation between the amount of communication and performance was first suggested by Foushee & Manos (1981) who found that better performing crews communicate more overall.

The importance of communication for efficiency and safety in aviation has been recognised for a long time. In the 1970's, several accidents had happened that had been mainly related to crew co-ordination, communication, and team-building factors in the cockpit, e.g. the crash of Eastern Airlines Flight 401 into the Everglades during its approach to Miami International Airport in 1972. This accident had resulted in part from a misunderstanding between controller and crew: The members of the flight crew were distracted by a landing-gear warning light and they didn't realise that the autopilot had disconnected and that the aircraft was descending. The approach controller had seen the aircraft's apparent decline in elevation indicated on radar. He wanted to check with the crew and asked: "How are things coming along out there?" In his utterance, he intended the word things to refer to the decline in elevation but the crew appears to have taken it to refer to the nose-gear problem they had been preoccupied with. The crew remained unaware of the declining elevation, and finally the plane crashed into the Everglades. The uncertainty about the reference of the indefinite noun things – that is, a linguistic ambiguity – had contributed directly to the accident (compare Cushing (1994: 18–19)).

Another key accident was the crash of United Airlines Flight 173 in Portland (Oregon) in 1978. In this accident, the poor use of crew resources played a crucial role. Because of a malfunction of the landing-gear warning system, preparation for an emergency landing preoccupied the captain and, despite warnings by other crew members about the low fuel level, he delayed the landing. The airplane crashed because of total fuel exhaustion, but a contributing factor was also "the failure of the other two flightcrew members either to fully comprehend the criticality of the fuel state or to successfully communicate their concern to the captain." (Kanki & Palmer (1993: 101)). In this respect, the accident resulted partly from the poor information sharing within the crew.

These two accidents contributed to a re-evaluation of cockpit organisation. As a result, the US National Transportation Safety Board (NTSB) has increasingly paid attention to the possible impact of crew communication and crew coordination on accident patterns. Increased efforts have been undertaken to raise the safety level by developing the concept of crew resource management (CRM) – a specific training program that focuses on interpersonal and communication skills.[3] The increased interest in language-related issues has led to a still growing volume of studies that investigate communication processes in the cockpit.

Communication research in aviation is mostly not interested in language as such, but in the social dimension of communication and the psychological categories behind actual language use. Language is understood as a behaviour marker. This means that communication patterns are interpreted as indicators of social aspects of behaviour, for instance as an indicator of a person's role, attention focus, and so on. In addition to the social component, this kind of research is also related to performance. It investigates which communicative

---

[3] For a description of CRM see Helmreich & Foushee (1993).

patterns contribute to effective teamwork, and whether differences in crew performance are reflected by particular communication patterns. One typical example for this approach is a study conducted by Kanki, Palmer & Veinott (1991), that analyses the links between a captain's personality, communication, and team performance.[4] We call this direction of research the psychologically-oriented approach.[5]

A different approach is taken by Steven Cushing. He is interested in the structural properties of language itself that might lead to misunderstandings, especially in situations of high cognitive workload. Cushing (1994) analyses language-related misunderstandings in air-ground communication that have been a crucial contributing factor in aviation accidents. We call this direction of research the linguistically-oriented approach.

This paper is indebted to both approaches. Studies in both lines of research yielded valuable results. They constitute the background to our own study.

2 Perspective, Goal, and Guiding Questions

The ultimate goal of aviation-related communication research is to apply the theoretical findings to the real aviation world in order to improve its safety. In other words, its aim is to "enable researchers, trainers, line pilots, government regulators, engineers, and designers to make recommendations that enhance the safe and efficient operation of aircraft." (Kanki & Palmer (1993: 126)). This application perspective includes the aspect of developing training patterns for aviation personnel – an aspect that constitutes a fundamental objective for researchers from the psychologically-oriented approach. Their studies try to crystallise those communication patterns that are associated with effective CRM principles, and they aim at transforming these findings into training programs. Those studies *presuppose* that effective communication patterns can be trained. But they don't take into consideration the impact of stress on human *ability* to communicate. Up to now, it is not clear how stress affects our ability to communicate and whether it impedes trained patterns. We do not know well enough the exact character of natural limitations which might inhibit human beings from communicating reliably under growing pressure. In order to draft appropriate training programmes, we not only need a fuller understanding of which communication skills *should* be trained but also whether they *can* be trained at all.

Therefore, we decided to take a different perspective: We investigate and describe linguistic performance under varying degrees of stress in order to find out whether linguistic patterns change in relation to the amount of workload.

---

[4] This study finds out that those captains who were characterised as having less achievement motivation in interpersonal and flying skills were also the captains who initiated communications the least and who lead crews that performed least well.

[5] The most important studies that belong to this approach are described in Kanki & Palmer (1993).

Our goal is to learn more about the effects of stress on the mechanisms that underlie communication. In order to achieve that goal, the following questions should be looked into:

– How does linguistic interaction vary in relation to the level of workload?

– Which elements of the utterances and which mechanism of language production do persist and which are eliminated under the conditions of high workload and danger?

Answers to these questions could serve as a basis to determine for which aspects of communication and for which situations training is possible, and for which it is not.

Our article does not, however, provide ready-made answers to these questions. Its main point is just to offer first hypotheses generated on the basis of empirical data. A lot of work is still required to convert the descriptive findings reported in this paper into substantial empirical evidence, including experimental tests of the hypotheses.

3 Data and Method

As Kanki & Palmer (1993) point out, cockpit-voice-recorder (CVR) data are a valuable source for communication research. Being real-time accounts of events unfolding, they are a primary resource for learning what happened in the accident sequence, and they often reveal what went wrong during the flight. The analysis of CVR-data identifies critical communication problem areas: "The communications contained in CVR data have pointed to a wide range of CRM problems related to command authority, maintenance of vigilance, monitoring and cross-checking, briefings, planning, and crisis management in addition to assertiveness and participative management." (Kanki & Palmer (1993: 102)).

Taking this into account, we decided to use authentic CVR data. From 20 authentic flight documentations, stemming for the most part from the US National Transportation Safety Board (NTSB), 14 typical examples were selected.[6] We applied the methods of Conversational Analysis[7] to identify potential stress-sensitive linguistic categories that show up in the selected transcripts. That is, we conducted a detailed analysis of each single transcript, of its formal and semantic structure. This method allowed us to detect utterances and passages that are conspicuous in some way, e.g. because of a strange structure or because of a content that does not fit into the thematic flow. Each transcript was screened for those marked passages, and we analysed what went wrong in these passages from a linguistic point of view. The following excerpt which is taken from the transcript of the Birgenair accident in 1996 might serve

---

[6] The criterion for selection was the completeness of the transcript.

[7] *Conversational Analysis* is a strictly empirical field of research that investigates the structure of conversation. Its major advocates are Sacks, Schegloff & Jefferson.

as a first example[8]. It illustrates communication under high workload conditions:

Example (1)
(1)	Captain:	There is something wrong, there are some problems.
(2)	Co-Pilot:	Direct Pokeg? [i.e.: "Should we head for the navigational fix POKEG"]
(3)	Captain:	Okay.
(4)	Captain:	There is something crazy, do you see it?
(5)	Co-Pilot:	There is something crazy there at this moment. Two hundred only is mine and decreasing, Sir. [i.e.: refers to the speed of the aircraft]

This passage is linguistically marked because of its communicational dynamics: In this segment, the co-pilot is confronted with a dual task situation. He has to solve two communicative tasks. One is standardised and the other unexpected: In (1) the captain informs him that a problem has just occurred. The co-pilot does not respond to this unexpected turn but continues in the standardised procedure which requires to determine the current heading (2) – that is, he solves first the communicative task that corresponds to the script. It is only after the captain refers to the problem again (4) that he takes up the unexpected topic.

This observation suggests that the capability to adjust readily to unexpected events might be hindered by the existence of competing standardised tasks. When faced with competing communicative demands we do not respond to the unexpected task but prefer the one that belongs to the script. To depart from the script requires higher processing capacity, which is particularly difficult in situations of already high cognitive workload. The potential stress-sensitive linguistic category revealed here is called responsiveness (cf. chapter 5.4).

This kind of text analysis was applied to the whole data base of 14 transcripts. As we looked at communicative behaviour in different types of situations we were able to find out which aspects of communication were impaired in situations of high workload and danger. The case-by-case study yielded altogether nine linguistic categories that were affected by stress. They will be introduced in chapter 5. After identifying these categories, we investigated how often each category was affected by high workload in the other transcripts. The results were quantified in order to find out which of the categories are stress-sensitive on a level beyond the single-case study. The above mentioned category responsiveness, for example, was not found to be affected by stress and danger in the other transcripts (cf. chapter 6.1.4).

---

[8] The complete transcript can be found in appendix (1).

4 Situation Types

We will now introduce the situation types that were relevant in our study. Although not all of the recordings span the entire flight (no recording exceeds 30 minutes) and not all flights include all types of situations, the data as a group do show a clear typology of five different situations: normal low workload, normal high workload, danger 1, danger 2, and danger 3. These different situation types are defined by external criteria: the amount of workload and the degree of danger.

- "Normal low workload" (N1) describes situations of normal working conditions and low cognitive workload. Typical examples are: taxi, cruise.
- "Normal high workload" (N2) refers to situations that are characterised by high cognitive workload under normal working conditions, for instance take-off, approach, and landing.
- "Danger 1" (D1) is marked by the occurrence of an unexpected incident, e.g. the malfunction of some minor instrument. The flight behaviour of the plane is not impaired, and there are no warning signals.
- "Danger 2" (D2) is a much more dangerous situation. The plane is difficult to control, its flight behaviour is impaired, and there are warning signals.
- "Danger 3" (D3) refers to highly critical situations. Vital systems of the airplane do not function any more and the plane is hardly controllable. The flight behaviour of the plane is seriously impaired, and there are several warning signals.

5 Linguistic Categories

This chapter introduces the linguistic categories that were found to be influenced by the high workload condition in the single-case studies. It explains to what aspect of communication each category refers and by which values they are characterised. If appropriate, examples will be included. The categories discussed under (5.1) and (5.2) are central concepts in the psychologically-oriented approach. Therefore, some of the major findings from that approach will be included.

5.1 Information Sharing

Our first category refers to the information flow within the cockpit crew. The transcripts were analysed with respect to the question of whether the individual crew members tell each other what they observe, think, and intend to do. The category was used to evaluate in how far external stimuli (events, situations) and internal stimuli (thoughts) prompted the crew members to produce an utterance. The category is characterised by the values [*yes*] and [*no*]. In a sense, this category reflects the decision whether or not to speak. The processes that guide this decision are located at a pre-linguistic, higher cognitive level.

The transfer of information within the crew is essential to establish shared knowledge of the current situation. It is particularly crucial in high-workload or dangerous situations because crew members must gather and use all available information in order to act upon a shared mental model if they want to resolve an ongoing or potential problem.

So far, it has been demonstrated that correlations between the amount of information sharing and performance outcomes exist: Foushee & Manos (1981), for example, found that increased performance was associated with increases in observations about flight status. Orasanu & Fischer (1991) show that crews perform best in a cockpit environment in which pilots share and acknowledge information about the state of the aircraft and thereby minimise the amount of uncertainty about communication. They conclude that in good-performing crews, captains create a context in which their commands and information requests take on meaning. These findings have been applied to the creation of training programs: One basic maxim in current CRM training is to communicate all relevant information to the other crew members. But so far, the effects of work overload on the ability to share all essential information with the crew members has not been investigated.

Our analysis of the transcript of the Birgenair crash has revealed that this ability can be impaired by high cognitive workload and danger, which is illustrated by the following segments:

Example (2)
Normal High Workload (N2)
   (1)   CO:[9]   power's set
   (2)   CA:[10]   okay checked

Danger 1 (D1)
   (3)   CA: my airspeed indicator's not working
   (4)   CO: yes, yours is not working
   (5)   CO: one twenty
   (6)   CA: is yours working?
   (7)   CO: yes sir
   (8)   CA: you tell me

Danger 2 (D2)
(sound of overspeed warning)
   (9)   CO: now it is three hundred and fifty yes
   (10)   CA: let's take that like this

---
[9] CO = Co-Pilot
[10] CA = Captain

Danger 3 (D3)
(11)   CA: thrust levers, thrust, thrust, thrust, thrust
(12)   CO: retard[11]

In the situation types N2, D1, and D2, problems of information transfer do not occur. The crew members inform each other about their actions (N2), about problems and strategies (D1), and about their perception of the situation (D2). Until then, they share a mental model even if this model is wrong: Both pilots assume that the plane has overspeed, whereas, in reality, it flies too slow. They have been misled about their actual speed by defective instruments and a false overspeed-warning.

But in D3, crucial information is not transferred. We can conclude from the transcript that the captain finally must have realised that they are too slow because he orders to increase speed. But he has failed to communicate this essential insight to his co-pilot, which leaves them with a fundamentally different conceptualisation of the situation. As a consequence, the crucial command "thrust levers" does not take on meaning for the co-pilot. It is in contradiction to his own mental model, and he demands the contrary action: "retard".

The question is why information transfer problems do arise. In a study on information transfer between pilots and controllers, Billings & Cheaney (1981) argue that such problems often arise because: "The person who had the information did not think it necessary to transfer it" (1981: 2). We think that in our case, this explanation does not hold. It is very unlikely that the captain consciously decided not to share his insight with his first officer. Our analysis has shown that the problem surfaced in the situation type that was characterised by the highest amount of workload and danger. This situation apparently impeded the captain to communicate with the co-pilot in greater detail as regards their actual speed. What remains to be investigated is whether this result of extreme overload and danger can be generalised, that is whether we can find similar tendencies in the other transcripts.

5.2   Initiation of Crew Resources

This category investigates the linguistic means (and their effects) that are used to organise teamwork within the crew. On the captain's side, we are interested in the style of directing the crew, how the crew's actions are coordinated, how tasks are distributed, and how the team members are involved in the process of problem-solving. On the co-pilot's and first officer's side, we are interested in how they contribute to this process. The category is characterised by four different values: [*activate resources*], [*react*], [*order*], and [*none*]. To [*activate resources*] means for the captain that language is used in a way that creates an

---

[11] For the full text, please refer to appendix (1).

open atmosphere – an environment in which each crew member feels free to seek and give suggestions. On the side of the subordinate crew members it means that suggestions are indeed provided. The label [*react*] is given to utterances of crew members who don't give any own suggestions but who only act out what has been stimulated by somebody else. Utterances that are not open for suggestions get the label [*order*], and [*none*] means that there is no linguistic interaction which aims at organising the teamwork.

There are various linguistic clues that indicate which label should be selected: the speech act, the sentence mode, and other formal features of the chosen construction. The speech acts express the communicative function of the utterance. They reveal the speaker's intention: whether the utterance is intended as a question, a request, or a command.[12] On the formal side, the following correlations between sentence mode (indicates the grammatical function) and category value exist: the interrogative mode correlates with the value [*activate*], and the imperative mode correlates with the value [*order*]. Other linguistic means indicate whether the speaker is open for suggestions: for instance question tags ("isn't it?", "will you?"), polite ("please", subjunctive) and informal (address by first name) forms.

Like information sharing, the category initiation of crew resources is crucial for effective teamwork. It is the aspect that is at the heart of the whole CRM concept. Researchers from the psychologically-oriented approach have conducted interesting studies into this category. They focus on the links between personality and performance, and between personality and communication. Chidester & Foushee (1988), for example, show that captains who are highly motivated, goal-oriented, and concerned with interpersonal aspects tend to lead crews at a high performance level in full-mission simulations. Kanki, Palmer & Veinott (1991) found out that captains who have less achievement motivation in interpersonal and flying skills are also the captains who initiate communications the least and who lead crews that performed least well.

But, again, the influence of the factor "workload" on the communicative behaviour has not been considered. It remains to be investigated in how far the ideal to involve team members in the process of problem resolution can be put into practice under conditions of threat and work-overload.

Our example illustrates some possible changes: In December 1995, a Boeing 747 was scheduled to fly from New York to Miami. Due to the wintry weather conditions, the runway was very slippery. The crew referred to its state as an "ice rink". The first phase of the take-off was normal, until suddenly the aircraft started to move to the left side of the runway. As corrections by the crew were ineffective, the captain aborted the take-off. The crew lost directional control over the airplane, and eventually they hit an obstacle. The following segments from the CVR transcript show how in this particular case the linguistic means

---

[12] For a classic account of speech acts, please refer to Searle (1969) and Searle (1975). A more recent theory of speech acts can be found in Vanderveken (1990).

used to organise the teamwork change in relation to the different situation types.[13]

Example (3)
Normal Low Workload (N1)
(1)   CA: Ralph, take a little walk and check the wings for me, will you?
(2)   FE:[14]   Sure.

Normal High Workload (N2)
(3)   CA: Set time, takeoff thrust.
(4)   FE: Set the takeoff thrust.

Danger 3 (D3)
(5)   FO:[15]   Going to the left.
(6)   ?:[16]   Going to the left.
(7)   FE: To the right.
(8)   FE: You're going off.
(9)   ?:   Going off.
(10)   CA: Aw #.[17]
(11)   CA: Easy guys.
(12)   CA: OK.
       CAM:[18]   [First sound of impact]

Let's first look at utterance (1) in the low workload condition – when the crew is waiting for the clearance to taxi to their runway. The underlying intention of (1) is: "x wants y to do z", that is: "CA wants FE to go and check the wings". The captain uses extensive linguistic means to convey this intention: In addition to the actual intention, his utterance includes the following elements: an informal address (first name), a periphrastic sequence, and a tag question. These additional elements make his utterance take on a polite form, so that it doesn't sound like a command but like a request. In this sense, (1) is a typical example for the value [activates resources]. In (2), the flight engineer expresses that he will comply. This utterance exemplifies the value [react].

As soon as the workload increases to the level of N2 – in our example, the crew has just received their take-off clearance – the linguistic means used to convey directive intentions change: The additional elements are omitted. The utterances are reduced to the "bare" expression of their underlying intention, and they take on the form of an [order], which is illustrated by utterance (3).

[13] The complete transcript can be found in appendix (2).
[14] FE = Flight Engineer
[15] FO = First Officer
[16] ? = unidentified voice
[17] # = expletive
[18] CAM = cockpit area microphone

In the D3 situation, the crew has lost directional control over the airplane. The communication that follows their loss of control does not contribute to organise team work. It consists mainly of observations (5, 6, 8, 9), swearwords (10), and attempts to calm down the situation (11). These utterances exemplify the value [none]. There is merely one utterance that initiates team work: In (7), the flight engineer says what should be done.

5.3 Receptiveness

In the cockpit, even under normal conditions, each crew member has to solve multiple tasks. In an emergency situation, the number of tasks dramatically increases: The crew has to fly the airplane, to find out what the problem is, to interpret technical information, to run emergency checklists, to decide on a strategy to solve the problem, to put the solution into practice, to talk to controllers, to change the flight plan – to name just a few. The majority of these tasks involve communication, at least to some degree. In such a situation it is particularly important to process information from different channels and to decide which is the most important one to answer.

The category receptiveness refers to language processing in such multi-task situations. We investigated how much information from different channels (crew members: cockpit crew, flight attendants; radio: controllers, other crews) can be processed under varying degrees of workload, and in how far the ability to react to those different channels varies in the different situation types. The category is characterised by four values: [broad] = to react to all incoming information, [focused] = to concentrate on those channels that are crucial in the current situation, [selective] = narrowed or reduced attention, choice of channel does not function appropriately, and [none] = no reaction.

Example (4) illustrates the value [focused]. It is also given for another reason: It serves to illustrate the switching between the different channels in order to make the reader better understand what is meant by a multi-task situation and what an enormous degree of attention is required to "function" in such a situation. Example (5) illustrates the value [selective]. Both examples are taken from the transcript of Atlantic Southeast Airlines Flight 529 from Atlanta to Gulfport in 1995.

First some background: Twenty minutes after take-off from Atlanta a serious problem occurred. One propeller blade separated due to a defect in the material. The separated blade destroyed the whole left propeller which made it extremely difficult to control the airplane.[19] In this situation it would have been essential to work as quickly as possible through particular checklists that determine what to do in such a situation: the engine-failure checklist and the single-engine checklist. At the same time, the radio communication had to be dealt with, which was the co-pilot's task.

---

[19] For a detailed description of the accident, please refer to the accident report NTSB/AAR-96/6.

The complete passage that contains the processing of the engine-failure checklist is much too long to be presented here in full detail.[20] But the selected short segment in example (4) already shows that the co-pilot constantly has to switch channels. We can see that – again and again – radio communication interferes with the crew's work on the checklist. As for this checklist, the co-pilot still succeeds to manage both channels: He responds to the ground and turns back to the checklist immediately afterwards. That is to say, so far his receptiveness can be characterised as [focused]. However, due to the required multi-tasking, the completion of the checklist was slowed down enormously.

Example (4)

Time	Cockpit Communication (between captain and co-pilot)	Radio Communication (between co-pilot and ground)
1246:38 CA	Let's get out the uh ... engine failure checklist, please.	
1246:47 CO	OK, I'll do it manually here.	
1246:55 CO	OK, engine failure in flight.	
1246:57 GRD		AC five twenty-nine, say heading.
1246:59 CO		Turnin' to about uh, three ten right now.
1247:01 CO	Power levers, flight idle.	
1247:03 GRD		AC five twenty-nine, roger. You need to be on about a zero three zero heading for West Georgia Regional, sir.
1247:07 CO		Roger, we'll prob'ly try to turn right. We're having uh, difficulty controlling right now.
1247:11 CO	OK, condition lever's, feather.	
1247:13 CA	All right.	
1247:14 CO	It did feather ... NP's showing zero.	
1247:18 CA	'K.	
1247:19 CO	OK.	
1247:20 GRD		AC five twenty-nine, when you can, it's zero four zero.
1247:22 CO		Zero four zero, AC five twenty-nine.

[20] The interested reader can consult appendix (3) for a longer excerpt from the transcript.

1247:25 CO	'K, electric, yeah OK it did feather. There's no fire.	
1247:27 CA	All right.	

The next step, after the crew has completed the engine-failure checklist, is the processing of the single-engine checklist, which is shown in example (5). If we compare examples (4) and (5), we can observe a change in the communicative behaviour of the co-pilot: He doesn't switch between the two channels of communication any longer. Again, the example shows only a short segment of the text.

Example (5)

Time	Cockpit communication (between captain and co-pilot)	Radio communication (between co-pilot and ground)
1249:45 CA	All right, single-engine checklist please.	
1249:48 GRD		AC five twenty-nine, I've lost your transponder. Say altitude.
1249:52 CO		We're out of four point five at this time.
1249:54 GRD		AC five twenty-nine, I've got you now and the airport's at your, say say your heading now sir.
1249:59 CO		Right now we're heading uh, zero eight zero.

The segment starts with the captain's request to go through the single-engine checklist. Immediately afterwards, a competing request is issued by the ground control. The co-pilot answers the controller's request. Afterwards, he remains in that channel of communication. He does not switch back to the checklist.

For the communication that follows, he remains in the radio channel until, finally, the captain tries to get his attention back to the checklist:

1251:17 CA	Sing, single, single-engine checklist, please.	
1251:28 CO	Where the # is it?	
1251:29 GRD		AC five twenty-nine, say altitude leaving.
1251:31 CO		We're out of nineteen hundred at this time.

The co-pilot's answer contains clearly emotional elements. It expresses that he cannot run the checklist right now because he cannot find it. In a way, his answer also indicates that the degree of workload and emotional stress has become so high that he cannot manage both tasks any more. Before he can continue his search for the checklist, the ground controller interferes again. From that point on he no longer searches for the list but concentrates exclusively on the radio communication. For the rest of the flight, the crew is occupied with navigation and with their attempt to bring the airplane down. But the plane is too difficult to control and the crew cannot avert the crash.

Examples (4) and (5) show how the co-pilot's receptiveness – in this particular case his ability to react to different channels – narrows down, how it changes from [focused] to [selective]. His reduced receptiveness, among other things[21], contributed to the fact that the running of the single-engine checklist was not performed and that the crew could not regain control over the airplane.

The next example demonstrates the value [none]. It is taken from the transcript of the Birgenair accident. Utterances 3–5 show how the argument between captain and co-pilot (cf. 5.1) continues.

Example (6)
(1) CA: Thrust levers, thrust, thrust, thrust, thrust!
(2) CO: Retard!
(3) CA: Thrust, don't pull back, don't pull back, don't pull back, don't pull back!
(4) CO: Okay, open, open.
(5) CA: Don't pull back, please don't pull back!

After initially contradicting the captain, the co-pilot finally complies with the captain's command to increase thrust, and he expresses his compliance verbally, see utterance (4). But the captain doesn't seem to register this utterance. He remains unaware of the co-pilot's approval and continues to ask him not to reduce the speed (5). His receptiveness – in this case already on the level of processing the given information – seems to be completely destroyed.

These examples suggest that the category receptiveness is impaired under high workload and danger conditions.

5.4 Responsiveness

This category looks into the ability to switch patterns, to adapt one's current behaviour to unexpected situational changes. It aims at higher cognitive pro-

---

[21] There are, of course, many different factors that contributed to the crash. The pilot who helped us to analyse this transcript emphasised that it would have been essential for the ground controller to reduce communication with the crew to a minimum. This, of course, was not the case. With his constant interference he hindered them from concentrating on the most essential task: to regain control over the airplane.

cesses, namely, how new information is integrated into established conceptualisations of the situation. In order to find out more about the influence of mental scripts on spontaneous communicative behaviour, we analysed how the crew members reacted to situational changes: whether they immediately adapted to sudden changes, or whether they remained in the routine course of events. The values of this category are simply [+ *responsive*] and [– *responsive*].

An example was already given in chapter 3. That example suggested that the capability to adjust readily to unexpected events might be hindered by the existence of competing standardised tasks. Based on that observation, we want to investigate in more detail which factors favour and which hinder a quick adaptation to new situations. In this context it is important to keep in mind that the language used in the cockpit is highly standardised. There are fixed phrases for standard procedures, standard call-outs, checklists, and radio communication. The standardised phraseology prescribes the exact wording and the dynamics of communication. In this sense aviation is what Clark (1996) calls a prescriptive setting: "The words actually spoken are completely, or largely, fixed beforehand." (Clark (1996: 5)).

Given that characteristic of aviation language, the question arises in how far the prescriptive nature of aviation language influences the category responsiveness. Does the prescription of communicational dynamics make it difficult to answer unexpected communicative demands?

If yes, might this particular trait of aviation language impede responsiveness in situations of sudden danger?

5.5 Relation to Task

In this case, the name of the category is already self-explaining: The category refers to the content of each single utterance – whether it contributes to the task of flying the airplane. It is specified by the values [+ *task-related*] and [– *task-related*]. Utterances are [+ *task-related*] if they refer to an event or to a condition related to that task, e.g. talk about technical details, checklists, or briefings. Pieces of small talk, jokes, or swear words get the value [– *task-related*].

In the example, we illustrate only the value [– *task-related*] because we have already seen many instances of task-related communication: Aside from utterance (10) in example (3), all the other utterances given so far exemplify the value [+ *task-related*].

The following short segments are taken again from the flight of the Boeing 747 from New York to Miami in December 1995 (compare example (3)).

Example (7)

Normal Low Workload: small talk
CA   Boy, they got some sick # at American West with their pay sheets, don't they?
FO   I tell you I ***[22]
JR[23] Shades of Braniff
        [sound of laughter]

Danger 3: swearing
CA: Aw #.

5.6 Coherence

This category relates to the communicational dynamics. It is characterised by the values [coherent] and [incoherent]. In order to decide which of the two values applies we investigated how the communicative interaction and the transition from turn to turn are organised, and whether the participants follow the conventionalised rules of linguistic interaction.

The transcripts were analysed according to the following criteria:

– Do the participants work on a shared communicative task?

– Do they answer questions directed to them by other crew members?

– Do they complete a current communicative task before opening a new turn?

– Do they let each other finish their utterances, or do they interrupt each other?

Example (8) shows a typical case of incoherent communication. It is taken from the accident report of a flight that was scheduled from Greensboro-High Point to Raleigh-Durham on December 13th, 1994.[24]

Example (8)

(1) 1833:45.2   CA: OK, uh
(2) 1833:46.0   FO: I'm gonna turn that
(3) 1833:46.5   CA: See if that, turn on the auto
(4) 1833:48.2   FO: I'm goin'to turn on, both uh ignitions, OK?
(5) 1833:51.5   CA: OK.

---

[22] * = unintelligible word
[23] JR = jumpseat rider
[24] Appendix (4) shows a longer excerpt from the transcript.

This segment received the value [*incoherent*] because it contains several interruptions: In (1), the captain starts an utterance. He is interrupted by the co-pilot who informs him about the next step he wants to perform (2). But the co-pilot, too, cannot finish his utterance due to an interruption that comes from the captain this time: In (3), the captain issues the command he presumably wanted to give in (1) already. And again, he is interrupted by the co-pilot before he has fully completed his utterance: The co-pilot suggests his next action[25] – without being interrupted (4). The captain agrees (5), and the segment finally comes to a successful end.

5.7 Information Quality

The coherence of communication does not allow conclusions about the quality of the individual utterances. An utterance that is coherent with regard to the communicational dynamics is not necessarily well-formed on the level of the single utterance: It can, for instance, contain deictically unclear references or grammatically ambiguous structures.

In other words, high workload might affect different levels of communication. The category information quality refers to the level of the single utterance. It is characterised by the values [+ *well-formed*] and [– *well-formed*]. We analysed whether the linguistic means used in the individual utterances were explicit and clear enough so that they would not evoke misunderstandings.

Example (9) contains two [– *well-formed*] utterances (8 and 10). It was chosen to illustrate that unclear information can indeed foster misunderstandings. The text stems from the transcript that was already used in examples (4) and (5).

The example sets in shortly after the problem occurred. In order to gain control over the situation, the crew tries to bring the destroyed propeller in a particular position, the so-called "feather position". The captain first informs the co-pilot about the problem (1), and he then goes on to give commands that specify the counter measures (2, 3, 5, 7).

Example (9)

(1) CA: We got a left engine out.
(2) CA: Left power lever. Flight idle.
(3) CA: Left condition lever. Left condition lever.
(4) CO: Yeah.
(5) CA: Feather.
(6) CA: Yeah we're feathered.
(7) CA: Left condition lever, fuel shut-off.

---

[25] It is not clear whether (4) is a new suggestion or a reformulation and completion of (2).

After they have brought the propeller in the desired feather position, the captain asks the co-pilot for help (8, 10). But he does not specify what he needs help for. Instead, he uses the ambiguous deictic expressions *here* and *on this*. As a consequence, the co-pilot does not know what these expressions refer to. He interprets the captain's call for assistance as referring to the feather-procedure they have just been occupied with.

(8) CA: I need some help *here*.
(9) CO: OK.
(10) CA: I need some help *on this*.
(11) ?: (You said it's) feathered?
(12) CA: Uh ...
(13) CO: It did feather.
(14) CA: It's feathered.
(15) CO: OK.

The captain now realises that his request for help was not understood properly. As he still needs assistance in controlling the airplane, he reformulates his call for help: This time he states explicitly what the problem is. He provides all the information needed by the co-pilot to understand his request. Consequently, the information quality of (16) and (17) is [+ *well-formed*].

(16) CA: I can't hold this thing.
(17) CA: Help me hold it.
(18) CO: OK.

5.8 Register

This category refers to the social component of language use. The choice of the appropriate register depends on a variety of different factors: the institutional frame, the hierarchic relation between the participants, their degree of familiarity and so on. The speakers' knowledge of these factors influences their choice of linguistic means. That is, speakers have a particular conception of their addressee, a so-called "hearer model". Usually, they select the linguistic means that correspond best to that model.

The category is characterised by the two values [*formal*] and [*informal*] language use. Which value applies was decided on the basis of the linguistic means used by the individual crew members. One important clue is the way in which they address each other: "Sir" correlates with [*formal*], first name with [*informal*]. Another clue is whether they stick to the standardised aviation language or whether they use sloppy formulations. The use of taboo and swear words is also typical for [*informal*] language use.

The question is whether the ability to adapt to the social norms of language use is influenced by different workload conditions: Is it more difficult to retrieve situational and hearer-related knowledge under high workload conditions, or does the register – once it is chosen – just remain stable, no matter what the workload conditions are?

5.9 Emotion

The previous categories have one thing in common: They refer to those communicational properties that are based on knowledge, e.g. situational knowledge, knowledge about norms and social rules of communicative interaction, and on conceptual thinking. That is, so far we have neglected the fact that communicative interaction also contains emotional elements. This neglect reflects the exclusion of emotions from the traditional fields of linguistic study.

We know, however, from everyday knowledge that conversations often include emotional elements. Emotions clearly affect the linguistic level, for instance the choice of lexical items and the intonation. Time pressure and danger – the two conditions relevant in our study – additionally provoke emotions and emotional responses. That is why we included "emotion" as a descriptive category. It is characterised by the values [calm] and [emphatic].

5.10 Synopsis of the Linguistic Categories and their Values

Before we present the quantitative findings, we give – for better orientation – a short summary of the linguistic categories and their values.

Category	Value
Information Sharing	[yes], [no]
Initiation of Crew Resources	[activate], [react], [order], [none]
Receptiveness	[broad], [focused], [selective], [no reaction]
Responsiveness	[+ responsive], [– responsive]
Relation to Task	[+ task-related], [– task-related]
Coherence	[coherent], [incoherent]
Information Quality	[+ well-formed], [– well-formed]
Register	[formal], [informal]
Emotion	[calm], [emphatic]

Figure (I): Synopsis of the linguistic categories and their values

6 Results

6.1 Results of the Quantitative Study

After identifying the linguistic categories introduced in (5), we investigated how often each category was affected by high workload and danger in the whole data set. In the following, we report the results. The diagrams show the distribution of the values of each linguistic category within the different situation types: normal low workload (N1), normal high workload (N2), danger 1 (D1), danger 2 (D2), and danger 3 (D3).

When looking at the results, we should, however, keep in mind that we are talking about a very small data set. Therefore, we have to be careful with drawing generalisations. Also, for reasons that will be described in chapter 7, the quality of this particular data set did not allow to conduct statistical tests in order to find out whether the observed changes are significant or not. Apart from these limitations, the results do show clear tendencies concerning the effects of high workload and danger on the different aspects of the ability to communicate.

6.1.1 Information Sharing

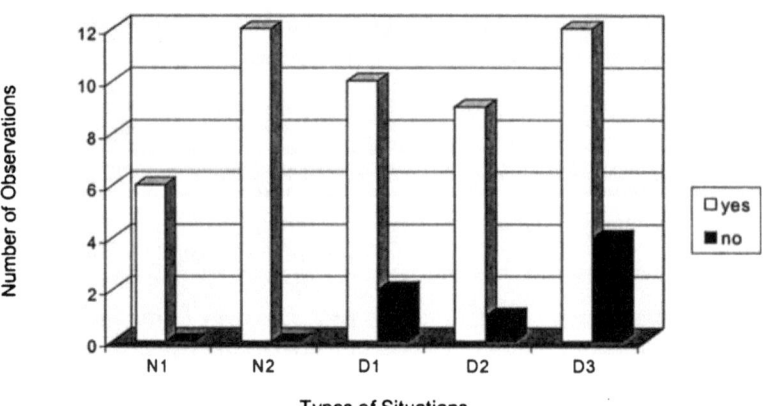

In our data, the category of information sharing was only slightly impaired under the influence of the danger condition. The diagram shows that under normal low and normal high workload all the crucial information was transferred, whereas in all three danger situation occurrences of a failure to transfer information could be observed. These results show that increasing danger slightly affects the ability to keep the information flow alive.

There is, however, a problem that should be mentioned briefly. It concerns the exact number of instances of the value [no]: In order to detect the instances in which information was not transferred we had to rely on certain clues that indicate missing information links. For instance, in one of the transcripts[26] the first officer had to constantly ask for information because the captain did not provide him with the relevant information which is illustrated by the two following short segments:

Example (10)
 FO: OK, you got it?
 CA: Yeah.
 FO: We lose an engine?
 CA: OK, yeah.
 FO: We lose that en' left one?
 CA: Yeah.
 FO: Watta you want me to do, you gonna continue?
 CA: OK, yeah. I'm gonna continue. Just back me up.

These sequences of turns were used as a clue for the value [no] on the captains side.[27] Other clues were missing answers on requests for information, and misunderstandings that arose out of a failure to share information, as in the case of the Birgenair accident, compare example (2).

The problem now is, that a failure to transfer information is not necessarily reflected in the text. So, if the text does not contain any of the clues mentioned above we have no chance to observe a missing information link and it just remains unnoticed. That is, the exact number of instances of the value [no] might be even higher than reported here.

---

[26] Compare example (8) in chapter 5.6. A longer excerpt from the transcript is given in appendix 4.
[27] But note the methodological considerations in chapter 7.

6.1.2 Initiation of Crew Resources

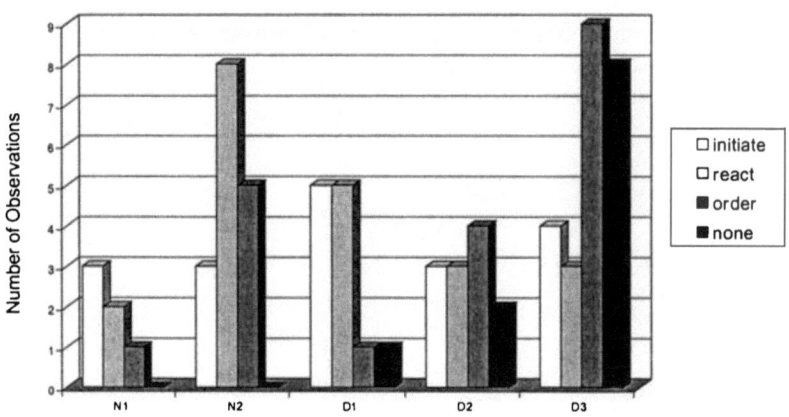

The category activation of crew resources was found to be strongly influenced by the danger condition in most of the transcripts. In N1, N2, and D1, the majority of cases got the values [*initiate*] and [*react*]. In N2, there is also a relatively high number of the value [*order*]. This is due to the fact that in this situation type, a lot of communication is prescribed by checklists. The most conspicuous result in the diagram is the clear increase in the values [*order*] and [*none*] compared to [*initiate*] and [*react*] in D2 and, even more so, in D3: In D3, the relation between [*initiate*] and [*react*] on the one side and [*order*] and [*none*] on the other side is clearly reversed. That is, those values increase that do not support the CRM-related goal to include the crew members in the process of problem solving.

The observed distribution of values shows that the ability to initiate crew resources is clearly impaired under the influence of time pressure and danger. It remains to be investigated what it is that causes these observed changes in the communicative behaviour. Do they result from insufficient training methods, or do they reflect regular mental processes evoked by dangerous conditions? How does the emotional component affect these results? What are the correlations between the observed changes and the actual properties of the linguistic structures used in the danger situations?

We can only report some observations concerning the last question: A detailed analysis of the linguistic structures in the D2 and D3 situations has shown that these situation types are characterised by very short and rudimentary utterances. Opinions and suggestions of the other crew members are not asked for, and we hardly find any tag questions, polite elements and "fillers" like, for instance, let's, please, would you please that indicate attempts to initiate crew resources. Instead, they contain a remarkably high number of orders. The utterances are reduced to their focus information, that is, only the most essential information is expressed. In the extreme cases, no linguistic interaction at all takes place.

That is, time pressure and danger evoke the use of very short linguistic structures that reduce the processing load to a minimum. All linguistic "ballast" is discarded. As logical as this may be, this tendency reduces the possibility to linguistically initiate crew resources. As a consequence, the CRM-related goal to include the whole team into the process of problem solving is hardly realisable in D2 and D3 situations.

6.1.3 Receptiveness

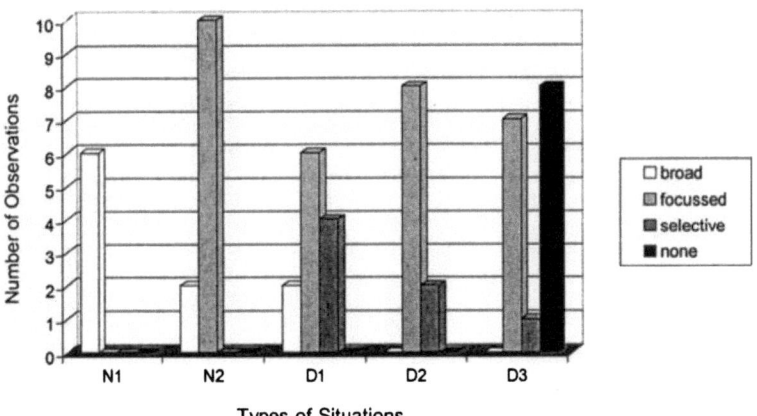

With regard to successfully managing the tasks in the cockpit, the four values that characterise the category receptiveness differ from each other along the following line: [broad] and [focused] contribute to the task management in a positive way whereas [selective] and [none] hinder the crew members from adequately coping with their situation, that is, [selective] and [none] have a negative effect.

The diagram shows that in N1 and N2, the receptiveness is completely on the positive side. In N1, it is exclusively characterised by the value [broad]. Due to the low workload, the crew members have enough capacity to react to all incoming channels. In N2, the value [focused] emerges. The increase of workload leads here to a concentration on the most essential channels. The crew members consciously choose those channels that are most relevant in their particular situation. That is, the shift from [broad] to [focused] reflects the increase of workload and it is conducive with respect to the management of the tasks.

In the danger conditions, we can observe a gradual shift towards the negative side. In D1, we still have instances of [broad] and [focused], but at the same time the value [selective] emerges. This trend continues in D2: There are no more instances of [*broad*], a high number of [*focused*], and some instances of [*selective*]. The shift towards the negative side becomes even more obvious in D3: In this situation type the instances of negative values outweigh the positive ones. Their majority is characterised by the value [*none*]. That is, in D3 the receptiveness is highly impaired.

To summarise we can say that the analysed transcripts reveal the following trend of development: The ability to process information from different channels and to adequately react to them changes from [*broad*] to [*focused*] to [*selective*] to [*none*]. These results suggest that the category receptiveness is systematically impaired under the influence of time pressure and danger.

6.1.4 Responsiveness

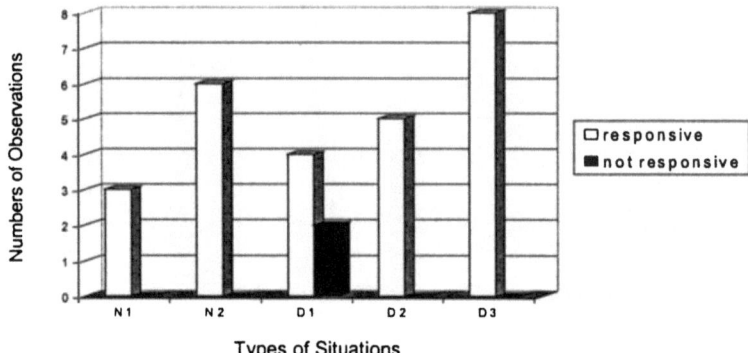

Types of Situations

The category of responsiveness was not found to be affected by stress and danger in the other transcripts. The diagram shows that there were only two cases in which the responsiveness was impaired, and these two instances occurred within the same crew. In all the other cases, the team members quickly adapted to situational changes. That is to say, in our data the ability to integrate new information into established conceptualisations of the situation was not impaired on a level above the single case study.

But again, we have to be careful with generalisations because this result might be due to the fact that – apart from example (1) – the situational changes did not occur while the crew was running strictly prescribed procedures. In other words, our data did not contain enough situations that allow us to investigate whether the prescriptive nature of aviation language affected the category responsiveness. That is, in order to answer this question it is necessary to conduct experimental studies because they allow us to evoke exactly these conditions.

6.1.5 Relation to Task

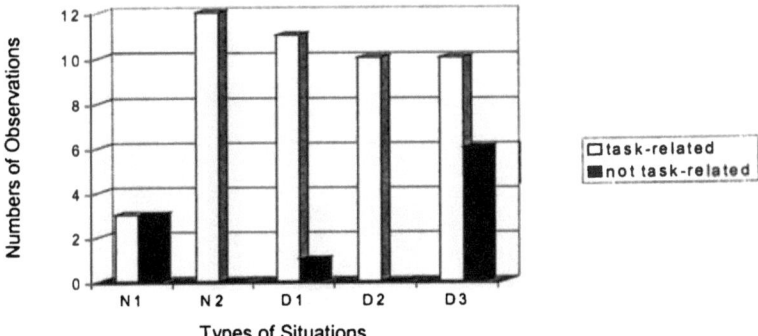

We can see in the diagram that instances of [*not task-related*] communication mainly occur in the two situation types that are characterised by the least and by the highest amount of workload and danger: in N1 and in D3. They differ, however, with regard to their content: In N1, the instances of [*not task-related*] communication consist of small talk, gossip about other crews, and jokes. The relation between [*task-related*] and [*not task-related*] in that situation type indicates that under normal low workload conditions, there is enough time for free conversation.

The instances of [*not task-related*] communication in D3 have, by contrast, a completely different meaning. They exemplify swearwords and other emotional exclamations. The relatively high number of [*not task-related*] utterances in D3 can be explained by the fact that in this situation type, danger and time pressure have increased to such a high degree that the crew members have to express their stress verbally.

6.1.6 Coherence

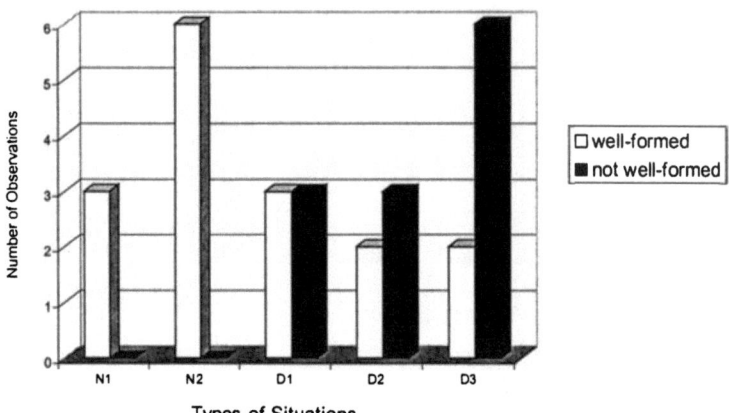

For the category of coherence, we see a clear effect of the danger condition. The diagram shows that communication is always coherent under normal low and normal high workload conditions. In contrast, all the three danger situations contain instances in which the communicational dynamics are disrupted: Questions are not answered, the crew members work on different communicative tasks and interrupt each other. These results suggest that the ability to produce coherent dialogic structures is impaired under the influence of time pressure and danger. That is, under the danger conditions it seems to become more difficult to include the utterances of the communicative partner into one's own planning processes.

6.1.7 Information Quality

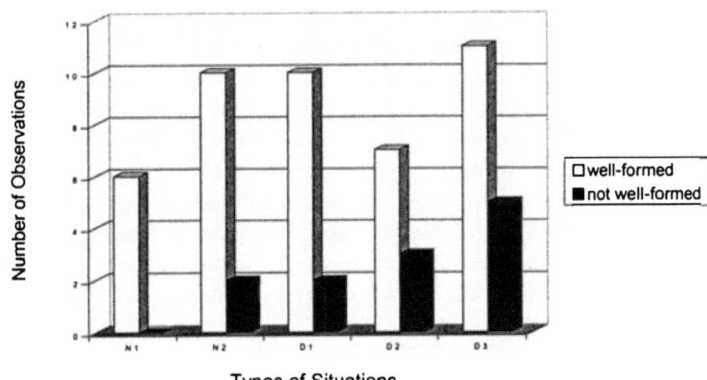

Compared to the category coherence, the influence of the danger condition on the information quality is less evident. The diagram shows that under normal low workload all the utterances were [*well-formed*]. In N2 and D1, there are some instances of [*not well-formed*] utterances. Their number slightly increases in the D2 and D3 situations, but even in these situation types there are much more [*well-formed*] than [*not well-formed*] utterances. These results suggest that increasing danger only slightly affects the quality of the individual utterances.

6.1.8 Register

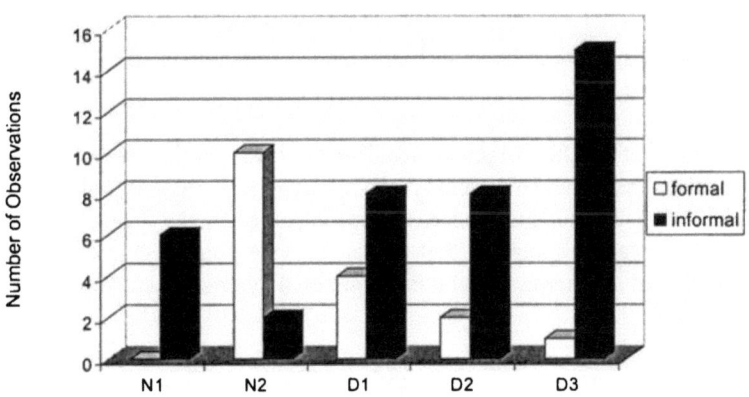

What is remarkable for this diagram is the surprisingly high number of instances of informal language use that can be observed in almost all situation types, except from N2. In N2, the dominant value is [*formal*]. The crews have to run many checklists, and the observed distribution of values shows that in the majority of cases the crew members stick to the fixed phraseology prescribed by the checklists. In all the other situation types, the dominant value is [*informal*].

One important factor that contributed to these results is the cultural background of the crews. Most of the transcripts in our data set stem from American crews. For them, a rather informal language use is generally accepted, and the choice of the informal register outside the checklist communication is consistent with the social norms. Consequently, their conversations contain many clues for the value [*informal*] across the different situation types: address by first name, sloppy forms, and taboo words. Taking this into account, it is not surprising that the diagram shows so many instances of informal communication.

This situation is completely different for crews from the Far East and from Moslem cultures. Crews from these cultures strictly stick to formal language use, even in situations as dangerous as D3. This is because the hierarchical structures are so deeply rooted in their cultures that it is unthinkable to give up the formal register, and a failure to choose the register according to the social conventions would equal a loss of face.[28] A very telling sequence happened during the crash of Japan Airlines flight 123 in 1985: The captain asked the co-pilot to stop using the formal register. But already his next order is again answered by the formal phrase "Yes, sir".

Example (11)
CA: Nose down. Lower nose.
CO: Yes, sir.
CA: Lower nose.
CO: Yes, sir.
CA: Lower nose.
CO: Yes, sir.
CA: Stop saying that. Do it with both hands, with both hands.
CO: Yes, sir.[29]

The transcript of the Birgenair accident contains another revealing example: Even under extremely dangerous conditions – just seconds before the plane crashes – the co-pilot's utterances are accompanied by the formal address "Sir". These two examples suggest that the category of politeness is conceptually so deeply rooted in the minds that it is not affected by time pressure and danger.

---

[28] According to Brown & Levinson (1987: 13), face is related to "the most fundamental cultural ideas about the nature of the social persona, honor and virtue, shame and redemption, and thus to religious concepts."

[29] The complete transcript can be found in MacPherson (1998: 64–68).

In sum, our analyses reveal the tendency for the chosen register to remain stable, no matter what the workload conditions are: For the American crews it remains [*informal*], and for crews from Moslem and Far Eastern cultures it remains [*formal*]. This conclusion cannot be drawn from the diagram, but it becomes evident in the single case studies.

6.1.9   Emotion

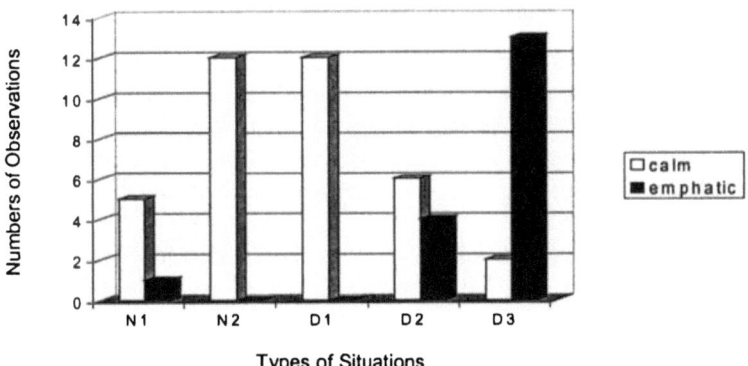

Types of Situations

For our last category – the category of emotion – there is an obvious effect of the danger condition. The diagram shows a clear increase of emphatic utterances in D2 and D3.

The effects of emotion on communication are multifold. The effects that we observed in the data are to be found on different linguistic levels. First, emotional forces effect various properties of the single utterances. On this level, we have to differentiate between semantic and syntactic effects.[30] Semantic effects include pejorative meaning components (e.g. swearwords). On the syntactic side, emotion can lead to elliptic structures, repetitions, imperatives and exclamatives. Second, emotional influences can lead to changes on the interactive level: There are emphatic utterances that don't answer a quaestio (they just express feelings), that follow no intention, that are not directed toward a particular addressee. All these effects on communication were increasingly observed in the transcripts in the situation types D2 and D3.

6.2   Other Results: Effects of Standardisation

Apart from the results concerning the effects of high workload and danger on the ability to communicate, our analysis of the linguistically marked passages

---

[30] Emotions may also have phonologic effects that concern suprasegmental features like prosody, rhythm, and rate of speaking. In our data, we could not observe these effects because we did not have access to the audio files.

has revealed another phenomenon that concerns the effects of standardisation on the mechanisms of language production. The following example shows the relevant segment. It stems again from the Birgenair accident.

Example (12)
(1) 0342:16   CO: power's set
(2) 0342:18   CA: okay checked
(3) 0342:23   CO: eighty knots [announces the current speed]
(4) 0342:24   CA: checked [confirms visual control of speed]
(5) 0342:26   CA: my airspeed indicator's not working

The example shows a short segment of crew communication during the acceleration phase. The plane is still on the runway, but it is only seconds before it is going to take off. The crew is highly occupied with preparations for the take-off. That is, they are in a typical N2-situation. The actions that have to be performed in that situation and the communication connected with these actions are highly prescribed.

What makes this segment linguistically marked is utterance (5). In (3), the co-pilot announces that they have reached a speed of 80 knots. This 80-knots call-out is prescribed by the script. In (4), the captain says "checked", an utterance that is also prescribed by the script. It is meant to express that he has visually checked the speed. But – and now comes the utterance that is interesting for us – two seconds later he informs the co-pilot that his airspeed indicator is not working. That is, in (4) he has confirmed an action that he cannot have carried out. This sequence of turns suggests the following scenario: The captain looked at his speed indicator and automatically produced the word "checked" without carrying out that action, and only afterwards he realised that his instrument did not work.

The analysis of example (12) suggests that prescribed phraseology might be automatically retrieved from the mental lexicon before the controlled conceptual processes set in. On the basis of our example it seems reasonable to assume that the processes that guide the production of standardised phraseology are sometimes faster than thought processes.

To sum up: In addition to the observed impairment of various aspects of the ability to communicate reported in (6.1), we also found evidence in the data suggesting that the standardisation of aviation language can lead to an unwanted side-effect on the mechanisms of language production: The fixed phraseology may be automatically retrieved from the lexicon, so that it would not go through the conceptual stages of language production.

Although we found only the one instance presented in example (12) to support that hypothesis, we think that it is still a relevant observation, and that it would be worthwhile to test that hypothesis, either by searching for other instances in a bigger data set or by conducting an experimental study.

7 Methodological Problems

In this chapter we want to describe why we have to be careful with drawing generalisations from the quantitative study. The main problem is connected with the nature of authentic aviation data: The CVR-recordings never exceed thirty minutes. Consequently, many recordings don't span the entire flight, and often they contain only communication that was exchanged after the problem occurred. That is, for many crews we don't know how they communicated under normal conditions, and in these cases we don't know whether the observed communicational problems are in fact due to the danger condition or whether they just reflect individual personality factors.

We want to illustrate this for the category of information sharing: In example (2), we have seen that information was always transferred in the situation types N2, D1, and D2. But in D3, a failure to transfer information could be observed. In this particular case, we can conclude that the linguistic behaviour changed in relation to the situation type. This is different for example (10) because in that case we have no data for the situation types N1, N2, and D1. The transcript begins in the moment when the captain has just realised that a problem exists. That is, we don't know how he communicated before the problem occurred. Consequently, we can't be certain that his obvious lack of information sharing is indeed related to the situation type and not just an individual trait of his personality.

Although we can still observe the changes that occur in the different danger conditions, these limitations in the data make the quantitative results rather unreliable. In order to avoid the confounding personality factor it would be essential to have access to data that show the communicational behaviour in all five situation types.

Also, the method of comparing the communicational behaviour in the five different situation types between the crews is not really "clean" if it is applied to authentic data because there is such a huge amount of variability between the conditions of the individual flights, be it the personality of the crew members, the nature of the problem, the weather conditions, specifics of the flight route, and so on.

These specifics of the authentic data did not allow to conduct statistical tests in order to find out whether the observed distributions of values deviate significantly from the chance distributions. Consequently, we could not validate the results from the single case studies on a statistical level. For these reasons, it would be important to used simulator data in the follow-up studies.

8 Summary

This chapter gives a short summary of the results and briefly relates them to the mechanisms of language processing and language production:

(1) Our analyses reveal nine linguistic parameters that were impaired by high workload and danger in individual transcripts: information sharing, initiation of crew resources, receptiveness, responsiveness, relation to task, coherence, information quality, register, and emotion.

(2) The quantitative analysis shows how often each category was impaired in the whole data set. The observed distribution of values indicates whether the category in question is systematically influenced by workload and danger. The diagrams also reveal how strong the influence of these conditions is – whether a linguistic category is more or less likely to be impaired under the influence of high workload and danger. The following figure summarises the strength of influence on the individual categories as observed in our data set.

Strength of influence	Category
only in the single case studies	register responsiveness
slightly influenced categories (more positive than negative values in the danger conditions)	information quality information sharing relation to task
strongly influenced categories (more negative than positive values in at least one of the danger conditions)	coherence emotion initiation of crew resources receptiveness

Figure (II): Strength of influence on the individual linguistic categories

(3) Apart from the quantitative results, we also developed hypotheses concerning the effects of standardisation:

(3.1) Prescribed phraseology is automatically retrieved, compare example (12).

(3.2) Highly standardised situational scripts can hinder the adjustment to situational changes, compare example (1).

With these results in mind, we want to briefly consider the question: Which mechanisms of language processing and production persist and which are impaired under the condition of high workload and danger? If we relate the findings that are shown in Figure (II) to a model of language production[31] we can formulate the following hypotheses:

- Let's first consider the *processing side*: The strong influence of the danger condition on the category of *receptiveness* suggests that the mechanisms of language processing are highly impaired under these conditions.
- Let's now look at the *production side*: The other eight categories have to be placed on a relatively high level in the production process. They belong to the conceptual stage – the level where the so-called "preverbal message" is

---

[31] I refer to Levelt's model of language production as described in Levelt (1989).

generated. That is, the processes that are likely to be impaired under the danger condition are the controlled conceptual processes.
- There seems to be a tendency for those categories that require a high degree of hearer-related planning, like e.g. *coherence* and *initiation of crew resources*, to be more strongly impaired than categories that do not require such a high degree of hearer-related considerations, like e.g. *information quality*.
- The utterances as such were grammatically correct. We didn't find any syntactic mistakes and only few slips of the tongue. This means that – in contrast to the controlled processes – the automatic syntactic processes seem to persist under the condition of high workload and danger.

We now want to look back to our initial research questions. We began our study with the following questions in mind:[32]

- How does linguistic interaction vary in relation to the level of workload?
- Which elements of the utterances and which mechanism of language production do persist and which are eliminated under the conditions of high workload and danger?

As already emphasised in chapter 2, the goal this article was not to provide answers to these questions. The focus of our study was clearly exploratory in many respects, and we hardly need to emphasise the preliminary nature of certain ideas and results presented here. First and foremost our study served to formulate hypotheses. These hypotheses concern:
(a) the effects of high workload and danger on different aspects of language use,
(b) the location of the impaired processes in a model of language processing and production and
(c) the effects of standardisation on language production.

A huge amount of work is still required to convert these hypotheses into substantial empirical evidence. So, instead of presenting solutions and answers, this article offers many questions, ideas, and starting points for further investigations.

---

[32] These questions were already given in chapter 2, but they are repeated here for the reader's convenience.

Appendices

Appendix 1

Birgenair B757 Accident
Intra-Cockpit Communication, (released 18.3.1996)

HOT 1 = captain
HOT 2 = co-pilot
CAM 3 = relief pilot
CAM = cockpit area microphone

* = unintelligible word
[ ] = editorial insertion

Time	Source	Content
0341:40 (42:02)	HOT-2	have a nice flight
0342:08 (42:30)	CAM	[sound of increasing engine noise]
0342:09 (42:31)	HOT-1	EPR select
0342:10 (42:32)	HOT-2	EPR
0342:16 (42:38)	HOT-2	power's set
0342:18 (42:40)	HOT-1	okay checked
0342:23 (42:45)	HOT-2	eighty knots
0342:24 (42:46)	HOT-1	checked
0342:26 (42:48)	HOT-1	my airspeed indicator's not working
0342:28 (42:50)	HOT-2	yes
0342:29 (42:51)	HOT-2	yours is not working
0342:30 (42:52)	HOT-2	one twenty
0342:32 (42:54)	HOT-1	is yours working?
0342:32 (42:54)	HOT-2	yes sir
0342:33 (42:55)	HOT-1	you tell me
0342:35 (42:57)	HOT-2	Vee one
0342:36 (42:58)	HOT-2	rotate
0342:43 (43:05)	HOT-1	Positive climb gear up
0342:43 (43:05)	HOT-2	positive climb
0342:44 (43:06)	CAM	[sound of landing gear handle being moved]
0342:46 (43:08)	HOT-2	gear is up
0342:50 (43:12)	HOT-2	LNAV
0342:51 (43:13)	HOT-1	yes please
0342:52 (43:14)	HOT-2	LNAV
0342:59 (43:21)	HOT-1	yes

0343:00 (43:22)	HOT-2		it began to operate
0343:02 (43:24)	HOT-1		is it possible to turn off the wipers
0343:03 (43:25)	HOT-2		okay wipers off
0343:05 (43:27)	CAM		[sound of windshield wipers stops]
0343:08 (43:30)	HOT-1		climb thrust
0343:09 (43:31)	HOT-2		climb thrust
0343:10 (43:32)	HOT-1		VNAV
0343:11 (43:33)	HOT-2		VNAV
0343:16 (43:38)	HOT-2		okay flap speed
0343:17 (43:39)	HOT-1		flaps five
0343:24 (43:46)	HOT-1		flaps one
0343:25 (43:47)	HOT-2		flaps to one
0343:30 (43:52)	HOT-1		gear handle off
0343:32 (43:54)	HOT-2		gear handle's off
0343:33 (43:55)	HOT-1		flaps up
0343:34 (43:56)	HOT-2		flaps up
0343:36 (43:58)	HOT-1		after takeoff checklist
0343:38 (44:00)	HOT-2		after takeoff checklist landing gear up and off, flaps are up checked up, altimeters later, after takeoff completed
0343:47 (44:09)	HOT-1		okay
0344:07 (44:29)	HOT-1		center autopilot on please
0344:08 (44:30)	HOT-2		center autopilot is on command
0344:10 (44:32)	HOT-1		thank you
0344:12 (44:34)	HOT-1		one zero one three
0344:13 (44:35)	HOT-2		one zero one three
0344:25 (44:47)	HOT-1		rudder ratio, mach airspeed trim
0344:27 (44:49)	HOT-2		yes trim
0344:28 (44:50)	HOT-1		there is something wrong there are some problems
0344:43 (45:05)	HOT-2		direct Pokeg
0344:44 (45:06)	HOT-1		okay there is something crazy do you see it
0344:46 (45:08)	HOT-2		there is something crazy there at this moment two hundred only is mine and decreasing sir
0344:52 (45:14)	HOT-1		both of them are wrong. what can we do?
0344:54 (45:16)	HOT-1		let's check their circuit breakers
0344:55 (45:17)	HOT-2		yes
0344:57 (45:19)	HOT-1		alternate is correct
0344:59 (45:21)	HOT-2		the alternate one is correct
0345:04 (45:26)	HOT-1		as aircraft was not flying and on ground something happening is usual
0345:07 (45:29)	HOT-1		such as elevator asymmetry and other things
0345:11 (45:33)	HOT-1		we don't believe them
0345:23 (45:45)	CAM-3		shall I reset its circuit breaker

0345:24 (45:46)	HOT-1	yes reset it	
0345:25 (45:47)	CAM-3	to understand the reason	
0345:27 (45:49)	HOT-1	yeah	
0345:28 (45:50)	CAM	[sound of aircraft overspeed warning]	
0345:30 (45:52)	HOT-1	okay it's no matter	
0345:39 (46:01)	HOT-1	pull the airspeed we will see	
0345:39 (46:01)	CAM	[overspeed warning stops]	
0345:40 (46:02)	HOT-2	now it is three hundred and fifty yes	
0345:47 (46:09)	HOT-1	let's take that like this	
0345:50 (46:12)	CAM	[sound of four warning alert tones]	
0345:52 (46:14)	CAM	[sound of stick shaker starts and continues to end of recording]	
0345:56 (46:18)	CAM	[sound of four warning alert tones]	
0345:56 (46:18)	HOT-1	****	
0345:57 (46:19)	HOT-2	****	
0345:59 (46:21)	HOT-2	sir	
0346:00 (46:22)	CAM-3	*ADI	
0346:05 (46:27)	HOT-1	****	
0346:07 (46:29)	HOT-2	nose down	
0346:19 (46:41)	HOT-2	****	
0346:22 (46:44)	CAM-3	now*	
0346:23 (46:45)	HOT-2	thrust	
0346:25 (46:47)	HOT-1	disconnect the auto-pilot, is autopilot disconnected?	
0346:25 (46:47)	HOT-2	already disconnected, disconnected sir	
0346:31 (46:53)	CAM-3	*ADI*	
0346:39 (47:01)	HOT-1	not climb? what am I to do?	
0346:43 (47:05)	HOT-2	you may level off, altitude okay, I am selecting the altitude hold sir	
0346:47 (47:09)	HOT-1	select select	
0346:48 (47:10)	HOT-2	altitude hold	
0346:51 (47:13)	HOT-2	okay, five thousand feet	
0346:52 (47:14)	HOT-1	thrust levers, thrust thrust thrust thrust	
0346:54 (47:16)	HOT-2	retard	
0346:54 (47:16)	HOT-1	thrust, don't pull back, don't pull back, don't pull back, don't pull back	
0346:56 (47:18)	HOT-2	okay open open	
0346:57 (47:19)	HOT-1	don't pull back, please don't pull back	
0346:59 (47:21)	HOT-2	open sir, open	
0347:01 (47:23)	HOT-2	****	
0347:02 (47:24)	CAM-3	sir pull up	
0347:03 (47:25)	HOT-1	what's happening	
0347:05 (47:27)	HOT-2	oh what's happening	
0347:06 (47:28)	CAM-3	*	

0347:09 (47:31)		GPWS	[sink rate whoop whoop pull up warning starts and continues until the end]
0347:13 (47:35)		HOT-2	let's do like this
0347:14 (47:36)		CAM-3	*
0347:17 (47:39)			[end of recording]

Copyright 1996, 1997 Harro Ranter/Aviation Safety Web Pages;
Updated: 26.10.1997

Appendix 2

Flight FF 41 scheduled from New York (John F. Kennedy Airport) to Miami, Boeing 747, 20.12.95

CAM = cockpit-area microphone voice or sound source
RDO = radio transmission from accident aircraft
GND = radio transmission from JFK ground control
TWR = radio transmission from JFK local control
-1 = voice identified as captain
-2 = voice identified as first officer
-3 = voice identified as flight engineer
-6 = voice identified as jumpseat rider
-? = voice unidentified
 * = unintelligible word
 # = expletive
[ ] = editorial insertion

Time	Source	Content
1122:56	CAM-1:	I'm gonna uh, stop and run these engines right here.
1123:00	CAM-2:	OK.
1123:09	CAM-1:	Mike, keep your eye outside. If we start to move let me know.
1123:13	CAM-2:	** tell ground what we're doing?
1123:14	CAM-1:	Naw.
1123:16	CAM:	[Sound similar to increase in engine RPM]
1123:20	CAM-2:	Feels like we're moving.
1123:21	CAM:	[Sound of click]
1123:23	CAM:	[Sound similar to decrease in engine RPM]
1123:25	CAM-6:	It started to move.
1123:26	CAM-?:	Yep.
1123:27	CAM-6:	Slippery out there.
1123:35	CAM-1:	It's an ice rink here.

1124:24	GND:	Tower forty-one heavy, you can stay on the inner. Cross three one left at Kilo.
1124:29	RDO-2:	Inner to three one left at Kilo, thank you, Tower forty-one.
1125:45	CAM-1:	Boy they got some sick # at America West with their pay sheets, don't they?
1125:49	CAM-2:	I tell you I ***.
1125:52	CAM-6:	Shades of Braniff.
1125:53	CAM:	[Sound of laughter]
1125:55	CAM:	[Sound similar to electric seat motion]
1125:58	CAM-?:	***.
1126:05	GND:	Tower forty-one heavy, cross runway three one left. On the other side monitor nineteen one, good day.
1126:10	RDO-2:	Tower forty-one, we'll monitor on the other side. Thanks.
1128:50	CAM-?:	***.
1129:04	CAM-2:	*** body gear steering.
1129:35	CAM-?:	* right.
1129:49	CAM-1:	Get around the corner here. Ralph take a little walk and check the wings for me will you?
1129:53	CAM-3:	Sure.
1130:06	CAM:	[Sound of clicks similar to crew harness release]
1130:42	CAM-1:	OK?
1130:42	CAM-3:	OK.
1130:46	CAM:	[Sliding sound similar to seat adjustment]
1130:55	CAM:	[Sound of clicks similar to cockpit door operating]
1131:59	CAM:	[Sound similar to cockpit door opening]
1132:01	CAM-3:	It's very clean out there.
1132:03	CAM-1:	OK.
1132:03	CAM-3:	**.
1132:07	TWR:	Tower forty-one heavy, four left, taxi into position and hold. Traffic down field right to left.
1132:11	CAM-1:	Right.
1132:13	RDO-2:	Position and hold ni ... four left, Tower Air forty-one heavy.
1132:15	CAM-1:	Position and hold, before-takeoff checklist.
1132:16	CAM-3:	Before-takeoff checklist.
1132:23	CAM-3:	Flight attendants please be seated for takeoff. Thank you.
1132:35	CAM-3:	Takeoff announcement is complete.
1132:47	CAM-3:	Air condition packs off.
1132:52	CAM:	[Sound of three clicks]
1132:53	CAM-3:	Ignition, flight start.
1132:54	CAM-3:	Transponder and radar?

1132:56	CAM-2:	On and on.
1132:58	CAM-3:	And stand by for body gear steering.
1134:26	CAM-2:	I don't guess you'll be able to get much of a run-up.
1134:29	CAM-1:	No. Just do the best we can. If it starts to move, we're going to take it.
1134:34	CAM-?:	Okay.
1134:35	CAM:	[Sound similar to crew seat operation]
1135:09	CAM-2:	I see an airplane looks like it's clear down the end.
1135:12	CAM-?:	Hold on.
1135:18	CAM-3:	Body gear steer?
1135:22	CAM:	[Sound of click]
1135:22	CAM-3:	Disarmed, before-takeoff checklist complete.
1135:25	CAM-?:	OK.
1135:26	RDO-2:	Tower Air forty-one is in position four left.
1135:29	TWR:	Yes sir, just continue holding.
1135:34	CAM-1:	Try a run-up here and see what happens.
1135:39	CAM:	[Sound similar to increase in engine RPM]
1135:47	CAM-1:	Start your clock **.
1135:49	CAM-?:	**.
1135:52	CAM-3:	It's about forty-five right there.
1136:02	CAM-2:	It's about fifteen.
1136:04	CAM:	[Sound of click and sound similar to decrease in engine RPM]
1136:15	CAM-1:	Pretty good uh, crosswind from the *.
1136:25	TWR:	Tower forty-one heavy, wind three three zero at one one, runway four left, RVR's one thousand eight hundred, cleared for takeoff.
1136:31	RDO-2:	Cleared for takeoff four left, Tower Air forty-one.
1136:34	CAM-1:	Checklist is complete?
1136:35	CAM-3:	Yes, checklist is complete.
1136:39	CAM:	[Sound of click similar to parking brake release]
1136:40	CAM:	[Sound similar to increase in engine RPM]
1136:44	CAM-3:	Power's stable.
1136:48	CAM:	[Sound similar to crew seat operation]
1137:00	CAM:	[Low-frequency sound similar to further increase in engine RPM]
1137:04	CAM-1:	Set time, takeoff thrust.
1137:05	CAM-3:	Set the takeoff thrust.
1137:10	CAM-?:	Watch it.
1137:10	CAM-?:	Watch it.
1137:11	CAM:	[Sound of click]
1137:11	CAM:	[Low-frequency sound similar to engine noise can no longer be heard.]
1137:12	CAM-3:	OK, losing it.

1137:12	CAM-2:	Going to the left.
1137:13	CAM-?:	Going to the left.
1137:13	CAM-3:	To the right.
1137:14	CAM-3:	You're going off.
1137:15	CAM-?:	Going off.
1137:16	CAM-1:	Aw #.
1137:17	CAM-1:	Easy guys.
1137:18	CAM-1:	OK.
1137:19	CAM:	[First sound of impact]
1137:20	CAM-?:	Pull up. Pull up.
1137:21	CAM:	[Second sound of impact]

Copyright 1996, 1997 Harro Ranter/Aviation Safety Web Pages;
Updated: 19.8.1997

Appendix 3

Atlantic Southeast Airlines, Flight 529, scheduled from Atlanta to Gulfport, 21.8.1995

HOT = crew member "hot" microphone voice or sound source
HOT-M = aircraft mechanical voice heard on all channels
RDO = radio transmission from accident aircraft
CAM = cockpit-area microphone
INT = transmission over aircraft interphone system
CTR = radio transmission from Atlanta ARTCC
ATLA = radio transmission from Atlanta approach control
UNK = radio transmission received from unidentified aircraft
-B = sounds heard through both pilots' "hot" microphone systems
-1 = voice identified as captain
-2 = voice identified as first officer
-3 = voice identified as flight attendant
-? = voice unidentified
* = unintelligible word
# = expletive
( ) = questionable insertion
[ ] = editorial insertion
... = pause

Time	Source	Content
1243:25	CAM:	[Sound of several thuds]
1243:26	CAM-1:	****.
		[Three chimes similar to master warning]

Time	Source	Content
1243:28	CAM:	Autopilot, engine control, oil [and continues to repeat.]
1243:29	CAM-?:	*.
1243:32	CAM-2:	Pack off.
1243:34	CAM-1:	*.
1243:38	CAM-1:	We got a left engine out. Left power lever. Flight idle.
1243:45	CAM:	[Shaking sound starts and continues for 33 seconds.]
1243:46	CAM-1:	Left condition lever. Left condition lever.
1243:48	CAM-2:	Yeah.
1243:49	CAM-1:	Feather.
1243:51	HOT-B:	[Series of rapid beeps for one second similar to engine fire warning]
1243:54	CAM-1:	Yeah we're feathered. Left condition lever, fuel shut-off.
1243:59	CAM-1:	I need some help here.
1244:02	CAM:	[Mechanical voice messages for engine control and oil cease. Chimes and autopilot warning continue.]
1244:03	CAM-2:	OK.
1244:03	CAM-1:	I need some help on this.
1244:05	CAM-?:	(You said it's) feathered?
1244:06	CAM-1:	Uh ...
1244:07	CAM-2:	It did feather.
1244:07	CAM-1:	It's feathered.
1244:09	CAM-2:	OK.
1244:09	CAM:	[Master warning chimes and voice warning continues.]
1244:10	CAM-1:	What the hell's going on with this thing.
1244:13	CAM-2:	I don't know ... got this detector inop.
1244:16	CAM-1:	OK ***.
1244:18	CAM-?:	OK, let's put our headsets on.
1244:20	CAM-1:	I can't hold this thing.
1244:23	CAM-1:	Help me hold it.
1244:24	HOT-2:	OK.
1244:26	CAM-1:	All right comin' on headset.
1244:26	RDO-2:	Atlanta center. AC five twenty-nine, declaring an emergency. We've had an engine failure. We're out of fourteen two at this time.
1244:31	CTR:	AC five twenty-nine, roger, left turn direct Atlanta.
1244:33	HOT-1:	# damn.
1244:34	RDO-2:	Left turn direct Atlanta, AC five twenty nine.
1244:36	HOT-?:	[Sound of heavy breathing]
1244:41	HOT-?:	** back **.
1244:57	HOT-?:	[Sound of squeal]
1245:01	CAM:	[Tone similar to master caution cancel button being activated. All warnings cease.]
1245:03	HOT-1:	All right turn your speaker off. Oh, we got it. Its ...
1245:07	HOT-1:	I pulled the power back.

1245:10	CTR:	AC five twenty-nine, say altitude descending to.
1245:12	RDO-2:	We're out of eleven six at this time. AC five twenty-nine.
1245:17	HOT-1:	All right, it's, it's getting more controllable here ... the engine ... let's watch our speed.
1245:32	HOT-1:	All right, we've trimmed completely here.
1245:38	HOT-2:	I'll tell Robin what's goin' on.
1245:39	HOT-1:	Yeah.
1245:44	HOT-B:	[Sound of two chimes similar to cabin call button being activated]
1245:45	INT-3:	Yes sir.
1245:46	INT-2:	OK, we had an engine failure Robin. We declared an emergency, we're diverting back into Atlanta. Go ahead and uh, brief the passengers. This will be an emergency landing back in.
1245:55	INT-3:	All right. Thank you.
1245:56	HOT-1:	Tell 'em we want ...
1245:58	CTR:	AC five twenty-nine, say altitude leaving.
1246:01	RDO-2:	AC five twenty-nine's out of ten point three at this time.
1246:03	CTR:	AC five twenty-nine roger, can you level off or do you need to keep descending?
1246:09	HOT-1:	We ca ... We're gonna need to keep con ... descending. We need a airport quick.
1246:13	RDO-2:	OK, we uh, we're going to need to keep descending. We need an airport quick and uh, roll the trucks and everything for us.
1246:20	CTR:	AC five twenty-nine, West Georgia, the regional airport is at your ... ten o'clock position and about ten miles.
1246:28	RDO-2:	Understand ten o'clock and ten miles. AC five twenty-nine.
1246:30	CTR:	's correct.
1246:36	HOT-1:	(* give me) [whispered]
1246:38	HOT-1:	Let's get out the uh ... engine failure checklist, please.
1246:47	HOT-2:	OK, I'll do it manually here.
1246:55	HOT-2:	OK, engine failure in flight.
1246:57	CTR:	AC five twenty-nine, say heading.
1246:59	RDO-2:	Turnin' to about uh, three ten right now.
1247:01	HOT-2:	Power levers, flight idle.
1247:03	CTR:	AC five twenty-nine, roger. You need to be on about a zero three zero heading for West Georgia Regional, sir.
1247:07	RDO-2:	Roger, we'll ("prob'ly," or possibly, "try ta") turn right. We're having uh, difficulty controlling right now.
1247:11	HOT-2:	OK, condition lever's, feather.
1247:13	HOT-1:	All right.

1247:14	HOT-2:	It did feather ... NP's showing zero.
1247:18	HOT-1:	'K.
1247:19	HOT-2:	OK.
1247:20	CTR:	AC five twenty-nine, when you can, it's zero four zero.
1247:22	RDO-2:	Zero four zero, AC five twenty-nine.
1247:25	HOT-2:	'K, electric, yeah OK it did feather. There's no fire.
1247:27	HOT-1:	All right.
1247:28	HOT-2:	OK.
1247:32	HOT-2:	Main auxiliary generators of the failed engine off.
1247:35	HOT-1:	'K. I got that.
1247:40	HOT-2:	'K, APU ... if available, start. Want me to start it?
1247:45	HOT-1:	We gotta, bring this down, bring those. Put the that off. Bring the ice off ...
1247:54	HOT-B:	[Sound of chime similar to master caution starts and repeats at six-second intervals until the end of the recording.]
1247:56	HOT-?:	*.
1247:56	CTR:	AC five twenty-nine uh, say your altitude now sir.
1247:59	RDO-2:	Out of seven thousand, AC five twenty-nine.
1248:00	HOT-B:	[Sound of three chimes followed by voice message] Trim fail. [Warning starts and continues.]
1248:04	HOT-1:	Good start.
1248:04	CTR:	AC five twenty-nine, I missed that, I'm sorry.
1248:06	RDO-2:	We're outta six point nine right now, AC five twenty-nine.
1248:09	CTR:	AC five twenty-nine roger, West Georgia Regional, heading zero seven zero.
1248:13	RDO-2:	Zero seven zero, AC five twenty-nine.
1248:20	HOT-B:	[Sound of single beep]
1248:33	HOT-2:	OK, it's up and running, Ed.
1248:34	HOT-1:	All right, go ahead.
1248:35	CTR:	AC five twenty-nine, West Georgia Regional is your closest airport. The other one's uh, Anniston and that's about thirty miles to your west, sir.
1248:40	HOT-1:	How long, how far West Georgia Reg ... What kind of a runway they got.
1248:44	RDO-2:	What kind of runway's West Georgia Regional got?
1248:54	HOT-1:	Go ahead and finish the checklist.
1248:58	CTR:	West Georgia Regional is uh, five say one six and three four and it's five thousand feet ...
1249:01	HOT-2:	OK, APU started. OK, prop sync, off. Prop sync's comin' off.
1249:03	HOT-1:	OK.
1249:04	HOT-2:	Fuel pumps failed engine. You want uh, max on this?

1249:07	HOT-1:	Go ahead, please.
1249:08	HOT-2:	OK.
1249:09	CAM:	[Sound similar to propeller increasing in RPM]
1249:09	CTR:	And it is asphalt sir.
1249:11	HOT-2:	Hydraulic pump, failed engine? As required. Put it to the on position?
1249:15	HOT-1:	Correct.
1249:17	HOT-2:	'K. Engine bleed failed engine is closed and the pack is off.
1249:19	HOT-1:	'K.
1249:26	HOT-2:	'K, cross-bleed open.
1249:29	HOT-1:	'K.
1249:32	HOT-2:	Electrical load, below four thousand amps.
1249:38	HOT-1:	It is. Put the ice ba ... (well you) don't need to do that just leave that alone.
1249:45	HOT-1:	All right, single-engine checklist please.
1249:48	CTR:	AC five twenty-nine, I've lost your transponder. Say altitude.
1249:52	RDO-2:	We're out of four point five at this time.
1249:54	CTR:	AC five twenty-nine, I've got you now and the airport's at your, say say your heading now sir.
1249:59	RDO-2:	Right now we're heading uh, zero eight zero.
1250:01	CTR:	Roger, you need about ten degrees left. Should be twelve o'clock and about eight miles.
1250:05	RDO-2:	Ten left, twelve 'n eight miles and uh, do we got a, ILS to this runway?
1250:10	CTR:	I'll tell you what. Let me put you on the approach. He works that airport and he will be able to give you more information. Contact Atlanta approach on one two one point zero, sir.
1250:15	HOT-1:	We can get in on a visual.
1250:17	RDO-2:	One more time on the freq ...
1250:20	RDO-1:	Say again on the frequency?
1250:22	CTR:	Atlanta approach one two one point zero.
1250:24	RDO-2:	Twenty one zero, see ya.
1250:26	UNK-?:	Good luck guys.
1250:27	RDO-2:	'preciate it.
1250:28	HOT-B:	[Single beep similar to radio frequency change]
1250:29	RDO-2:	Atlanta approach, AC five twenty-nine's with you out of three point four.
1250:36	HOT-1:	Engine's exploded. It's just hanging out there.
1250:43	RDO-2:	Atlanta approach, AC five twenty-nine.
1250:45	ATLA:	AC five twenty-nine, Atlanta approach.

1250:48	RDO-2:	Yes sir, we're with you declaring an emergency. AC five twenty-nine, roger.
1250:49	ATLA:	Expect localizer runway three four approach and uh, could you fly heading one eight zero uh no sorry, one six zero?
1250:56	RDO-2:	Yeah we can do that. Give me the loc freq ...
1250:59	ATLA:	Localizer frequency, runway three four localizer frequency is uh, one one one point seven.
1251:05	HOT-1:	We can get in on a visual. Just give us vectors.
1251:07	RDO-2:	One one one point seven. ... Just give us vectors. We'll go the visual.
1251:17	HOT-1:	Sing, single, single-engine checklist, please.
1251:28	HOT-2:	Where the # is it?
1251:29	ATLA:	AC five twenty-nine, say altitude leaving.
1251:31	RDO-2:	We're out of nineteen hundred at this time.
1251:33	HOT-1:	We're below the clouds. Tell 'm ...
1251:35	ATLA:	You're out of nineteen hundred now?
1251:36	RDO-2:	'K we're uh, VFR at this time. Give us a vector to the airport.
1251:39	ATLA:	AC five twenty-nine. Turn left uh, fly heading zero four zero. Bear, the uh, airport's at your about ten o'clock and six miles sir. Radar contact lost at this time.
1251:47	RDO-2:	Zero four zero, AC five twenty-nine.
1252:07	HOT-M:	Five hundred.
1252:10	HOT-M:	Too low gear. [Starts and repeats.]
1252:11	ATLA:	AC five twenty-nine, if able, change to my frequency, one one eight point seven. The airport uh, in the vicinity of your ten o'clock at twelve o'clock and about four miles or so.
1252:20	HOT-1:	Help me, help me hold it, help me hold, help me hold it.
1252:56	ATLA:	AC five twenty-nine, change frequency, one one eight point seven if able.
1252:32	HOT-B:	Too low gear. [Warning stops.]
1252:32	HOT-B:	[Series of rapid beeps similar to aural stall warning]
1252:32	CAM:	[Vibrating sound similar to aircraft stick shaker starts and continues for four seconds.]
1252:36	CAM:	[Vibrating sound similar to aircraft stick shaker starts again and continues to impact.]
1252:37	HOT-2:	Amy, I love you.
1252:40	HOT-B:	Landing gear.
1252:41	CAM-?:	[Sound of grunting]
1252:45	CAM:	[Sound of impact]

1252:46	HOT-B:	Landing gear.	
1252:46	CAM:	[Sound of impact]	
1252:46		[End of recording]	

Source: NTSB/AAR-96/06

Appendix 4

Flight AA3379, scheduled from Greensboro-High Point IAP – Raleigh-Durham APT, British Aerospace 3201 Jetstream 32, American Eagle/Flagship Airlines, 13.12.94

CA = captain
FO = first officer
CAM = cockpit area microphone
* = unintelligible word;
... = pause
HOT-B = sounds heard through both pilots' hot microphone systems

Time	Source	Content
1833:33.3	CA	Why's that ignition light on? We just had a flame-out?
1833:38.4	FO	I'm not sure what's goin' on with it.
1833:39.8	CA	We had a flame-out.
1833:40.7	CAM	[Low-frequency beat sound similar to propellers rotating out of synchronisation starts and continues for approximately eight seconds.]
1833:41.4	FO	OK, you got it?
1833:42.5	CA	Yeah.
1833:42.8	FO	We lose an engine?
1833:43.6	CA	OK, yeah.
1833:45.2	CA	OK, uh ...
1833:46.0	FO	I'm gonna turn that ...
1833:46.5	CA	See if that, turn on the auto ...
1833:48.2	FO	I'm goin' to turn on, both uh ... ignitions, OK?
1833:51.5	CA	OK.
1833:54.2	FO	We lose that en' left one?
1833:55.9	CA	Yeah.
1833:58.9	FO	Watta you want me to do, you gonna continue?
1834:00.1	CA	OK, yeah. I'm gonna continue. Just back me up.
1834:03.1	FO	All right, I'm gonna ...
1834:03.7	CAM	[Low-frequency beat sound similar to propellers rotating out of synchronisation starts and continues for approximately three seconds.]

1834:03.9	CA	* lets go missed approach.
1834:05.0	FO	All right. **.
1834:05.3	CAM	[Sound similar to single stall warning horn starts and continues for 0.7 seconds.]
1834:05.7	CA	Set max power.
1834:06.1	CAM	[Sound similar to single stall warning horn starts and continues for 0.3 seconds.]
1834:06.5	FO	Lower the nose, lower the nose, lower the nose.
1834:09.4	CAM	[Sound similar to single stall warning starts.]
1834:09.6	CAM	[Sound similar to dual stall warning horns starts.]
1834:09.8	FO	You got it?
1834:10.8	CA	Yeah.
1834:12.2	FO	Lower the nose.
1834:13.0	CAM	[Unidentified rattling sound]
1834:13.2	FO	It's the wrong, wrong foot, wrong engine *.
1834:14.7	CAM	[Sound similar to dual stall warning horns stops.]
1834:14.8	CAM	[Low-frequency beat sound similar to propellers rotating out of synchronisation starts and continues for approximately four seconds.]
1834:14.9	CAM	[Sound similar to single stall warning stops.]
1834:16.1	CAM	[Sound similar to dual stall warning horns starts.]
1834:16.3	HOT-B	[Sound of heavy breathing]
1834:17.6	CAM	[Sound similar to dual stall warning horns stops and single horn continues.]
1834:18.2	CAM	[Sound similar to dual stall warning horns starts.]
1834:18.9	FO	Here.
1834:19.6	CAM	[Sound similar to dual stall warning stops.]
1834:22.3	CAM	[Sound similar to dual stall warning horns start and continues to impact.]
1834:24.4	CAM	[Sound of impact.]

Copyright 1996, 1997 Harro Ranter/Aviation Safety Web Pages;
Updated: 30.12.1997
Source: NTSB/AAR-95/07

References

Billings, C. E. & Cheaney, E. S. (Eds.) (1981): "Information transfer problems in the aviation system". (NASA Technical Paper 1875). Moffett Field, CA: NASA-Ames Research Center.

Blackwell, A. & Bates, E. (1995): "Inducing Agrammatic Profiles in Normals: Evidence for the Selective Vulnerability of Morphology under Cognitive Resource Limitation". In: Journal of Cognitive Neuroscience, 7 (2). 228–257.

Brown, P. & Levinson, S. C. (1987): Politeness: Some Universals in Language Use. Cambridge: Cambridge University Press.

Chidester, T. R. & Foushee, H. C. (1988): "Leader personality and crew effectiveness: Factors influencing performance in full-mission air transport simulation". In: Proceedings of the 66th Meeting of the Aerospace Medical Panel on Human Behavior in High Stress Situations in Aerospace Operations. The Hague, Netherlands: Advisory Group for Aerospace Research and Development.

Clark, H. (1996): Using Language. Cambridge: Cambridge University Press.

Cushing, Steven (1994): Fatal Words. Communication Clashes and Aircraft Crashes. Chicago and London: The University of Chicago Press.

Foushee, H. C. (1984): "Dyads and Triads at 35,000 Feet. Factors Affecting Group Process and Aircrew Performance." In: American Psychologist, Vol.39 (8). 885–893.

Foushee, H. C. & Manos, K. (1981): "Information transfer within the cockpit: Problems in intra-cockpit communications". In: C. E. Billings & E. S. Cheaney (Eds.): Information transfer problems in the aviation system (NASA Technical Paper 1875). Moffett Field, CA: NASA-Ames Research Center.

Helmreich, R. L. & Foushee, H. C. (1993): "Why Crew Resource Management? Empirical and theoretical bases of human factors training in aviation". In: E. Wiener, B. Kanki & R. Helmreich (Eds.): Cockpit Resource Management. San Diego, CA: Academic Press. 3–45.

Kanki, B. G. & Palmer, M. T. (1993): "Communication and Crew Resource Management". In: E. Wiener, B. Kanki & R. Helmreich (Eds.): Cockpit Resource Management. San Diego, CA: Academic Press. 99–137.

Kanki, B. G., Palmer, M. T. & Veinott, E. (1991): "Communication variations related to leader personality". In: Proceedings of the Sixth International Symposium on Aviation Psychology. Columbus, Ohio: The Ohio State University. 253–259.

Levelt, W. J. M. (1989): Speaking: From Intention to Articulation. Cambridge, MA: MIT Press.

MacPherson, M. (1998) (Ed.): The Black Box: All-New Cockpit Voice Recorder Accounts of In-flight Accidents. New York.

Orasanu, J. & Fischer, U. (1991): "Information transfer and shared mental models for decision making". In: R. S. Jenson (Ed.): Proceedings of the Sixth International Symposium of Aviation Psychology. Columbus, Ohio: The Ohio State University.

US National Transportation and Safety Board: Aircraft Accident Reports. Report No. NTSB/AAR-95/07.

US National Transportation and Safety Board: Aircraft Accident Reports. Report No. NTSB/AAR-96/06.

Searle, J. (1969): Speech Acts. Cambridge: Cambridge University Press.

Searle, J. (1975): "Indirect Speech Acts". In: P. Cole & J. Morgan (Eds.): Syntax and Semantics 3: Speech Acts. New York: Academic Press. 59–82.

Sexton, J. B. & Helmreich, R. L. (1999): "Analyzing Cockpit Communication: The Links between Language, Performance, Error and Workload". In: Proceedings of the Tenth International Symposium of Aviation Psychology. Columbus, Ohio: The Ohio State University. 689–695.

Vanderveken, D. (1990): Meaning and Speech Acts. Vol.1. Cambridge: Cambridge University Press.

Berlin   Dagmar Silberstein and Rainer Dietrich

Humboldt University at Berlin, Institut für Deutsche Sprache und Linguistik, Unter den Linden 6, 10099 Berlin, Rainer.Dietrich@rz.hu-berlin.de

Using Language in the Cockpit: Relationships with Workload and Performance

J. Bryan Sexton and Robert L. Helmreich[1]

Overview

Few events attract as much international attention as an accident involving a commercial jumbo jet airplane. The public, the airlines, the airplane manufacturers, and particularly the friends and family of passengers demand answers. The work presented here illustrates the importance of flight deck communication in flight safety through a simulator study of *how* and *what* pilots communicate. This investigation utilized a computer-based linguistic method of text analysis as well as a micro-coding of communication content. Analyses of simulator transcripts demonstrated that several language dimensions were associated with higher performance, fewer errors, and better communication. The ways in which pilots used language varied as a function of crew position and level of workload. Additionally, language use in the first flight of a crew pairing was associated with performance in subsequent flights.

1 Communication in Aviation

NASA researchers analyzed the causes of jet transport accidents and incidents between 1968 and 1976 (Cooper, White & Lauber 1980; Murphy 1980 as cited in Cooper et al.) and concluded that pilot error was more likely to reflect failures in team communication and coordination than deficiencies in technical proficiency. In fact, human factors issues related to interpersonal communication have been implicated in approximately 70% to 80% of all accidents over the past 20 years. Correspondingly, over 70% of the first 28,000 reports made to NASA's Aviation Safety Reporting System (which allows pilots to confidentially report aviation incidents) were found to be related to communication problems (Connell 1995). Communication is critical in order for cockpit crewmembers to share a "mental model", or common understanding of the nature of events relevant to the safety and efficiency of the flight. This is not to say that

---

[1] Research reported here was conducted with the support of FAA Grants 92-G-017, 99-G-004, and a grant from the Daimler-Benz Stiftung, Robert Helmreich, Principal Investigator. Thanks are due to research assistants Kathrine Kirby, Anne-Marie Deville, Renee Mauldin, C. J. Winkler, and Dolly Dimke for their many "less than exciting" hours of transcription, and to John A. Wilhelm and Steven C. Predmore for their assistance in acquiring the simulator data and maintaining the archival database.

effective communication can overcome inadequate technical flying proficiency, but rather the contrary: that good "stick & rudder" skills can not overcome the adverse effects of poor communication. Ruffell Smith's (1979) landmark full-mission simulator study showed that crew performance was more closely associated with the quality of crew communication than with the technical proficiency of individual pilots or increased physiological arousal as a result of higher environmental workload. No differences were found between the severity of the errors made by effective and ineffective crews, rather, it was the ability of the effective crews to communicate that kept their errors from developing into undesirable outcomes. Interestingly, such findings are not unique to aviation, as similar results have emerged in other safety-critical systems such as surgical operating rooms and medical intensive care units. Medical researchers have found evidence that it is not the technical or medical proficiency of healthcare providers, but rather the quality of their interactions which predicts outcomes (Young, Charns, Daley, Forbes, Henderson & Khuri 1997; Knaus, Draper, Wagner & Zimmerman 1986; Donchin, Gopher, Olin, Badihi, Biesky, Sprung, Pizov & Cotev 1995).

1.1 Language in the Cockpit

Researchers at NASA (Kanki 1995) have reported that the interdependent nature of the cockpit crew requires the effective use of language to issue commands, acknowledge commands, conduct briefings, perform standard callouts, state intentions, ask questions, and convey information (Figure 1).

> **Language is used in the Cockpit to:**
>
> - Issue commands
> - Acknowledge commands
> - Conduct briefings
> - Perform standard callouts
> - State intentions
> - Ask questions
> - Convey information

Figure 1: Using language in the cockpit

Historically, the role of language use in communication processes has been neglected, but researchers have recognized the need for a deeper understanding of the workings and characteristics of language (Orasanu & Fischer 1991; Cushing 1997). There is a growing body of Cockpit Voice Recorder (CVR) data from high fidelity simulations, and from commercial aviation accidents – both of which detail the verbal interactions of crewmembers. Contemporary methods of content-coding simulation and/or accident transcripts have provided valuable insights into communication processes (e.g., Orasanu & Fischer 1991; Predmore 1991).

An automated system of linguistic analysis that could quickly and efficiently identify patterns in communication as well as provide a new level of insight into language use in aviation, would be a valuable tool to complement current methods of investigation. To this end, the present research examined the use of a computer-based linguistic analysis of aviation communication, in addition to the relatively more common analysis of content through the micro-coding technique.

1.1.1 Language Analyses

Research conducted in the language lab of Professor James W. Pennebaker at The University of Texas at Austin has shown that linguistic styles can be considered individual difference markers, i.e., individuals appear to have a distinct "language-use fingerprint" which is relatively stable across time and situations (Pennebaker & King 1999). He has identified language dimensions to be internally consistent, and modestly correlated to objective and self-reported health and performance measures at rates comparable to or greater than traditional trait markers of personality such as the "big five" (McCrae & Costa 1987).

In order to provide an efficient and practical method for studying the various emotional, cognitive, structural, and process components present in individuals' language use, Pennebaker and Francis developed and validated a computer-based text analysis program called Linguistic Inquiry and Word Count (LIWC: Francis & Pennebaker 1993; Pennebaker & Francis 1999). In essence, LIWC analyzes written or transcribed verbal text files by looking for dictionary matches to words in the text file. LIWC does this on a word by word basis by calculating the percentage of words in the text that match a particular dimension of language. Standard linguistic dimensions include categories such as word count, sentence punctuation, 1st person plural (we, our, us), negations (no, never, not), and assents (yes, OK, mmhmm). Dimensions of psychological processes include categories such as positive emotions (happy, pretty, good), anger (hate, resent, pissed), and cognitive processes (cause, know, effect, maybe, would, should). Other categories include swear words, nonfluencies (uh, er, um), and fillers (you know, I mean). In addition to using LIWC, micro-coding of content was conducted using a method pioneered by The University of Texas Human Factors Research Project (Predmore 1991). Using the micro-coding technique, individual utterances were classified into action-decision sequences (ADS), which are task-related communication categories centered on events and issues requiring coordinated action among crew members. One such category is Problem Solving: communications dealing with corrective action, completing abnormal checklists, dumping fuel, etc. Problem solving communications are the verbal embodiment of threat and error management in the cockpit, which is currently accepted as the focus of flight safety assessments and training initiatives endorsed by the United Nations (Helmreich, Merritt & Wilhelm 1999; Helmreich, Klinect & Wilhelm, in press).

1.2 The Simulator Study

The cockpit communication data discussed here were collected at the NASA-Ames Research Center during an investigation into the effects of captain personality on crew performance (see Chidester, Kanki, Foushee, Dickinson & Bowles 1990 for a detailed description). These data involved a three person crew (captains, first officers, and second officers) flying a simulated Boeing 727 during a 5 segment flight over two days. Transcripts were made available for 12 crews across the last four flight segments (A, B, C, and D), and for 14 crews for the last two flight segments (C and D). Segments A and C were routine (low workload), and segments B and D were abnormal (high workload). As part of the data collection process in the original simulator study, an expert pilot observer was present in the simulator. Flight outcome data regarding individual performance, individual errors, and individual communication skill were recorded by this observer for each pilot by segment.

Analyses were performed using LIWC and micro-coding to codify the data from each transcript into a database delineating crews, flight segments, and crewmember positions (captains, first officers, second officers). To classify ADS utterances a 727 captain was trained in the techniques of micro-coding and assigned ADS categories to every utterance of the 14 crews for which segment C and segment D data were available.

1.3 Workload and Performance

In investigations of cockpit communication variables, it is important to understand the critical role of workload on pilot performance. Fortunately, for the flying public, the vast majority (75–80%) of cockpit crew performance can be classified as *good* or *outstanding*[2] during routine flights with normal workload. During abnormal flights, however, the proportion of cockpit crews rated as *good* decreases and the proportion rated as *outstanding* increases (see Figure 2.). Similarly, very few crews (0–1.5%) are rated as *poor* performers during routine flights, but there is a significant rise in the proportion *poor* performers in abnormal flights. In other words, when workload is high, the proportion of crews rated as "good performers" decreases and the proportion of crews rated as *outstanding* or as *poor* increases. These data are not inconsistent with arousal theory, which suggests that some pilots would perform better under stressful conditions than under normal conditions, whereas others will succumb to the stress resulting in worse performance (as a function of individual differences).

[2] These ratings refers to the 4-point scale: 1=Poor, 2=Minimal, 3=Good and 4=Outstanding.

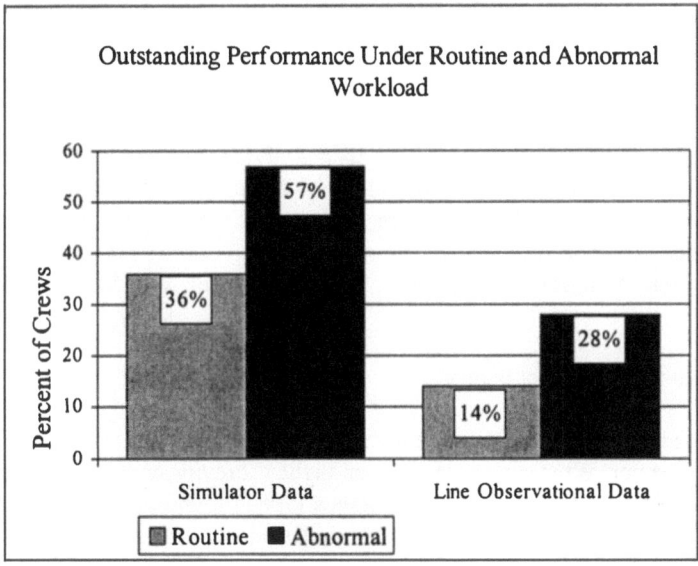

Figure 2: Performance differences as a function of workload

The data in the above figure come from the present simulator study and an archive of line observations which is maintained by the LOSA Collaborative at The University of Texas at Austin. Both the simulator data and the observations of regularly scheduled flights (n=3,241) show that the percentage of crews who are rated as "outstanding performers" is higher during abnormal[3] flights than during routine flights. Accordingly, research into cockpit communication should carefully consider the role of workload relative to outstanding performance:

Unlike the data typically derived from accident and incident studies, simulator studies and line observations provide researchers with examples of outstanding performance. These "superior examples" help researchers to understand what pilots do well, rather than focusing on what happens when pilots do poorly. In the present study, we pay particularly close attention to the language use of pilots with outstanding performance, in an effort to better understand the components of effective cockpit communication.

---

[3] In the simulator study, abnormal flight scenarios were designed to be physically and mentally taxing on the entire crew. For the line observational data, a 4-point complexity scale (1=low complexity ... 4=high complexity) was used to classify flights rated 1 or 2 as "routine" whereas flights rated 3 or a 4 were considered "abnormal".

2 Context of the Current Study

Foushee (1984) observed that most of the research studies of team performance have ignored communication as a process variable moderating the relationship between input (e.g. team size, team structure, composition) and output factors (e.g., quality, errors, efficiency). The data analyses reported here were investigations of the structure (i.e., linguistic) and content of individual crewmember utterances. These analyses explore the use of language as an individual differences variable in cockpit communication processes. For a more detailed explanation of the statistical analyses, please see Sexton & Helmreich 1999.

2.1 Number of Words Spoken

A fundamental aspect of communication is *quantity*, or how much is verbalized by the speaker. What makes for a safer flight – brevity or verbosity? In a previous simulator study, Foushee and Manos (1981) found that better performing crews communicated more overall. This relationship between performance and quantity of verbal communication was also documented in a Bell Aeronautics Company study in 1962 (Siskel & Flexman) and replicated in Foushee, Lauber, Beatge & Acomb (1986). In addition, there is some evidence for differences in quantity of communication as a function of workload and cockpit position. Veinott and Irwin (1995) reported simulator data demonstrating that captains talked more than first officers and that there was more communication during the abnormal phases than the normal phases. Taken together, results from previous studies indicate that the amount of communication may be associated with performance, workload and the crewmember position of the speaker.

For the purposes of the current study, the quantity of language used in the cockpit was readily captured by the LIWC category WORDCOUNT (overall number of words spoken). In general, crews communicated about twice to three times as much during abnormal flight segments as during routine flights segments[4] (Figure 3).

---

[4] The same pattern of results was also present in the number of utterances as analyzed by the micro-coding technique.

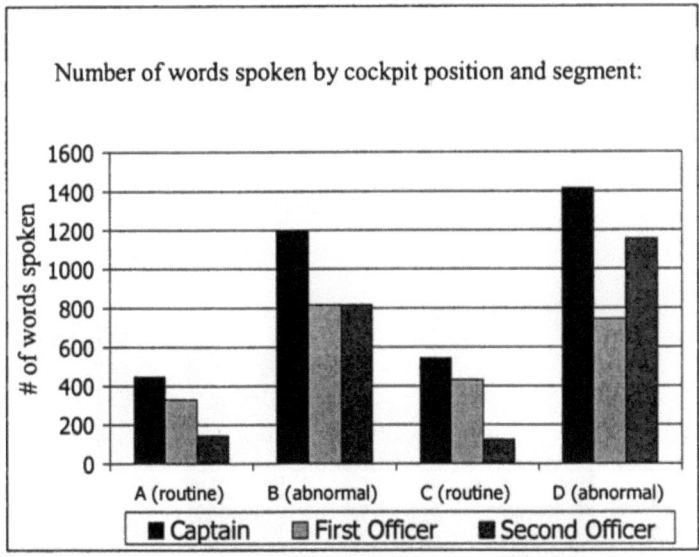

Figure 3: Number of words spoken by cockpit position and flight segment

The number of words spoken was associated with higher performance and lower rates of error. In other words, when it comes to cockpit communication – it appears to be the case that more is better. Pilots spoke more during high workload flights than during routine workload flights, and captains spoke more than first officers and second officers. Individuals are likely to communicate more during periods of high workload due to the inherent multi-tasking involved in flight deck management.

2.2 Crewmember Familiarity

In a review of major accidents from 1978 to 1990, the National Transportation Safety Board (1994) found that 73% of commercial aviation accidents occur on the first day of a crew paring (relative to the baserates of 7–30% of flights that are an initial crew pairing) and that 44% of accidents occur on the first flight of a crew paring (baserates 3–10%). These results have been interpreted as an indication of crewmember familiarity with one another, such that the more crewmembers fly together, the better they will be able to anticipate and respond to each others' actions. Foushee, Lauber, Beatge & Acomb (1986) found conceptually similar results, such that fatigued crewmembers who had previous experience flying together outperformed well-rested crews who had no previous experience flying together. This notion of crewmember familiarity may manifest itself as a function of crewmembers referring to themselves in the first person plural. The first person plural is a linguistic dimension captured by the LIWC category WE (e.g., we, our, us). In the present study, a pattern of increasing use of the first person plural emerged across the four simulated flights (see Figure 4). Perhaps this indicates an increasing sense of familiarity among the crewmembers or an increase in their team perspective.

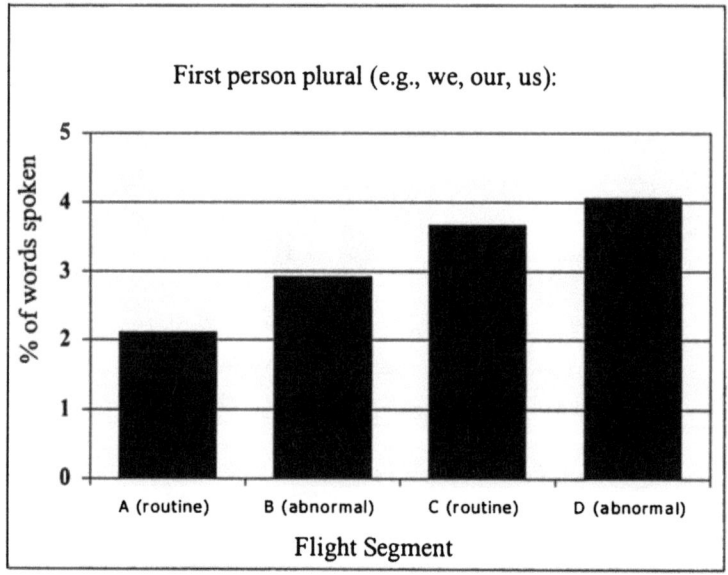

Figure 4: First person plural by flight segment

In the past, the use of the first person plural has been interpreted as a collective or team perspective by the speaker (McGreevy 1996; White & Lippitt 1960). Recent research by Driskell, Salas & Johnston (1999) found that team perspective was a significant predictor of team performance. In the present study, the use of first person plural by a pilot was positively correlated to performance, and negatively correlated to the number of errors. Use of the first person plural also appeared to differ as a function of position the cockpit (see Figure 5.). In a pattern similar to the cockpit position results of WORDCOUNT, use of the first person plural was most common in captains, followed by first officers and second officers. It could be the case that the hierarchy of cockpit positions is what dictates the extent of first person plural use by a given crewmember.

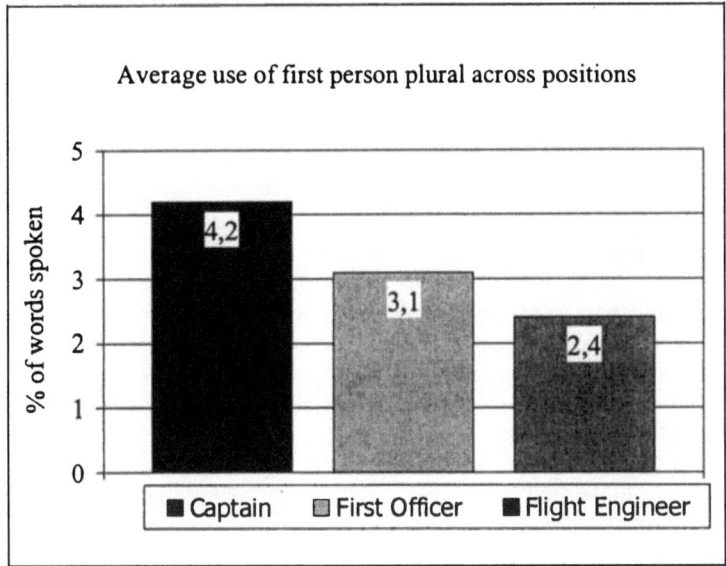

Figure 5: First person plural by cockpit position

2.3 Cockpit Position Differences

Further differences as a function of crewmember position were found in the LIWC dimension which counted the number of questions asked. In fact, captains were significantly less likely to ask questions than first officers and second officers (Figure 6).

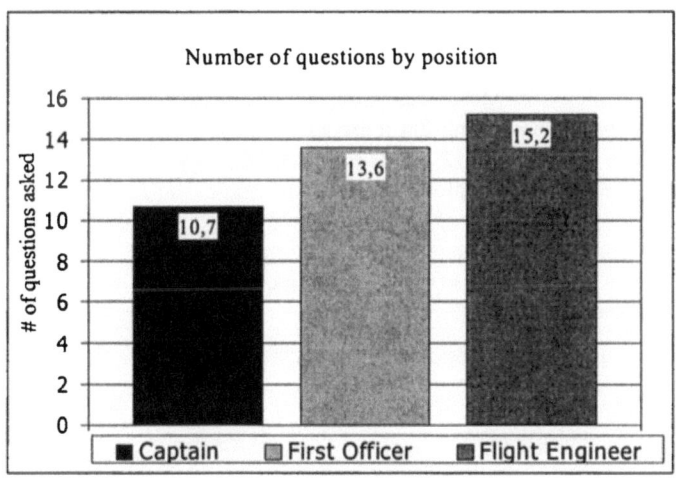

Figure 6: Number of questions asked by cockpit position

In addition to position differences, the number of questions asked in the initial flight was positively correlated to performance in subsequent flights. In other words, crews who asked a lot of questions initially (thereby clarifying uncertainties) had higher subsequent performance than crews who did not ask questions. Asking questions was not correlated to performance within the same flight, rather, initial inquiry was correlated to subsequent performance. It appears to be the case that clarifying uncertainties is best accomplished in an initial flight rather than waiting to ask questions later.

In general, WORDCOUNT, WE and the number of questions indicated that language may serve as an indicator of status, as the pattern of results was always different for the captain versus the other crewmembers. Captains consistently used more words, used more first person plural, and asked fewer questions than the other two crewmembers. Captains also used more present tense than first officers and second officers.

Individual language use was moderately to highly associated with individual performance, individual error rates, and ratings of individual communication skills. In sum, WORDCOUNT, first person plural, and number of questions asked in the first flight were positively related to performance and communication, but negatively related to rates of error. A similar pattern of results was found for use of the present tense and discrepancy words "would, should and could." Present tense usage is probably a marker of verbalization, such that pilots who verbalize their actions more, use more present tense, and that linguistic dimension is related to flight outcomes. Pilot use of discrepancies could be an indicator of linguistic politeness in the cockpit, such that better performance is associated with pilots who say, e.g., "we should get out the checklist," versus "get out the checklist." An overview of the linguistic results related to performance is outlined in Figure 7 below.

Linguistic results

As the rates of each of the following language categories increased, positive flight outcomes (better performance and fewer errors) increased
– Word Count (# words spoken)
– First person plural (we, our, us)
– Questions (# of questions asked)
– Present Tense (is, flying, turning, dialing, etc.)
– Discrepancies (would, should, could, etc.)

Figure 7: Overview of linguistic results related to performance

2.4 Initial Language Use Predicts Subsequent Performance

Prior research has demonstrated that shared mental models and predictable patterns of behavior are imperative to laying the groundwork for effective teamwork and communication in the cockpit. Ginnett (1987) has shown that initial crewmember interactions set the tone for the team and can predict subsequent team performance. Similarly, Hines (1998) demonstrated that the best predictors of line performance are captain leadership and pre-flight briefing content. In this vein, one of the goals of the current study was to investigate the extent to which initial language use is related to subsequent performance and error ratings. In fact, the relationships between language use and flight outcome measures were strongest between segment A language use, and subsequent (B, C, and D) performance and error measures. This is indeed similar to the relationship between initial interpersonal interactions and subsequent performance identified by Ginnett (1987) and Hines (1998).

2.5 Micro-coding of Problem Solving Utterances

Problem Solving communications regard corrective actions such as completing abnormal checklists and dumping fuel. In the decade that has passed since the original micro-coding investigation of Steven Predmore at The University of Texas Human Factors Research Project, very little attention has been focused upon the content code of *problem solving*. Recently, the commercial aviation industry has embraced the notion of assessing pilot ability to manage threats and errors in order to achieve safe and efficient flight, and problem solving communications are the verbal manifestation of threat and error management. Figure 8. below provides eight separate examples of problem solving utterances from the current study.

> **Problem Solving Utterance Examples**
> - "So you might want to determine what they want us to do if we lose ATC communications."
> - "And if we execute a missed approach, we have two procedures we could follow."
> - "Okay, ask him, uh, what kind of weather trends he has got going there, if it is going down."
> - "Okay, what do we have for gas?"
> - "You can tell them, if you get a chance to talk tell them, we got a hydraulic problem."
> - "I don't want to dump any fuel, in case we might need it."
> - "Got a little bit of cross wind, not much, 240 at 8 I believe he said,"
> - "I want to see if that gear works early enough, though."

Figure 8: Examples of problem solving utterances

As the above examples illustrate, *problem solving* communications are task-related communications regarding the management of threats and errors during a flight. Perhaps not surprisingly, flights with higher workload appeared to have more problems which needed to be "solved", such that there were many more problem solving utterances during abnormal flights than during routine flights (Figure 9).

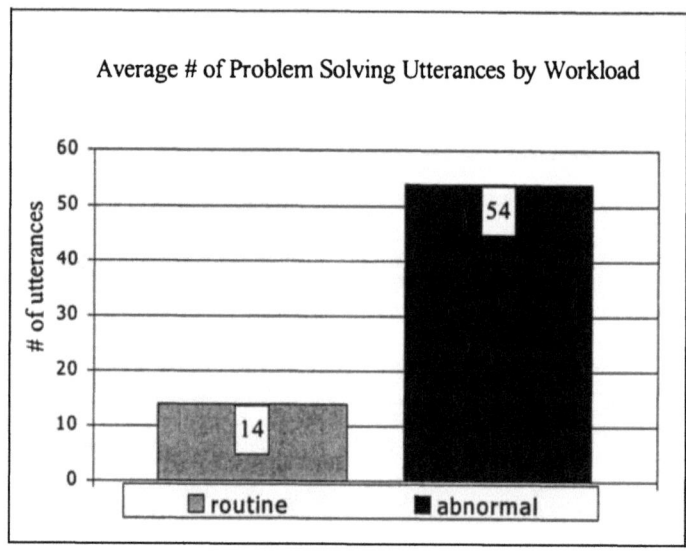

Figure 9: Number of problem solving utterances by workload

However, there were important differences in the use of problem solving utterances as a function of pilot performance. Recall that in the earlier discussion of performance and workload in the cockpit, one of the critical areas around which to focus research investigations is upon what effective pilots do well (rather than what ineffective pilots do poorly). Problem solving communications are a prime example of what distinguishes effective performance from ineffective performance. For example, captains with outstanding performance used problem solving utterances seven to eight times more often than their poor performing counterparts. Furthermore, there were no differences in how *outstanding* captains used problem solving utterances as a function of workload. Outstanding captains consistently devoted a third of their utterances to problem solving, whether it was a routine or an abnormal flight. These results are illustrated in Figure 10 below.

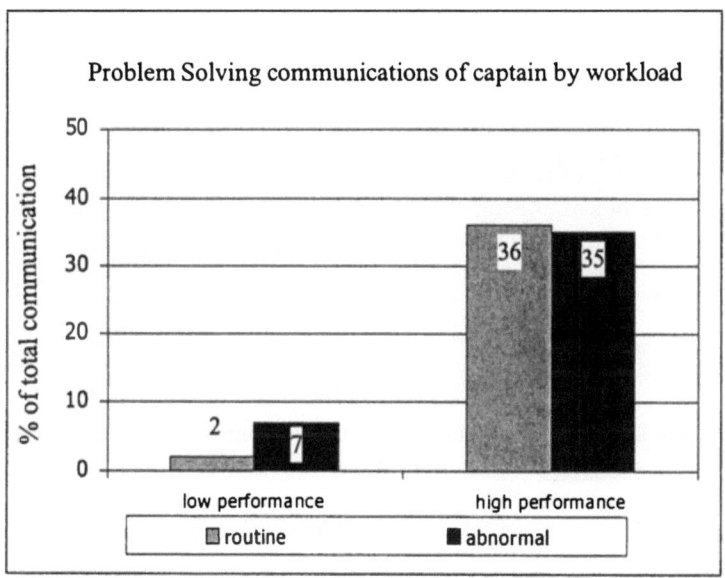

Figure 10: Captain problem solving utterances by workload and performance

In fact, the more frequent use of problem solving utterances was not unique to outstanding captains – outstanding first officers and second officers used problems solving utterances in approximately one third of their communications overall (see Figure 11 below).

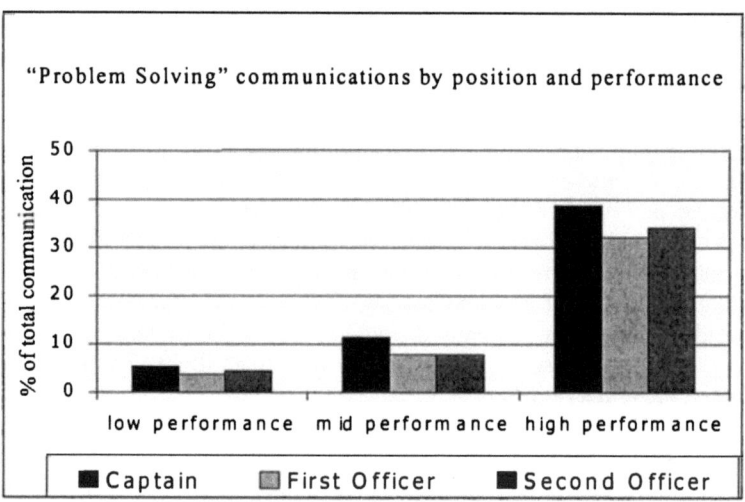

Figure 11: Captain problem solving utterances by position and performance

The above pattern of results is striking in that there is a substantial difference in the use of problem solving utterances between outstanding pilots and both average and poor pilots. The best pilots simply talk more about their task related problems and how to solve them – the essence of threat and error management.

3 Discussion

Why should language use be considered as a variable of interest in crew factors? Language is a coping mechanism in that it helps individuals lessen and manage both the causes and the effects of stress. This is perhaps the reason that there are links between pilot language use and flight outcome measures in the present study.

Language use is dynamic, as it is sensitive to both workload and position, and varies systematically with flight outcome measures. This is in contrast to a more static measure such as "paper and pencil" measurements of personality, which are stable across time and situation. Furthermore, research into language use has the potential to yield a clearer understanding of thought processes involved during communication. Linking "online communication" to personality test results collected at a different time is difficult, if at all possible. Such personality tests are also difficult to link to pilot communication captured by accident CVR's. In contrast, LIWC and content coding variables are easily extracted from CVR transcripts, and could potentially add a new level of insight into what took place in the minds of the crewmembers.

Without making a causal statement, it is important to consider the potential implications that language use could have for training. Perhaps the use of more effective language styles is trainable, whereas personality interventions (aside from selection) are generally futile. The findings of Siegel & Federman (1973), indicate that it is possible to isolate aspects of effective communication and to train those aspects successfully (in this case using anti-submarine helicopter crews). Chidester, Helmreich, Gregorich & Geis (1990) have assessed the trainability of specific behaviors and have found that human factors training produces measurable improvements in communication skills.

A possible limitation of the present study is that these results may not generalize to two-person crews, where the social structure is conceptually different from the more hierarchical, and more formal three-person crews. Also, small sample size is a limiting factor in this study, and these results need to be replicated as a test of their generalizability. Despite these limitations, the results reported here, were significant, consistent, interpretable, and based on a large number of utterances (over 10,000) from the small number of crews.

The performance and error outcomes of cockpit crews are multiply determined, and language use is just one of the many group process factors which can impact flight outcomes. The results of this exploratory study indicate that the language use of pilots varies as a function of who is talking (captain, first officer, or second officer) and as a function of workload. The relationships between the LIWC/problem solving categories and flight outcome measures of safety such as performance, error, and communication skill serve as a form of convergent validity for the utility of linguistic and content analyses. The problem solving results also indicate that the current human factors emphasis on threat and error management in the cockpit is warranted and justifiable.

The current study replicated findings of previous research and provided additional levels of insight into how pilots use language and what they communicate relative to their performance, position, and workload. These results are important because poor communication is commonly equated to an obstinate captain or unassertive first officer, whereas the current study demonstrates specific aspects of language use relevant to flight outcome and to workload. Cockpit communication is a rich area of study for language investigators, and it has been relatively underresearched given the critical role it plays in flight safety.

References

Cannon-Bowers, J. A., Tannenbaum, S. I., Salas, E. & Volpe C. E. (1995): "Defining team competencies and establishing team training requirements". In: R. Guzzo & E. Salas (Eds.): Team effectiveness and decision making in organizations. (pp. 333–380). San Francisco: Jossey Bass.

Chidester, T. R., Helmreich, R. L., Gregorich, S. E. & Geis, C. (1990): "Pilot personality and crew coordination: Implications for training and selection". International Journal of Aviation Psychology, 1. 23–42.

Chidester, T. R., Kanki, B. G., Foushee, H. C., Dickinson, C. L. & Bowles, S. V. (1990): Personality factors in flight operations: Volume 1. Leader characteristics and crew performance in a full-mission air transport simulation (NASA Technical Memorandum 102259). Moffett Field, CA: NASA-Ames Research Center.

Connell, L. (1995): "Pilot and controller communications issues". In: B. G. Kanki & O. V. Prinzo (Eds.): Proceedings of the Methods & Metrics of Voice Communication Workshop.

Cooper, G. E., White, M. D. & Lauber, J. K. (Eds.) (1980): "Resource management on the flightdeck: Proceedings of a NASA/Industry workshop" (NASA CP-2120). Moffett Field, CA: NASA-Ames Research Center.

Cushing, S. (1997): "Language differences in aviation communication: Problems and solutions". In: P. Quigley & P. McElwain (Eds.): Proceedings of the Aviation Communication: A Multi-Cultural Forum.

Donchin, Y., Gopher, D., Olin, M., Badihi, Y., Biesky, M., Sprung, C. L., Pizov, R. & Cotev, S. (1995): "A look into the nature and causes of human errors in the intensive care unit." Critical Care Medicine, 23. 294–300.

Driskell, J. E., Salas, E. & Johnston, J. (1999): "Does stress lead to a loss of team perspective?" Group Dynamics: Theory, Research, and Practice, 3 (4). 291–302.

Foushee, H. C. (1984): "Dyads and Triads at 35,000 feet: Factors affecting group processes and aircrew performance". American Psychologist, 39 (8). 885–893.

Foushee, H. C. & Helmreich, R. L. (1989): "Group interaction and Flight Crew performance". In: E. L. Wiener & D. C. Nagel (Eds.): Human Factors in Modern Aviation. San Diego: Academic Press.

Foushee, H. C., Lauber, J. K., Beatge, M. M. & Acomb, D. B. (1986): "Crew Performance as a function of exposure to high density, short-haul duty cycles". (NASA Technical Memorandum 88322). Moffet Field, CA: NASA-Ames Research Center.

Foushee, H. C. & Manos, K. L. (1981): "Information transfer within the cockpit: Problems in intracockpit communications". In: C. E. Billings & E. S. Cheaney (Eds.): Information transfer problems in the aviation system (NASA TP-1875). Moffet Field, CA: NASA-Ames Research Center.

Francis, M. E. & Pennebaker, J. W. (1993): LIWC: Linguistic Inquiry and Word Count. Technical Report. Dallas, TX: Southern Methodist University.

Ginnett, R. C. (1987): First Encounters of the Close Kind: The Formation Process of Airline Flight Crews. Yale University: Doctoral dissertation.

Helmreich, R. L., Klinect, J. R. & Wilhelm J. A. (in press): "Models of threat, error, and CRM in flight operations". In: Proceedings of the Tenth International Symposium on Aviation Psychology: The Ohio State University.

Helmreich, R. L., Merritt, A. C. & Wilhelm, J. A. (1999): "The evolution of Crew Resource Management training in commercial aviation". International Journal of Aviation Psychology, 9 (1). 19–32.

Hines, W. E. (1998): Teams and technology: Flight crew performance in standard and automated aircraft. The University of Texas at Austin: Unpublished doctoral dissertation.

Kanki, B. G. (1995): "A Training Perspective: Enhancing Team Performance Through Effective Communication". In: B. G. Kanki & O. V. Prinzo (Eds.): Proceedings of the Methods & Metrics of Voice Communication Workshop.

Knaus, W. A., Draper, E. A., Wagner, D. P. & Zimmerman, J. E. (1986): "An evaluation of outcome from intensive care in major medical centers". Annals of Internal Medicine, 104 (3). 410–418.

McCrae, R. R. & Costa P. T. Jr. (1987): "Validation of the five factor model across instruments and observers". Journal of Personality and Social Psychology, 52. 81–90.

NTSB (1994): A review of flight-crew-involved major accidents of U.S. air carriers, 1978–1990. National Transportation Safety Board Safety Study, Washington D.C.

McGreevy, M. W. (1996): "Reporter Concerns in 300 Mode-Related Incident Reports from NASA's Aviation Safety Reporting System". (NASA Technical Memorandum 110413). Moffett Field, CA: NASA-Ames Research Center.

Orasanu, J. & Fischer, U. (1991): "Information transfer and shared mental models for decision making". In: R. S. Jenson (Ed.): Proceedings of the Sixth International Symposium of Aviation Psychology. Columbus, Ohio: The Ohio State University.

Pennebaker, J. W. & Francis, M. E. (1999): Linguistic Inquiry and Word Count (LIWC). Mahmah, N. J.: Erlbaum Publishing.

Pennebaker J. W. & King, L. A. (1999): Linguistic styles: Language use as an individual difference. Manuscript submitted for publication.

Predmore, S. C. (1991): "Microcoding of communications in accident investigation: Crew coordination in United 811 and United 232". In: R. S. Jenson (Ed.): Proceedings of the Sixth International Symposium of Aviation Psychology (pp. 350–355). Columbus, Ohio: The Ohio State University.

Ruffell Smith, H. P. (1979): "A simulator study of the interaction of pilot workload with errors, vigilance, an decisions". (NASA Technical Memorandum 78482). Moffett Field, CA: NASA-Ames Research Center.

Sexton, J. B. & Helmreich, R. L. (1999): "Analyzing cockpit communication: The links between language, performance, error and workload". In: Proceedings of the Tenth International Symposium on Aviation Psychology: The Ohio State University.

Siegel, I. & Federman, P. J. (1973): "Communication Content Training as an Ingredient in Effective Team Performance". Ergonomics, 16 (4). 403–416.

Siskel, M. & Flexman, R. (1962): Study of effectiveness of a flight simulator for training complex aircrew skills. Bell Aeronautics Company.

Veinott, E. S. & Irwin, C. M. (1995): "Communication methodology issues in aviation simulation research". In: B. G. Kanki & O. V. Prinzo (Eds.): Proceedings of the Methods & Metrics of Voice Communication Workshop.

White, R. & Lippitt, R. (1960): "Leader Behavior and Member Reaction in Three 'Social Climates'". Autocracy and Democracy. New York: Harper.

Young, G. J., Charns, M. P., Daley, J., Forbes, M. G., Henderson, W. & Khuri, S. F. (1997): "Best practices for managing surgical services: the role of coordination". Health Care Management Review, 22. 72–81.

Austin, Texas USA   J. Bryan Sexton and Robert L. Helmreich

The University of Texas at Austin, Department of Psychology, The University of Texas Human Factors Research Project, Room 4.110, The Seay Building, Mail Code A8000, 108 East Dean Keeton St., Austin, Texas 78713, helmreich@psy.utexas.edu; sexton@psy.utexas.edu

Group Interaction in the Cockpit: Some Linguistic Factors[1]

Manfred Krifka, Silka Martens, and Florian Schwarz

For a number of years it has been recognized that the social dynamics of group interaction is an import factor in the origin of accidents and in the way how accidents or accident-prone situations are handled in aviation (cf. Helmreich 1997a, 1997b). Factors related to interpersonal communication have been implicated in up to 80% of all aviation accidents over the past 20 years. As a reaction to this, Crew Resource Management (CRM) has been developed with the goal of rating and improving crew performance in aviation and in other fields in which professional groups interact in situations of high taskload and potential risk (cf. Helmreich ea. 1999). As far as this can be estimated at all, installing CRM techniques in the major American and European airlines has resulted in a definite improvement in the safety of commercial aviation. In spite of this success of CRM, practitioners in the field feel that, beyond the general social dynamics of group interaction, there might be potential problems relating to language and communication in such settings.

In this article, we first summarize some aspects of previous research in this area. Then we report findings from a project that one of us, Manfred Krifka, has carried out, using transcripts of flight simulator sessions with pilots of a commercial American airline. We will discuss some of the problems of this project. Finally, we describe an ongoing continuation of that project that uses flight simulator sessions with pilots of a commercial German airline.

1 Previous Research

Communication in situations with high task load and its problems can be described from various angles. In particular, the following two perspectives come to mind: First, we can investigate properties of the language that serves as the medium of communication. Certain features of language may be detrimental to the goals of a group in situations of high task load, and they may be improved

---

[1] Work on this project is supported by the Gottfried Daimler- und Karl Benz- Stiftung, in the context of the project *Group Interaction in High Risk Environments*. We thank the members of this project for extensive discussion, especially Bryan Sexton for providing the data for the first part of the project, Dagmar Silberstein for help with discussing and analyzing the data, and Gerhard Fahnenbruck for the ingenious design of the simulator situation of the second project and for providing us with the data.

by carefully designing appropriate terminology and rules of language use. Secondly, we can investigate whether the social structure in the group leads to certain biases in the communication within the group that impede proper group interaction. Professionals then could be trained to recognize these biases and their danger to the flow of information within the group. In the following, we will describe two prominent examples of these types of research in the general area of aviation.

1.1 Problems of language

As for potential problems of language, investigations of accident reports in aviation have indeed uncovered that structural properties of language can lead to misunderstandings, especially in situations in which the cognitive resources of participants are limited because of high task load.

Cushing (1994) has collected a number of cases, from reports of the National Transportation Safety Board (NTSB) and especially from informal reports of the pilots newsletter Callback, in which properties of language and language use caused accidents or near-accidents in aviation. Typically, such cases arise because the cognitive apparatus of the pilots is preoccupied and overloaded with paying attention to problems such as equipment failure or adverse weather conditions; also, communication can be severely impeded in the noisy cockpit or in the radio talk with the air traffic control (ATC).

Cushing identifies several types of cases in which structural properties of language, and aviation language in particular, may lead to problems or actually have led to problems. A particularly important problem is ambiguity of language. Ambiguity was arguably involved in the most severe accident in commercial aviation, the collision of two airplanes at the Tenerife airport in 1977. In this event, the pilot of the starting KLM plane reported to the ATC 'We are now at takeoff', and got the reply 'OK ... Stand by for takeoff', which was partly masked by noise. Clearly, the pilot meant to say 'we are now on the takeoff roll', or 'we are now taking off', whereas ATC understood it as 'we are waiting at the takeoff point'. There are a number of such word ambiguities or structural ambiguities in aviation language – Cushing mentions, for example, the verb hold, which means in aviation parlance 'stop what you are now doing', but in ordinary English also, 'continue what you are now doing', or the use of PD as 'pilot's discretion' or 'profile descent'. While such instances of ambiguity could be eliminated by improving the terminology of aviation English, others are more deeply rooted in the natural language, English, on which it is based. For example, Cushing reports a case that nearly led a midair collision that was caused by the phonological similarity of two and to: A pilot misunderstood the command climb two five zero as climb to five zero.

In addition to lexical ambiguities, and often in connection with them, structural ambiguities of language play a role, and it is difficult to see how they could be eliminated or even reduced. Cushing mentions a case in which back on the power could be parsed as [back on] [the power] or as [back] [on the power].

Perhaps even more important than lexical and structural ambiguities are ambiguities that are related to the use of pronouns and other anaphoric devices of language, such as contextual ellipses. One could imagine trying to avoid such anaphoric expressions if possible; but on the other hand they have developed to make human language more efficient. A rule like "avoid pronouns" or "avoid ellipsis" would very likely be counter-productive in making communication too verbose and slowing it down. However, it is feasible that awareness of the potential dangers of pronoun use and ellipsis could improve communication in the cockpit.

1.2 Problems of Communication

In addition to the problems that in one way or other relate to structural problems of language and its relation to situations in the world, there are specific problems of communication in the cockpit (see, e.g., Sexton & Helmreich 2000; Nevile 2001; Silberstein 2001). These can arise, again, due to overload of the cognitive system of the pilots in situations of high taskload or danger, or because of the specific social situation in the cockpit with one experienced pilot with higher status and legal power, and one typically less experienced first officer with lower status (and, formerly, a flight engineer with yet fewer rights and lesser status).

Problems stemming from the asymmetric social situation in the cockpit have been analyzed by Goguen & Linde (1983), see also Linde (1988). In a detailed analysis of NTSB transcripts, Goguen & Linde showed: (i) Speech acts by the First Officer are often mitigated, that is, more indirect, and often belittling potential or real problems, than speech acts by the Captain. (ii) Speech acts that do not lead to their intended effect are more often mitigated than speech acts that do. Goguen & Linde explicitly discuss the United Airlines accident in Portland of 1978, in which the officers failed to communicate the growing emergency of the fuel situation to the captain. For example, when the captain requests from the engineer a projection for the fuel situation for the next fifteen minutes, which he estimates to be 3000 or 4000 pounds, the engineer answers: "Not enough. Fifteen minutes is gonna – really run us low on fuel here." When, later, the captain reports the fuel situation by showing a thousand or better, the first officer challenges this just by: "I don't think it's in there." When the fuel is, as a matter of fact, nearly used up, the flight engineer reports: "Not very much more fuel." Five minutes later, the engines stopped.

Goguen & Linde analyzed flight recorder tapes of real accidents using analytic categories derived from speech act theory. The main interest was on mitigation and aggravation of speech acts, on speech acts of planning and explanation, and on the topic success or topic failure of speech acts. The speech act categories used were rather coarse. Goguen & Linde distinguish the following types: Requests (which includes orders, requests, suggestions, and questions), reports (which includes simple reports, supporting and challenging reports, and psycho-ostensive reports), declarations (like declarations of emergency) and acknowledgements. The data, which were from real accidents as transcribed from flight recorders by the NTSB, certainly were authentic; however, the type and development of the accidents were naturally very different.

2 The First Project Phase

2.1 General Description

In 1999 one of us (Manfred Krifka, then University of Texas at Austin) started a project of investigating the fine structure of linguistic communication in the cockpit. The general aim was to look at properties of language use, in the general tradition of Linde and Goguen. However, we intended to use a more fine-grained and linguistically informed set of categories. Secondly, the data investigated should be more comparable, which meant investigating flight simulator transcripts of simulated flights that follow a comparable scenario. The project was carried out with Carrie Clarady as an assistant. It was supported by the Gottfried Daimler- and Carl Benz-Stiftung within the setting of the GIHRE project. The data we worked with were transcripts of flight simulator recordings on B-727 aircraft of a study on the effect of captain personality on crew performance carried out by NASA-Ames Research Center in 1987 (see Chidester ea. (1990) for a description). The transcripts of the video and audio recordings were done by Robert L. Helmreich and J. Bryan Sexton of the Texas Aerospace Crew Research Project.

The data available consisted of 17 transcribed simulation flights. The flights followed roughly a similar scenario, even though the reactions of the pilots could lead to quite different situations. There were five segments to each flight. A first segment was, unfortunately, not recorded; the four following segments were labeled A, B, C and D. Segments A and C were segments with, roughly, medium task load; segments B and D were segments with high task load. Segment A consisted of a climbout from San Francisco Airport and a descent and landing into Sacramento Airport. Segment B consisted of a descent and landing at Los Angeles Airport, with simulated events like a jammed stabilizer and low oil pressure. Segment C simulated a descent to Sacramento Airport, with a missed approach. In Segment D, the plain was diverted to San Jose Airport, with simulated events like hydraulic malfunction and a split flap malfunction. The performance of the crews was independently rated. In the limited time available for this project (April 1999 to July 2000) we could investigate altogether 5 flight simulator sessions completely, were we picked the two best-rated crews and the three worst-rated crews. Altogether, we investigated 6900 "thought units", or units of speech as provided by the transcribers, which we tried to follow in order to secure comparability with potential other research using the same material. This was altogether about 9 hours of conversation.

Our goal was to investigate whether there are features of communication that correlate with, on the one hand, the well-performing crews and the poorly performing crews, and, on the other, with situations of medium task load and of high task load or potential danger. It was obvious early on that given the nature of the material, in which the scenarios differed quite substantially, and our limited project resources, we could not hope to arrive at assertions that could attain a level of statistical significance. Rather, we intended to find out whether there are phenomena that could be investigated later in a more rigorous way.

The data set analyzed here is a subset of the one that was analyzed by Sexton & Helmreich (2001), using the Linguistic Inquiry and Word Count (LIWC) program described in Pennebaker & Francis (1999). The main findings in this study were: Captains used a higher number of words per segment; the numbers of words were higher in segments of high task load; Captains more often referred to the group by 'we', especially in segments of high task load; large words (greater than six letters) was negatively related to performance and positively related to error.

2.2 Analysis and Findings

We investigated the material in a number of dimensions. First, we were interested in the actual involvement in conversation. The crew consisted, as it was common in the 1980's on commercial aircraft of this size, of three members, the Captain (CA), the First Officer (FO) and the Flight Engineer (FE); in addition, there is the Air Traffic Controller (ATC).

2.2.1 General Characteristics

The following chart (Figure 1) gives a typical picture of the communication density during a simulation flight (here, the flight of the "good" crew 8). The number of contributions of each participant of a particular flight, which were called "thought units" by the transcribers, were added for each minute during the whole duration of the flight. We see that communication density is higher in the difficult segments B and D, that the captain in general has the most contributions, and that the flight engineer has more contributions in the difficult segments B and D (see Figure 1).

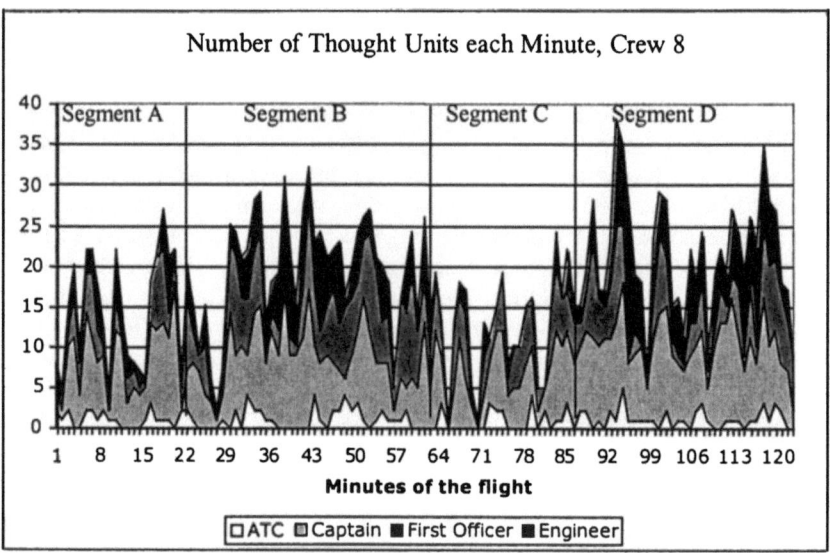

Figure 1: Number of thought units for each minute of the flight, crew 8

In the following charts, Segments A and C are combined to the "Medium" Taskload Segments, and Segments B and D to the "High" Taskload segments. Also, Crews 3 and 4 are combined to the "Poor" crews, and Crews 5, 8 and 13 to the "Good" crews. "PoorM" refers to the medium task load segments of the poorly performing crews, "PoorH" to the high task load segments of the poorly performing crews, and "GoodM" and "GoodH" refers to the medium and high segments of the well performing crews. The charts give average values, and indicate standard deviations.

In general, high taskload segments were longer than medium taskload segments. Abstracting from the duration of the segments, there were more utterances per minute in the segments of high workload, and the utterances were longer, leading to a substantial difference of speech time per minute (see arrows, Figure 2). There was no clear relation to the performance level of the crews.

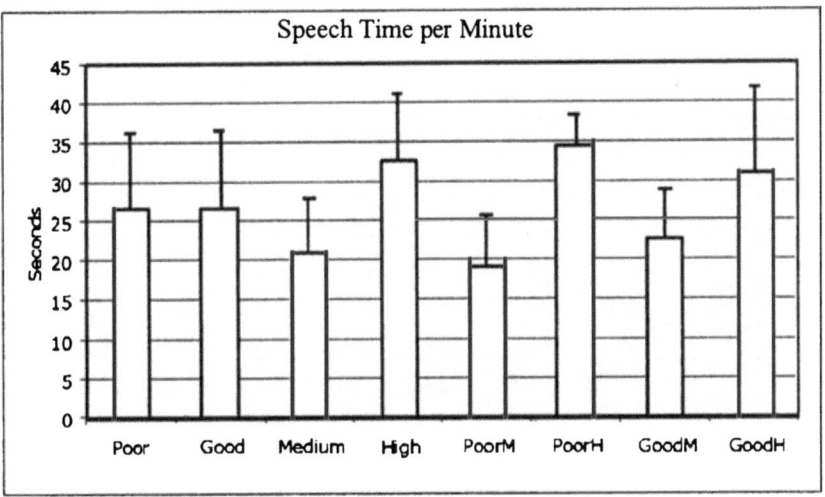

Figure 2: Speech time per minute, in seconds
(for lack of complete data, crew 13 is excluded)

The segments also differed with respect to speakers. While the captain assumed the speaker role most often overall (typically, about 40%), the engineer assumed the role of speaker more often in high task-load segments. The engineer was more often the addressee in the difficult segments, again with no clear differences between crews. Figure 3 and Figure 4 show the speaker and addressee role per thought unit (The figures for the addressee role do not add up to 100% as the addressee of some utterances cannot be identified properly, or is the whole crew).

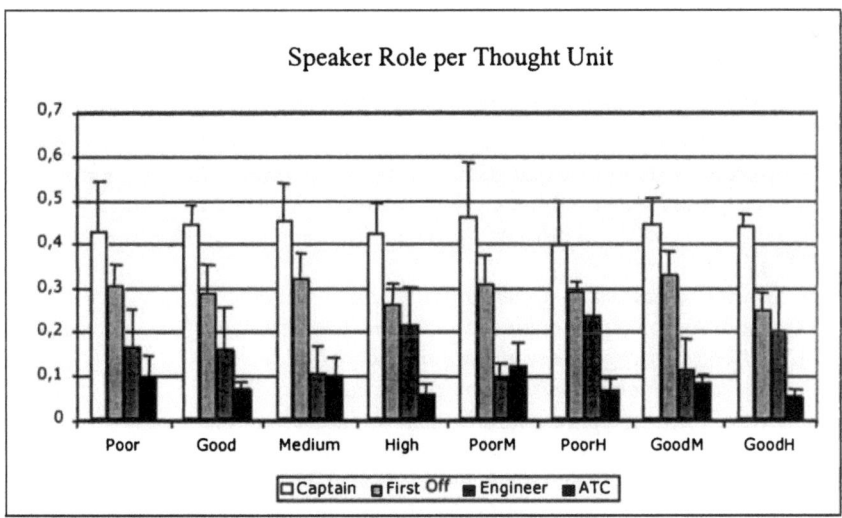

Figure 3: Speaker role (Captain, First Officer, Engineer,
Air Traffic Control) per thought unit

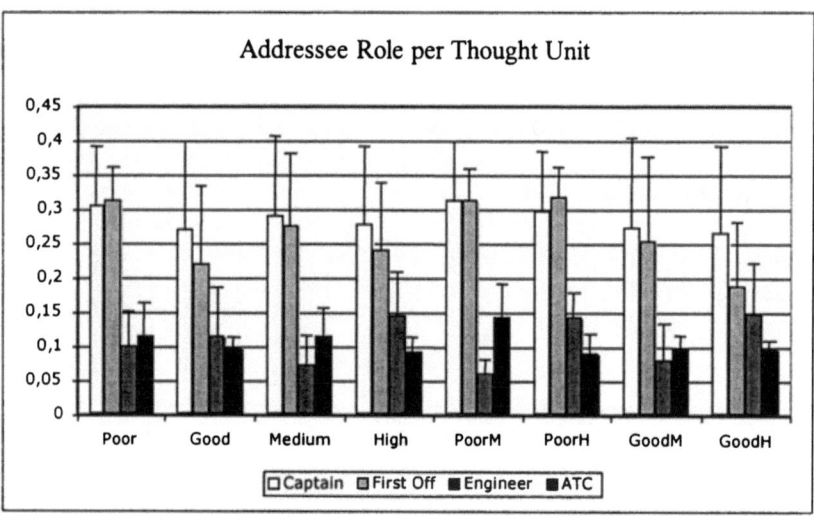

Figure 4: Addressee role per thought unit

2.2.2 Speech Act Analysis

Our major efforts concentrated on an analysis of the utterance types informed by speech act theory because we hoped that in this area we could find differences between crews and task loads in the types of speech acts used, and that recommendations concerning the use of particular speech act types could conceivably become part of training programs for pilots. Our categories were inspired by the classical work on speech act theory, most notably Searle (1975), but we felt that the specific area of cockpit communication required more detailed speech act categories in particular areas. We decided to use the following categories (with examples added from Crews 4 and 8). In the transcript, *abc 801* refers to the plane.

– Status Reports (report current state of equipment, weather, location, etc.)
   [4.17] *uh roger uh we are out at 1443 and off at 53 from san Francisco*
   [4.62] *uh, abc 801, be adviced the meter locator outer marker is unreliable, i'll call you at meter*
   [8.28] *we have an underexcited fault light on, uh, number 3*
– Reports of Action (speaker gives a report his own action
   [4.75] *i keep looking for the altitude right here and see 801*
   [4.111] *i'll put it on the missed approach altitude*
– Reports of Report (rephrase information expressed before)
   [4.461] *well, he told us be ready for ils 24 right*
– Prognoses (express likely future course of events)
   [4.373] *okay, so i think if we do the two engine, the two generator operation that'll be uh, the next thing.*

[8.214] *he's setting you up it almost looks like for a lot of bracketing here, bob, so...*
[814] *we dump fuel it makes the, uh, out of trim situation worse though.*
– Diagnoses (express likely cause of past events)
   [8.92] *i think we drifted up.*
   [8.111] *i think what that light was, was when that field relay tripped.*
   [8.1926] *so we just weren' going far enough.*
– Commands (request an action by addressee)
   [8.94] *hey, with this fault light, would you switch essential power off of number 3, please for me*
   [8.212] *abc 801, that turn looks like it's going to take you through, so continue the right*
   [8.356] *press on*
   [8.64] *okay, now you fly the airplane*
   [8.224] *why don't you make it 190.*
   [8.305] *final flaps should be 30*
– Permissions (give permission to perform action to addressee)
   [8.19] *abc 801's cleared for traffic. you can descent at pilot's discretion.*
   [8.15] *oh, whatever you want to do here, bob*
– Complies (verbalizes an action that is performed to carry out a command)
   [8.414] *[how about that brake? now try it.] no.*
– Reports of Intention (express intention to act in a certain way)
   [8.32] *meanwhile i'll take care of the approach/descent here*
   [8.63] *we'll ... we'll take care of that*
– Expressives (express an emotional state of the hearer)
   [4.185] *uh, shit*
   [8.639] *little devil*
   [8.904] *boy that is a lot of pressure*
   [8.989] *great, excellent, no, excellent*
   [8.1019] *come on, baby, come around here*
– Acknowledgements (express that preceding speech act was understood)
   [4.13] *[abc 801, expect ils 16 approach to sacramento] okay.*
   [8.410] *[i'll just crank it and you tell me when to stop]. yeah.*
– Affirmations (acknowledge and affirm a preceding speech act)
   [8.1075] *[well we got ... we're committed to the right] that's right*
   [8.1120] *[cant't do it] no [as an agreement].*
   [8.1169] *[shouldn't be that much of a problem]. nope, no no no.*
– Rephrases (acknowledge and rephrase preceding speech act)
   [8.50] *[one six right, approach.] one six right, yeah.*
   [8.1640] *[ground spoilers, out spoilers] out spoilers.*

This classification combines speech act types with content features (e.g., status reports, prognoses, diagnoses are all assertive speech acts that differ in their content). The last three categories concerned with the proper flow of information in conversation are often neglected in speech act theory, but we considered them to be of potential importance in the present context. In general, speech act theory (as opposed to discourse analysis) underestimates that many speech acts are parts of well-defined sequences (e.g., acknowledgements of statements, verbal complies to commands, etc.).

Certain generally recognized speech act types do not form separate categories, but rather cross-classify other categories. This is most obvious with questions and answers that can be related to assertive speech acts, i.e. state reports that can be true or false, or to commands. For example, 'You got any problems?' was classified as a Status report / Question, as the answer would count as an assertion, or Status Report, whereas 'You want me to brief with you?' was classified as Command / Question, as a positive answer would count as a command. The question 'Was that what screwed it up?' was classified as Diagnosis / Question, and the answer 'Might have.' as Diagnosis / Answer. The speech act of Command (and Comply to Command) could also have been cross-classified; a command like 'Tell me about the weather condition.' requests a linguistic action, and hence is equivalent to a question. However, we didn't do so as such commands appeared to be quite rare.

A well-known problem for the classification of utterances into speech act types is that the linguistic form often does not determine the act type. A command can be expressed directly, by an imperative, 'Close the door!', or more indirectly, by a modal declarative statement, 'The door should be closed.', or a question, 'Why don't you close the door?'. We would classify such utterances as commands. Only a very indirect speech acts that require inferencing, e.g. 'It is cold in here.', would have been classified directly (here, as a status report), as it would not be clear whether the speaker intended this as an assertion or as a command.

Another problem was that the segmented utterances in the transcripts (the "thought units") quite often comprised more than one speech act. As we wanted to maintain the integrity of the transcripts to ensure comparability with other studies, we did not break up such utterances. Nevertheless, we were forced to classify each utterance as belonging to one speech act. For example, the utterance ABC 801, 'That turn looks like it's going to take you through, so continue to the right turn to 180.' could have been broken up into a status report and command, but was classified as a command (the first part can be seen as a motivation for the command). Take another example, 'I'm on the air, so you get it.' This could be analyzed as a command, or as an assertion and a command, or perhaps as a new speech act, "motivated command". Again, as the main function of this utterance seems to be to get the addressee to do something, we classified it as a command.

2.2.3 Other Features of Communication

Beyond the analysis of speech acts we looked at a number of other features that appeared likely candidates for the correlation with the quality of the crew or the task load.

- Explicit reference to addressee, speaker, or group
  [8.31] *why don't WE go to the book and see what YOU can do on it.*
  [8.32] *meanwhile I'll take care of the approach/descent here*
  [8.41] *YOU got any problems at all, bob, back there with that?*
- Correction of previous information
  [8.175-177] *[lots of gas. about 29] 28.*
  [8.266] *do you want abc 801 to the MARKER er... TOWER?*
- Evidence for misunderstanding
  [4.45-46] *[atc: abc 801, contact sacramento approach on 1256.] CA: 801, uh, 276, roger.*
- Hesitation
  [4.121] *abc 801 is meter, UH, inbound.*
- Hedges (sort of, I think, etc.)
  [4.156] *WELL, that is true.*
  [4.164] *I THINK what he was saying was be prepared for a fillmore 4 and uh a.*
- Encouragement
  [8.134] *looking good, bob.*
  [8.190] *this is excellent.*
  [8.552] *you can fly it ... hold it ...*
- Emotional words
  [8.620] *we don't have a hell of a lot of gas to screw around with either.*
  [8.640] *little devil.*
  [8.905] *boy is that a lot of pressure.*
  [8.82] *ah, shit*
- Politeness
  [8.94] *hey, with this fault light, would you switch essential power off of number 3, please for me.*
  [8.105] *yessir, we just heard some other voices in the background, thank you.*
  [8.905] *pull back just a touch please.*

2.2.4 Results

We now report some of our findings. One should keep in mind that the numbers of cases we are working with are too low to achieve statistical significance, which is also clear by looking at the large standard deviations in many cases. But we do hope that some of the results may lead to worthwhile hypotheses for future work.

First, we found more prognoses and diagnoses in good crews and, to a lesser degree, under high task load (Figure 5). In particular, speech acts that can be thought of prognoses of one's own future behavior, which we called "report of intention", and which were not counted as prognoses, were more frequent in the good crews and, less dramatically so, in the segments of high task load (Figure 6).

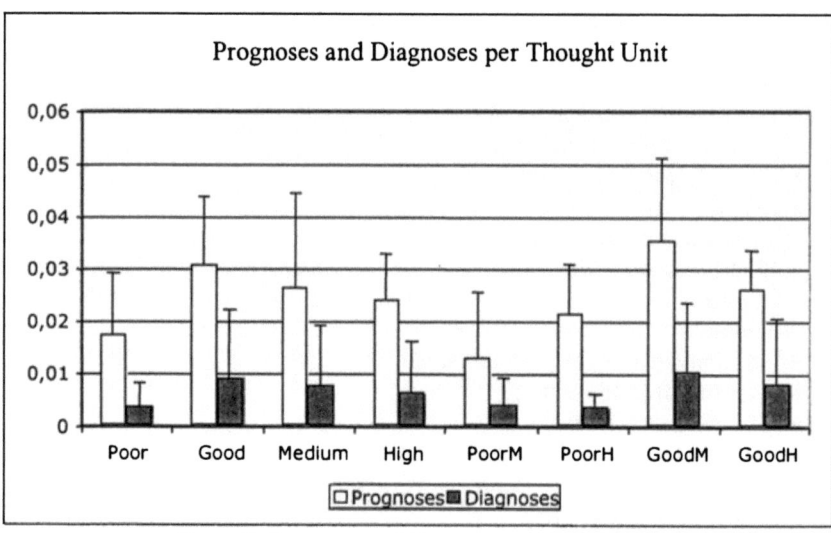

Figure 5: Prognoses and diagnoses per thought unit

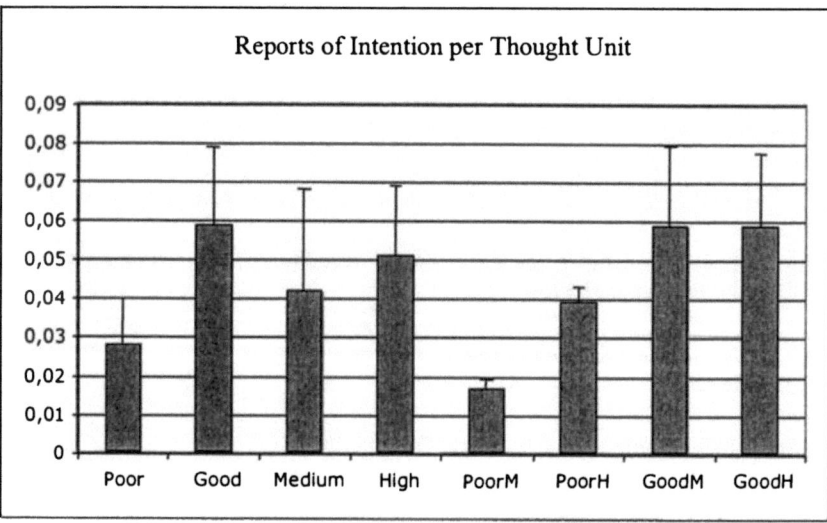

Figure 6: Reports of intention per thought unit

Questions occurred slightly more frequently in the good crews, and the proportion of questions that were answered was considerably higher there. Interestingly, poor crews had more questions in the high task load segments, whereas good crews had more questions in the medium task load segments (see Figure 7).

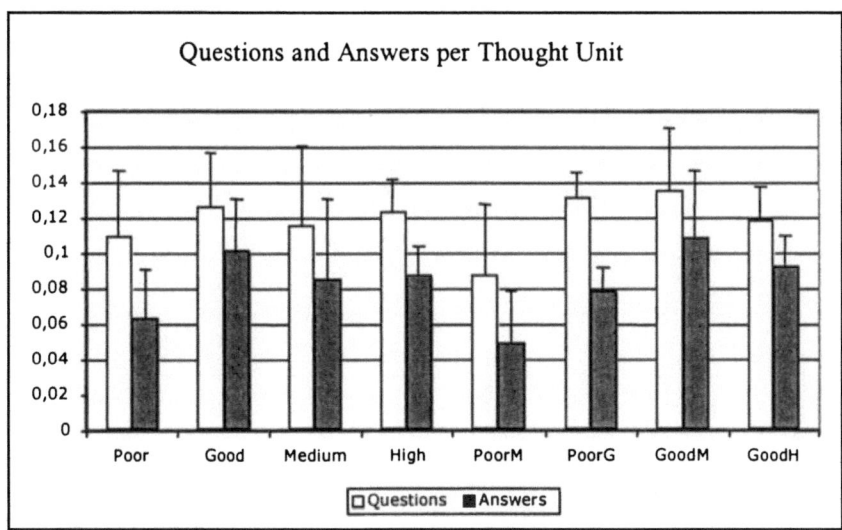

Figure 7: Questions and answers per thought unit

Commands occurred more frequently in the poor crews, as well as overt linguistic verbalizations that commands are carried out. There was no relation with task load (see Figure 8).

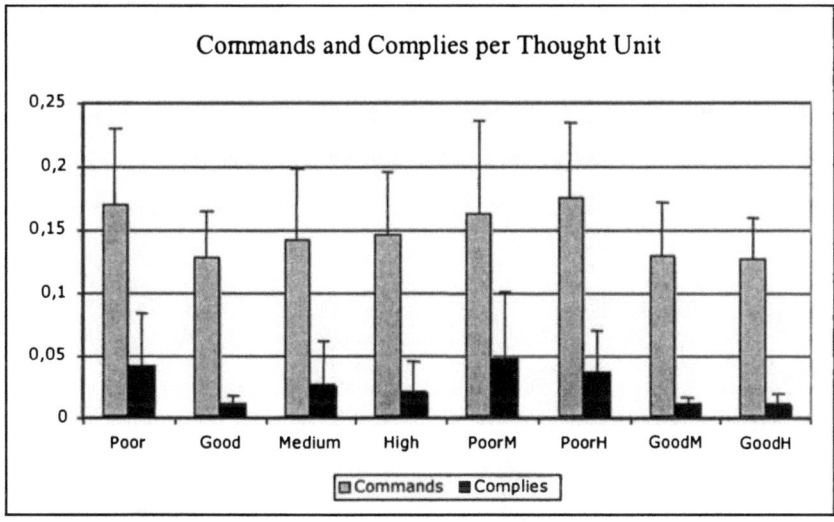

Figure 8: Commands and complies to commands per thought unit

As for the speech act types that acknowledge or confirm another speech act type, which are quite characteristic for cockpit talk, we find generally more simple acknowledgements in the good crews, and fewer in the segments with high task load (Figure 9).

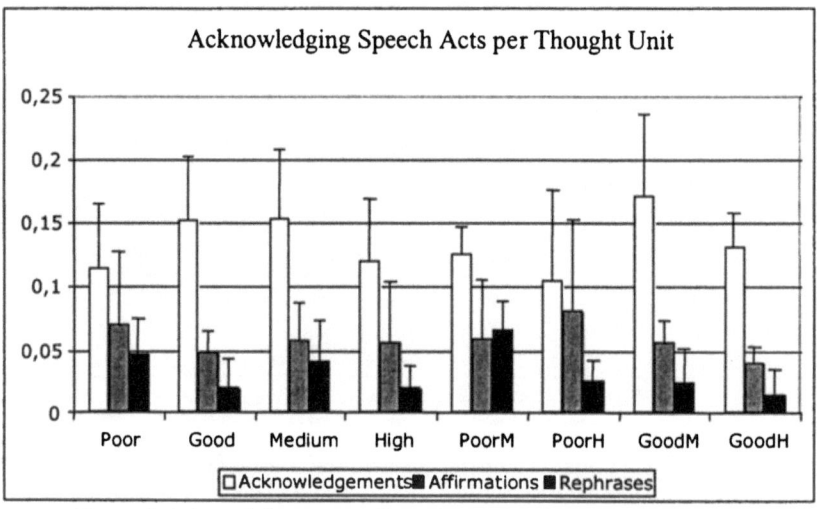

Figure 9: Acknowledgements, affirmation and rephrases per thought unit

Expressive speech acts and emotion words occur more frequently in the poor crews. Interestingly, in those crews segments of high task load showed fewer expressive speech acts and emotion words (see Figure 10).

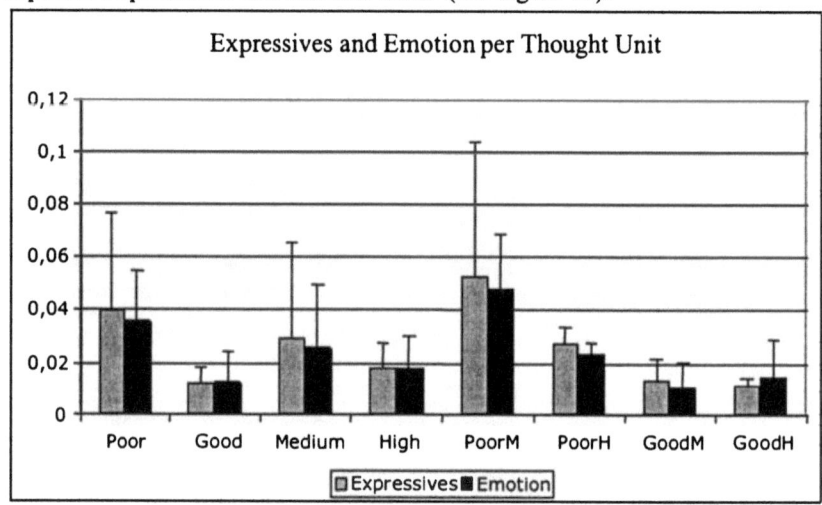

Figure 10: Expressive speech acts and emotional expressions per thought unit

Linguistic evidence for misunderstandings was found especially in one poor group, more frequently in segments of medium task load. Evidence for corrections occurs in all segments and crews about equally (Figure 11).

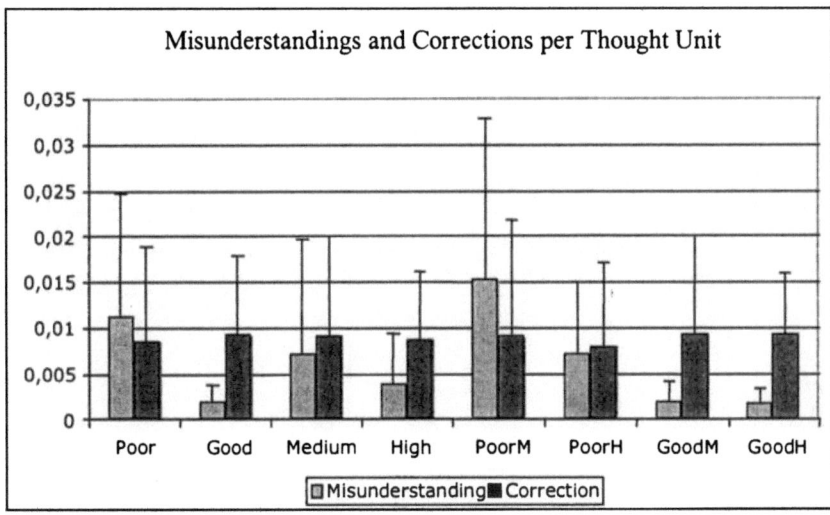

Figure 11: Evidence for misunderstandings and corrections per thought unit

With hesitations and hedges we find the following picture: Hesitations occurred slightly more frequently with the poor crews. In these crews, the incidence of both hesitations and hedges increased with high taskload (Figure 12).

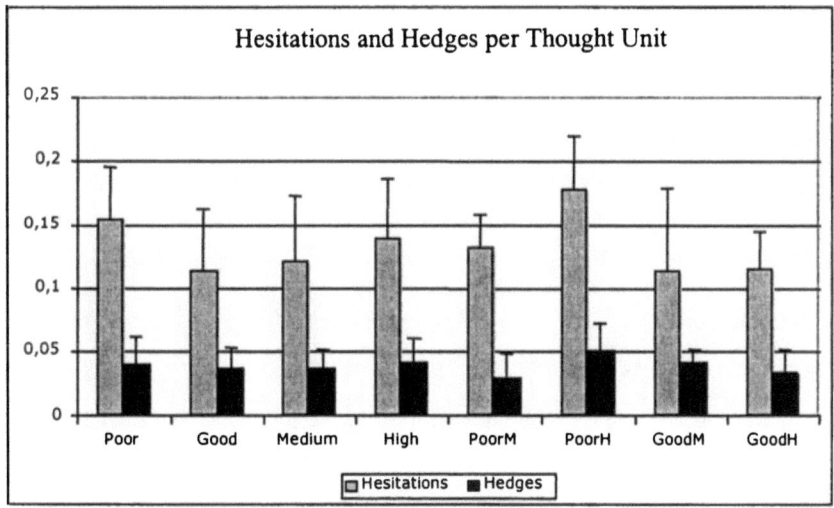

Figure 12: Hesitations and hedges per thought unit

Politeness elements occur slightly more often in good crews. Interestingly, good crews have fewer politeness elements in segments of high task load, just the opposite to poor crews (see Figure 13).

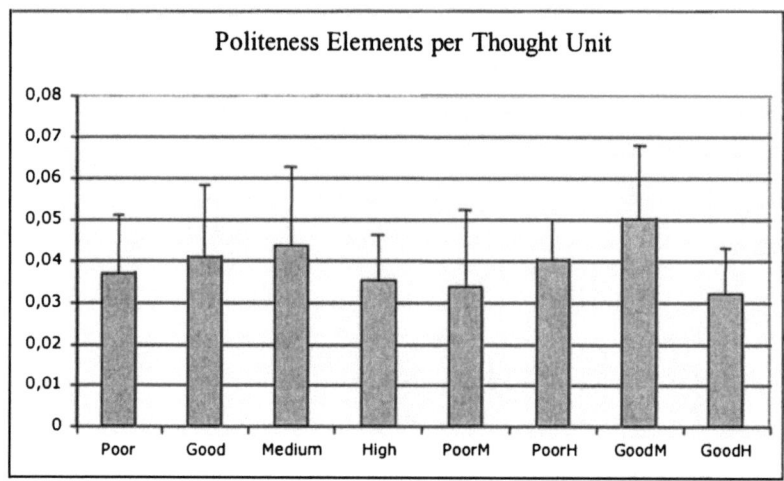

Figure 13: Politeness elements per thought unit

We also counted explicit references to the speaker, the addressee and the group (see Figure 14). Especially reference to groups can be considered a group-building measure, Sexton & Helmreich (2001) found out that reference to the group increases over the life of a crew, and that captains use more reference to crews than first officers or engineers. They all occur somewhat less frequently with poor crews in medium task load segments, but increase in high task load segments. For good crews, they stay about the same.

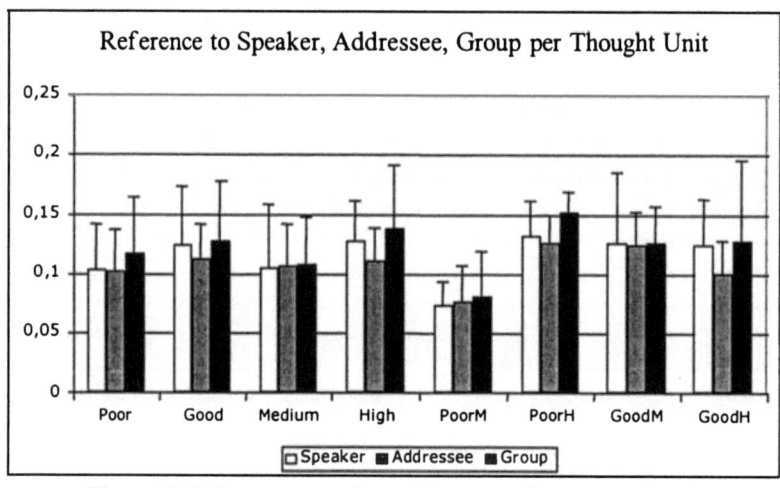

Figure 14: Reference to speaker, addressee, and group per thought unit

Of the other features that we investigated, we would like to mention encouragement. This category occurred quite frequently in the best-performing crew (in about 5% of the thought units, more frequently in those with medium task load), and not at all in the worst-performing crew.

2.2.5 Limitations

The scope of the first part of the project was more limited than originally envisioned (we planned to analyze more flight transcripts), and therefore the results of this part have to be understood as indicators of tendencies at best. Nevertheless, we could identify some linguistic dimensions in which there is a relatively clear influence of workload and crew performance. For some cases, like the category of reports of intention and of prognoses in general, which was higher in difficult segments and with good crews, one could develop specific advice for crew resource management training.

But it also became clear in the course of the study that this type of research could be improved in a number of ways, some of which are listed below.
- The classification of segments A/C and B/D as low workload vs. high workload does not capture the fact that high workload stretches also occur in A/C, and low workload stretches occur in B/D. Thus, the correlation of workload with linguistic behavior may appear less pronounced in our analysis than they actually are.
- The number of crews that were analyzed is far too low to arrive at statistically significant conclusions with respect to crew performance. This is also reflected in the standard variation in the charts, which often is quite high.
- The complete analysis of simulation flights (about 7 hours), which included relatively routine stretches like checklists, was, in hindsight, not the most efficient way to apply the limited resources of the project.
- The quality of the transcripts we worked with was rather varied, e.g. in the recording of hesitation signs or other paralinguistic behavior.
- The information available about the flight scenario and the precise timings of malfunctions was limited.
- We did not have the means for extensive independent classification of the communicative features, like the speech acts. Some informal sample tests showed an interrater consistency of 70% and higher, depending on the category.

We also had the impression that quite a few types of linguistic behavior were not identified by our system of categories. For example, the following acts quite obviously invoke crew resources; we found such passages often in the best Crew 8, and rarely, if at all, in the worst Crew 4:

[8.1511] you can, you can listen with me, I might misunderstand.
[8.2162] what else? what else have we missed?
[14.1118] Okay, do we have everything?

The technique that we have applied is particularly bad with coherent passages of discourse. For example, the following passage, a dialogue between captain and engineer, is remarkable because the interlocutors try to secure a precise understanding by asking back and forth:

[8.146] E-C: climb to 500 feet, proceed directly sacramento v-o-r hold south 180, radial 5,000 feet.
C-E: 5,000?
E-C: yeah.
C-E: after 5000, direct to v-o-r to hold?
E-C: right.
C-E: okay got it.

And in the following passage the captain focuses the crew resources in an admirable way:

[8.2007] F-C: i'm worried about the gas. we're pissin' out 15,000 pounds an hour.
C-F: don't worry.
C-F: don't worry.
F-C: ok.
C-F: i'll tell you when to worry.

One problem that is difficult to address is the issue of whether simulator data are representative of real data. While the participants in the simulated flights obviously took their job very seriously, there is evidence that they were frequently aware of the fact that they were operating in a simulator. We hope that, nevertheless, the communicative behavior in simulated situations is similar enough to real-life situations to make these analyses relevant for such situations.

3 The second project phase: an outlook

Due to the various problems in the first project phase several changes and improvements have been made in the second phase that started in May 2001. The improvements, which will be discussed in detail in the following, concern the scenario, the data corpus including the transcripts and the modified methods of analysis. At the time of writing of this article we are just beginning our analysis, as the technical organization of the data has taken extensive efforts. Therefore we can not yet present any results.

The new project phase differs from the first project phase not only in respect to the methods of investigation but also in terms of the points of emphasis within the investigation. The general goal of our research, however, remains the same: To identify specific linguistic features of cockpit communication that correlate with crew performance, especially under varying levels and types of taskload. All three parts of the flight-simulator scenario (description see below) are classified as medium to high task load segments, but the type of task load varies. One part, for example, is demanding mainly in terms of manual skills, while another requires analytical skills. All parts involve high time pressure.

Our goal is, as in the first project phase, to find out which concrete linguistic factors are crucial for the crew's communicative behavior and what differences there are relative to different types of task load and different crews. Comparability of the different crews, an essential factor, is ensured by the design of the new scenario, which is considerably more constrained and leaves less room for variation in the course of events. Furthermore, communication skills are crucial in resolving the occurring problems. In contrast to the first project phase, we do not know the performance ratings of aviation experts in advance, but we will compare our findings to find out if and in which ways crew performance and communication do correlate. Also, we will systematically test for interrater consistency.

3.1 The New Flight Simulator Scenario

The first point of improvement concerns the structure of the scenario: It is substantially more focused, more clearly oriented towards communication. It was developed by a group of aviation experts around Gerhard Fahnenbruck and carried out by Lufthansa CityLine on a CanadAir Regional Jet simulator.

The scenario consists of three parts: First, a so called circling approach, where the runway has to be approached with the wind from behind due to an instrumental landing system (ILS) failure on the ground. With the runway in sight, the crew has to circle around the airport in preparation to landing. The pilots have to brief and prepare for this particular type of approach. When they are about to land, another plane is blocking the runway and the crew has to fly a go around. In the second phase that begins at this point, the ILS has been repaired and a normal approach to the runway can be flown. During the approach, however, the glide slope, a part of the instrumental landing system, breaks down at 1500 feet. Constant communication about the altitude both within the crew as interactional partners and with the tower is necessary to be able to land under these conditions. After the landing the third section starts with a take-off. Shortly after the plane is in the air, an instrument failure occurs while the plane is in the clouds: The artificial horizon (pitch) on the captain's side and the compass (heading) on the first officer's side display incorrect values, the captain's instrument being far more important. This section is especially interesting from a linguistic point of view, as there is an increased need for communication in order to exchange the correct values of the defective instruments.

Since each crew goes through the same scenario, with the possibility of different developments within the course of events being quite limited, the degree of comparability is much higher than during the previous phase of the project.

3.2 Data Corpus and Transcripts

The next point of improvement is the quality of the data. We have a corpus of 16 simulator flights (video and audio data), all consisting of the same scenario. Differing from the previous project phase, the crews consist of only two members, the captain and the first officer, because there is no engineer on this type of plane. The shortest flight lasts about 27 minutes, the longest one hour and 28 minutes, the average length per flight is 53 minutes. The whole corpus consists of 14 hours and ten minutes. As it will not be possible to transcribe, let alone analyze, the entire 14 hours of data, certain well-defined segments will have to be chosen for our purposes. We intend to transcribe and analyze three comparable parts of each scenario in which different crews have to manage very similar tasks. In the third part of the scenario, for example, the segment to be analyzed starts at the moment a warning signal indicates an instrument failure to the crew and ends when their analysis of the problem is completed. Thereby we ensure that the objective tasks that the crew has to solve and the contexts in which they have to be solved are very similar, if not equal.

3.3 Methods

The methods used in the second project phase will be substantially different from the ones in the first phase. In addition to the (adjusted and changed) speech act theoretic investigation we will also apply methods from conversation analysis and try combining the two approaches. This means that our strategy will include quantitative analysis, since the occurrences of speech act types can be counted, as well as qualitative analysis.

3.3.1 Applied Speech Act Theory

Due to the better quality of the data corpus and by applying recent developments in applied speech act theory, we will be able to use a more fine-grained system of speech act types. Also, we will not rely on a previously determined dissection of the communicative events into sometimes relatively large "thought units" but will be able to assume a more fine-grained division, which will also enhance our ability to assign speech act types in an unambiguous manner. We will go beyond analyzing single, isolated speech acts by considering and developing types based on longer sequences of dialogue. These will also be organized in well-defined speech act classes, which will result in improved possibilities for quantification. We will determine more clearly how often well-defined speech act types occur in which kind of task load type and in which crews. This is essential for our goal of comparing the results with the performance ratings for the crews.

3.3.2 QVA and more fine-grained speech acts

The assignment of certain defined speech act types to utterances is a difficult task and should be valid and reliable. Working with "authentic" material (if we may consider simulator data authentic), this step of analysis should not simply rely on the researcher's intuitions, in order to guarantee reliability and validity. One method to operationalize this step is *Qualitative Verlaufsanalyse* (QVA, "Qualitative Progression Analysis"), as described in Diegritz & Fürst (1999). QVA is a successor of the so-called *Pragmatisch-dynamische Methodenkombination* (PDMK, "Pragmatic-Dynamic Method Combination") of Diegritz and Rosenbusch (see Diegritz & Rosenbusch 1995), developed to analyze the communication between teachers and students in the classroom. It combines different research approaches from linguistics and sociology (e.g. interaction research), with speech act theory playing a central role. It is currently the most manageable instrument to classify utterances into speech acts in a transparent and rater-consistent way. Diegritz & Fürst have developed a *Sprechakttypen-Inventar zur Analyse von Lehrerintentionen im Gruppenunterricht* (SALG, "a speech act inventory for the analysis of teacher's intentions in group lessons"). The goal of SALG is to achieve a sufficient level of objectivity and reliability for the analysis of speech acts in a specific context. In analogy to this we are developing an inventory of speech act types for the analysis of cockpit communication, namely a *Sprechakttypen-Inventar zur Analyse von Cockpit-Kommunikation* (STACK), that, we hope, should be useful for further investigations of cockpit communication.

Following QVA, the segmentation and classification of utterances into speech act types will be broken up in ten micro steps of analysis, as follows: Basic step 0: explication of relevant background knowledge; (1) which illocutionary indicators occur? (2) division of the utterance into speech acts; (3) verbal and non-verbal context, reading back and ahead (optional); (4) explicit interpretative verbalization of the utterance; (5) perlocutionary effects; (6) exploration of the institutional determination of the utterance; (7) explication of aspects of development of thematic progression, the development of relationships within the group and of the group process in general; (8) separation of illocution and proposition and the determination of the individual speech acts and their types; (9) explication and discussion of possible alternative acts and utterances the speaker could have chosen (this serves to explicate the speaker's intention more clearly). See Diegritz & Fürst 1999: 60–65 for a worked example. On the basis of this procedure, the role of particular speech act types in the interactional context of the cockpit can then be investigated qualitatively and quantitatively.

While much of research in speech act theory has been concerned with a global taxonomy for the classification of speech acts, there has also been an increasing interest in subdividing the major speech act classes into a more fine grained system of speech act types. This has been done, with a focus on German, by Rolf (1983) for informatives, by Hindelang (1978, 1981) for directives and questions, by Graffe (1990) for commissives and by Marten-Cleef (1991) and Zillig (1982) for expressives. For an overview of all of these, see Kohl & Kranz (1992). Such a fine-grained system is highly desirable for an empirical application of speech act theory. While it may be advantageous for theoretical purposes to establish a very general taxonomy, the analysis of authentic dialogue seems to benefit from a more fine grained system, since this seems more adequate to the vast variety of possible things that can be done with words.

One disadvantage of a large number of speech act types could be thought to be that the quantitative analysis does not lead to statistically relevant numbers of occurrences of a certain type. But then it is unlikely that all speech act types do occur in the cockpit. We will therefore, as already mentioned, create an inventory of types likely to occur in the cockpit. This inventory should contain a systematic and perspicuous explication of the relevant speech act types. The speech act types will also be organized in a hierarchical structure. This will allow for great flexibility in the level of abstraction used in the quantitative analysis. For example, we make a distinction, following Rolf (1983), between mitteilen ("informing") and melden ("reporting"), where the characteristic of mitteilen is that the speaker acts without obligation and assuming that the information conveyed should be of interest to the addressee, whereas what is characteristic for melden is that the speaker conveys the information under a certain obligation. If this does not lead to any interesting correlations, we can collapse this distinction and investigate whether the group of transmissive speech acts as a whole shows such a correlation.

3.3.3 Extended Speech Act Theory

One desideratum of classical speech act theory is that it doesn't consider sufficiently enough the conversational context in which speech acts are performed. Many speech acts can be uttered only in certain positions within a conversation. We will follow the distinction of Rolf (1983) between *initiative*, *reactive* and *reinitiative* speech act types. Initiative speech acts can be uttered independent of previous utterances; reactive speech acts can only be uttered in response to a previous speech act (by someone else); and reinitiative speech acts can only be uttered in response to a reactive speech act (see Kohl & Kranz 1992: 10–11). Typical pairs of initiative and reactive speech acts in aviation are *command* and (verbal) *comply* (see also command and control discourse in Goguen & Linde 1983: 39–46), as well as *statement* and *confirmation*. Other reactive types are problematic ones such as *expressing doubt* and rejective ones such as *refuting*.

The context-sensitive typology of speech acts introduces a level that goes beyond the single speech act. A systematic way of representing the structure of dialogue, in terms of an extended speech act theory, has been developed by Franke (1990). His approach attempts to account for the sequential embedding of speech acts in the communicative context. The basic unit on this level is the minimal dialogue. These minimal dialogues are then classified as a certain dialogue type, depending on the initial speech act.

The main idea of Franke's approach is as follows. With an initial speech act (ISA), speaker 1 (S1) states a communicative goal. Speaker 2 (S2) can accept or reject that goal. If, for example, S2's reaction did not constitute a minimal dialogue (that is, if S2 was not accepting S1's communicative goal, e.g. did not answer a question), S1 has three different options in the third move: (i) A retractive speech act: S1 gives up his original communicative goal; (ii) A revised speech act: S1 modifies his original communicative goal; (iii) a re-initiative speech act: S1 insists on his original goal and possibly attempts to reach it by different means. In the case of (i), the speech act constitutes a minimal dialogue. In the case of (ii) or (iii), the dialogue continues until one of the speakers has achieved his or her communicative goal or until it is clear that the other speaker does not accept it. Complex dialogues consist of a number of minimal dialogues.

This type of analysis, which takes into consideration the structure of minimal dialogues, allows for the quantitative analysis of aspects of cockpit communication that could not be described in terms of traditional speech act theory. It will enable us to test hypotheses that involve interesting aspects of the crew members' communicative behavior. For example, one could test how often crew members initiate dialogues, how often they give up their goals in a dialogue, how often they respond with a counter-initiative speech act, and how often (and perhaps also how quickly) they do (or do not) finish a dialogue, that is, constitute a minimal dialogue. In the end this, as in the first project phase, can then be related to crew performance and task load in order to find out whether there is a correlation.

3.3.4 Conversation Analysis (CA)

The extended speech act theory mentioned above should bridge the gap with another tradition of analysis of verbal interaction, Conversation Analysis. CA criticized Speech Act Theory as a tool for empirical research in a number of ways: For its tendency to isolate units without considering their context, for the fact that it is speaker-centered and does not consider the role of the addressee in an appropriate way, and for putting to much focus on the speaker's intentions: Asking questions like "what does the speaker really mean" to determine what a speaker really intended with an utterance seems to be a questionable approach when working with authentic material. Diegritz & Fürst therefore argue that a clear distinction needs to be made between the speech act as such, the illocution as speaker's intention and the communicative function of a speech act (see Diegritz & Fürst 1999: 43f.). All of these criticisms are ultimately connected to speech act theory's origins in theoretical philosophy, where constructed utterances are at the center of attention. Applying a type system that is based on constructed utterances to authentic dialogue is very difficult, if not close to impossible.

Because of these points of criticism we will use conversation analysis in addition to (extended) speech act theory as a second, equivalent method. Conversation analysis, as opposed to speech act theory, has always been a strictly empirical approach. Its main purpose is the investigation of social interaction as a process of creation and stabilization of social order (Bergmann 2000: 525), or the investigation of "interactional organization of social activities" (Hutchby & Wooffitt 2001: 14). These authors pointed out that even the key role of talk in broader institutional processes "takes the essential CA starting point that talk-in-interaction is to be seen as its own social process, governed by its own regularities." (Hutchby & Wooffitt 2001: 21). This is, of course, also valid for talk-in-interaction in the cockpit.

Due to its roots in ethnomethodology, CA is concerned with the reconstruction of data segments and not with psychological interpretations. Conversation or, respectively, talk-in-interaction is understood as a process, as a place in which social facts are produced. This process is always integrated into interaction – each single utterance is produced and modified by both interlocutors together. The speakers constitute their turns in interaction with the addressee.

If we want to investigate cockpit communication, this means that we will have to reconstruct the constitutive principles and mechanisms in the process of cockpit interaction during the simulator flight by analyzing it systematically, thereby exploring the structural principles which the individual crews follow. The social relationship between the crew members and the social order within the crew are important factors. We want to find out whether these structural principles are modified in relation to different types of task load and within crews and also in how far different structural principles of crews affect the interaction (and presumably the performance) in high task load situations. The goal is to reconstruct the practical methods the crews apply in solving interactional problems. The use of these methods generates the observable order within the interactional process in the cockpit. In other words: We do not describe homogeneous forms of behavior, but principles that represent real points of orientation for the acting individuals.

A basic interest of CA is the question, how it is possible for interactional participants to understand each other and to ensure that they do. This is an essential issue, especially in highly dangerous situations. Another topic concerns the organization of turn-takes and, relative to that, the activation of repair organization by the participants in a conversation, in cases where a problem of understanding occurs (see Schegloff, Jefferson & Sacks 1977). Consequently, the investigation of uptake and repair organization as a substantial factor in the turn-taking-system as well as of concepts of face and politeness (see Brown & Levinson 1987 and also Linde 1988 and Goguen & Linde 1983: 28–36 from a related speech act theoretic view) will be central to our analysis. After all, interaction in the cockpit takes place in a hierarchical setting and involves the creation and maintenance of social order, where these concepts play a rather significant role

Evidently cockpit communication differs from everyday conversation, as other forms of institutional communication, or rather: talk-in-interaction, do as well. Have (1999) writes about this difference "that for some institutional systems, there is a pre-established system of turn allocation, and quite often turn-type allocation" (Have 1999: 163). The institutional form can be seen as "more 'restricted'" than everyday conversation. The asymmetrical distribution of questions and answers might be an interesting example for that (see Have 1999: 164). Nevertheless, in institutional as well as in everyday talk-in-interaction the same principles are applied by the participants, even though the distribution may be different.

For our investigation of cockpit communication this means to reconstruct the process of cockpit interaction during the simulator flight through a comparative-systematic analysis, especially in respect to the social relationship, i.e. the social order within the crew, and to determine which structural principles are applied by the crew in which ways. What is to be found out is (i) whether the structural principles vary in relation to the type of task load (and if they do, how), and (ii) whether differences can be determined in terms of how different structural principles among crews influence the interaction in situations with different types of task load. The idea is to reconstruct the "practical methods" (Bergmann), which serve the crew as a solution for interactive problems. It is the use of those practical methods that generates the observable order in the cockpit-interaction. In other words: The point is not a "description of uniformities of behavior" but rather "in which way the participants themselves consider these formal principles in their utterances and actions" (Bergmann 2000: 533, translation by the authors). For the concrete goals of our investigation this means: Which variations are possible in the different types of task load, i.e. how and to what extent does the crew's behavior vary, and is there a particularly efficient form of communicative behavior or a successful strategy that could be determined, which would enable crews to solve aviation problems in a more result-oriented and therefore more successful way?

4 Conclusion

In this article, we reported some of the findings in a number of studies concerned with communication in aviation. There is evidence that linguistic features of communication correlate with the performance of crews and with the level of task load. We reported, in particular, results of a study based on flight simulator sessions done in the USA on a B-727, and the design and analysis of a new study, also based on flight simulator sessions done in Germany on a Canadair Regional Jet that promises to yield more definite results.

Literature

Bergmann, J. (2000): „Konversationsanalyse". In: Flick, U., von Kardorff, E. & Steinke, I., Hrsg. (2000). 524–537.

Brown, P. & Levinson, S. (1987): Politeness. Some Universals in Language Use. Cambridge: University Press.

Chidester, T. R., Kanki, G. G., Foushee, H. C., Dickinson, C. L. & Bowles, S. V. (1990): Personality factors in flight operations. Volume 1. Leader characteristics and crew performance in a full-mission air transport simulation (NASA Technical Memorandum 102259). Moffett Field, CA: NASA-Ames Research Center.

Diegritz, T. & Fürst, C. (1999): Empirische Sprechhandlungsforschung. Ansätze zur Analyse und Typisierung authentischer Äußerungen. Erlangen: Univ.-Bilbiothek.

Diegritz, T. & Rosenbusch, H. (1995): „Die pragmatisch-dynamische Methodenkombination (PDMK) zur Erforschung von Kommunikationsprozessen". In: König, E. & Zedler, P., Hrsg. (1995). 435–461.

Flick, U., von Kardorff, E. & Steinke, I., Hrsg. (2000): Qualitative Forschung. Ein Handbuch. Reinbek bei Hamburg: Rowohlt.

Franke, W. (1990): Elementare Dialogstrukturen. Tübingen: Niemeyer.

Fritz, G. & Hundsnurscher, F., Hrsg. (1994): Handbuch der Dialoganalyse. Tübingen: Niemeyer.

Goguen, J. A. & Linde, C. (1983): Linguistic Methodology for the Analysis of Aviation Accidents. Technical Report, Structural Semantics. Nasa Contractor Report 3741, Nasa Ames Research Center. National Aeronautics and Space Administration. Palo Alto, California.

Graffe, J. (1990): Sich festlegen und verpflichten: Die Untertypen kommissiver Sprechakte und ihre sprachlichen Realisierungsformen. Münster: Waxmann.

Have, P. ten (1999): Doing Conversation Analysis: A Practical Guide. London: Sage.

Helmreich, R. L. (1997a): "Managing human error in aviation". In: Scientific American, May issue. 62–97.

Helmreich, R. L. (1997b): „Kommunikationstraining gegen menschliches Versagen im Cockpit". In: Spektrum der Wissenschaft, July issue.

Helmreich, R. L., Merritt, A. C. & Wilhelm, J. A. (1999): "The evolution of Crew Resource Management training in commercial aviation". In: International Journal of Aviation Psychology 9. 283–301.

Hindelang, G. (1978): Auffordern. Die Untertypen des Auffordems und ihre sprachlichen Realisierungsformen. Göppingen: Kümmerle.

Hindelang, G. (1981): „Zur Klassifikation der Fragehandlungen". In: Hindelang, G. & Zillig, W., Hrsg. (1981). 215–225.

Hindelang, G. (1994): „Sprechakttheoretische Dialoganalyse". In: Fritz, G. & Hundsnurscher, F., Hrsg. (1994). 95–112.

Hindelang, G. (1995): „Frageklassifikation und Dialoganalyse". In: Hindelang, G., Rolf, E. & Zillig, W., Hrsg. (1995). 176–196.

Hindelang, G. & Zillig, W., Hrsg. (1981): Sprache: Verstehen und Handeln. Tübingen: Niemeyer.

Hindelang, G., Rolf, E. & Zillig, W., Hrsg. (1995): Der Gebrauch der Sprache. Festschrift für Franz Hundsnurscher zum 60. Geburtstag. Münster: LIT.

Hutchby, I. & Wooffitt, R. (2001): Conversation Analysis. Principles, Practices and Applications. 3rd ed. Cambridge: Polity Press.
Kohl, M. & Kranz, B. (1992): „Untermuster globaler Typen illokutionärer Akte. Zur Untergliederung von Sprechaktklassen und ihrer Beschreibung". In: König, P.-P. & Wiegers, H., Hrsg. (1992). 1–44.
König, E. & Zedler, P., Hrsg. (1995): Bilanz qualitativer Forschung. Band II: Methoden. Weinheim: Deutscher Studien Verlag.
König, P.-P. & Wiegers, H., Hrsg. (1992): Sprechakttheorie. Münster: LIT.
Linde, C. (1988): "The quantitative study of communicative success: Politeness and accidents in aviation discourse". In: Language in Society 17. 375 – 399.
Nevile, M. (2001): "Knowing who's who in the airline cockpit: pilot's pronominal choices and cockpit roles". In: McHoul, A. & Rapley, M. (2001).
Marten-Cleef, S. (1991): Gefühle ausdrücken. Die expressiven Sprechakte. Göppingen: Kümmerle.
McHoul, A. & Rapley, M. (2001): How to analyze talk in institutional settings. A casebook of methods. London & New York: Continuum.
Pennebaker, J. W. & Francis, M. E. (1999): Linguistic Inquiry and Word Count (LIWC). Mahmah, N.J.: Erlbaum Publishing.
Rolf, E. (1983): Sprachliche Informationshandlungen. Göppingen: Kümmerle.
Schegloff, E. A., Jefferson, G. & Sacks, H. (1977): "The preference for self-correction in the organization of repair in conversation". In: Language 53. 361–382.
Searle, J. (1975): "A classification of illocutionary acts." Language in Society 5. 1–23.
Sexton, J. B. & Helmreich, R. L. (2000). "Analyzing cockpit communication. The links between language, performance, error, and workload". In: Human Performance in Extreme Environments 5. 63–68.
Silberstein, D. (2001). Final Report of the Subproject "Initiating Crew Resources under High Cognitive Work Load", GIHRE project, http://www2.rz.hu-berlin.de/GIHRE/page/engl.html
Zillig, W. (1982): Bewerten: Sprechakttypen der bewertenden Rede. Tübingen: Niemeyer.

Berlin   Manfred Krifka, Silka Martens, and Florian Schwarz

Humboldt University at Berlin, Institut für Deutsche Sprache und Linguistik, Philosophische Fakultät II, Unter den Linden 6, 10099 Berlin, krifka@rz.hu-berlin.de; silkamartens@web.de; florentinoz@gmx.net

The Organisation of Coherence in Oral Communication

Rainer Dietrich and Patrick Grommes

Abstract

How do interlocutors manage to have their contribution to the discourse to be understood as coherent? Language use is a special case of a joint action performed by the speaker and the hearer in a situational setting. An essential subtask of the communicative interaction is making each turn a part of the whole. In this paper, we address the question of how the interlocuters adapt their linguistic behaviour to common ground factors established by the situational setting in the operating room and in the cockpit of an airplane. Authentic data from this type of institutional conversation under varying conditions of workload are analysed. The results show that under conditions of increased workload the balance between explicit linguistic coding of information and non-verbal communication is shifted in favour of the latter. This does not affect the success of the communication in the OR-setting, while it does affect the cockpit-setting. The difference is explained as a consequence of differences in the amount of shared focus of attention on the side of the interlocutors. A model of coherent performance is proposed that integrates theories of common ground, discourse production and structural properties of texts.

1 The Problem and Preliminary Remarks Concerning the Methods

Two substantial, if not central, tasks of a speaker in the production of a text are to bring understanding of the relevance of his/her talk to the addressee and, secondly, to ensure coherence, which is a central macro structural requirement for the clarity of speech. In the last decades, text linguistic investigations have looked at the linguistic conditions of coherence in text, both individually and within the framework of larger concepts, through which it has been identified and explicated. One of these conceptions, an extension of a psycholinguistic model of utterance production, has recently succeeded at modelling conditions of relevant and, at the same time, coherent text production. For an overview of the development of the research about questions of coherence, see Schwarz (2000: Chap. 2.3).

As is commonly known, a stronger theory is immediately faced with stronger questions. This is the case here as well. A model, which records relevance and coherence conditions in texts in a subtly differentiating and conceptually coherent manner, invites speculation as to whether or not it can lead to the recording of more complex phenomena such as exist in conditions of distributed text production in communication that involves several speakers/listeners. One way in which phenomena are more complex is that the communication partner has not only the task of shaping the individual contribution to the conversation in a relevant and coherent way, but, in addition, also has to organise the relevance and coherence within a sequence of texts while alternating between production and reception. That relevant and coherent communicating contains an additional task, as opposed to speaking in monologue, already follows from the observation that not every random sequence of distributivly produced texts, which are relevant and coherent within themselves, constitutes relevant and coherent communication. Consider the following example from act II of "Waiting for Godot" by Samuel Beckett:

Vladimir: I tell you his name is Pozzo.
Estragon: We'll soon see. (He reflects) Abel! Abel!
Pozzo: Help!
Estragon: Got it in one!
Vladimir: I begin to weary of this motif.
Estragon: Perhaps the other is called Cain. Cain! Cain!
Pozzo: Help!
Estragon: He's all Humanity. (Silence) Look at the little cloud.

Therefore, the first question is what more is there to successful communication than a sequence of individually relevant and coherent texts. We have to direct the search towards the question of how a contribution to a conversation is linked to proceeding contributions. If the connection is successful, the conversation, at this point, is understood as coherent.

Methodologically, this analysis can be seen from two different perspectives: from that of the recipients and from that of the producers. From the point of view of the recipients, it can be reconstructed whether the contribution to the conversation directed at the recipients connects to the contribution produced prior to it or not. Then the conditions of success or failure can be reconstructed, aposteriori. This is the basic approach of Gernsbacher & Givón (1995) and Givón (1995): "The measurable litmus test for success is then the readers' and listeners' coherent comprehension." (Gernsbacher & Givón 1995: viii).

An analysis that is directly aimed at the process and at the production of successful connection, is nearer to the cognitive mechanism of conversation coherence. Therefore, we have adopted this perspective. The theoretical framework of this analysis forms a model of speech production (Garrett 1980) that originally comes from the findings of analyses of speech errors. It was refined by the process and system of utterance production and, later, experimentally proven and further developed (Levelt, Roeloffs & Meyer 1999). In the end, it was supplemented by the principles for the production of coherent texts, and was, then, tested experimentally again (v. Stutterheim 1997; Kohlmann 1996).

As a first attempt to empirically analyse the organisation of coherence in conversation, it was desirable to have data that enabled the production of data analogous to the speech error data available at the time from Garrett's work. This data would be desirable in order to compare it to data that is as authentic as possible, but which is unsuccessful with respect to coherence in some cases and is otherwise similar to setting and all other relevant factors. A systematic and comparable analysis of specimens from these two groups of conversation should, actually, provide the chance to extract clues to the isolation of the decisive circumstances. In order to come to methodologically secure findings, four types of conversations are needed.

– Conversation Type 1 / Setting 1: coherent in terms of condition A

– Conversation Type 2 / Setting 1: incoherent in terms of condition A

– Conversation Type 1 / Setting 2: coherent in terms of condition B

– Conversation Type 2 / Setting 2: incoherent in terms of condition B

Such data actually exist in non-pathological fields as well and in settings in which people work together in teams and in which successfully dealing with a task requires verbal interaction. As far as circumstances change in terms of an increase in cognitive demand for the primary task, it could be that, as a result, the success of communication is impaired. Therefore, settings A and B were given. If one could find at least two types of conversations in which the strain from the primary task has different effects on communicative success, then the analysis of the difference should provide the insights that have been pursued.

Typical settings in which members of a common work group carry out one task that contains cognitive problem solving activities include the cockpit of an airplane, the control room of a nuclear power plant, a space shuttle, a large building site, the control centre for various groups of fire fighters, and a deep sea rescue team – to name a few. It is obvious that members of such work groups have to communicate, and it is easy to imagine that such work places are more or less burdened by circumstances that are changed, in terms of cognitive procedures, in regards to how the primary task is dealt with under time pressure, the pressure to do precise work, by the perceived risk of danger, by complications in the task to be completed, and by other complicating context conditions.

One needs only to think of driving a car through a large city that is familiar and then, in comparison, of driving through an unfamiliar large city, and, then, in both situations doing so one time with and one time without a talkative person in the passenger's seat. Here, communication doesn't play an instrumental roll in the driver's ability to cope with the situation unless the passenger has taken over navigation. Data from occupational contexts such as operating room teams and cockpit crews is suitable. The events in these situations and in similar work places that are connected to demands for heightened security are more and more frequently becoming the object of work and organisational psychological investigations. Still leading the way, in this regards, is the anthology from Weiner et al. (1993), to which a series of individual studies from Grote, Zala & Grommes refer (this volume, Chap. 4). Cushing (1994) provides a simple account, in layman's terms, that increases the ability to see a diagnose that is common to all of these studies and that experts and courts are increasingly concerned with: the so-called human error. The incidents at Tschernobyl, Eschede, and Puerto Plata (Birgen Air-Crash) are additional and telling examples.

In view of the goal of our investigation, we offer data samples from operating rooms and cockpit communication, identified above as settings 1 and 2. Members of a work group co-operate to perform the activities of carrying out an operation and of flying an airline jet. A fundamental task is the management of the cognitive process. The task load is variable in the standard procedure as well as in the appearance of unexpected disturbances. The team leader communicates while dealing with his/her task, and the coherence of communication is influenced differently by higher task load. Under circumstances such as are found in operating room settings, coherence is maintained under high task pressure, whereas, in the cockpit, coherence is impaired cf. Grommes & Dietrich (2002).

In the following section, the issue of how coherence in monological talk is cognitively organised will be recapitulated. Moving on from these processes, an assumption about how interlocutors cognitively control coherence over the span of several turns in a conversation will be developed. The empirical part of this article will exemplary test this concept in the manner discussed above.

2 Communication and other activities

Communication is a joint activity among two or more people. Any activity of a given group is determined by a certain goal which is jointly pursued by the group members. Any activity consists of single events comprising certain participants, specific situational conditions, and strong restrictions on the allowable contributions of the participants (Levinson 1992, 69). Flying an airplane from A to B is an activity of this kind. The goal is to reach the scheduled destination in time and without damage. The participants act jointly in a pre-defined manner on a joint task, at the same time, and at the same place. Any flight is comprised of identifiable events or segments: preparatory briefing of the crew, take-off briefing at the parking position, seating of the passengers, requesting clearance for take-off, taxiing, take-off, climbing, and so on. All of these action are subject to certain constraints, e.g. seating the passengers lies within the responsibilities of the flight attendants, whereas the cockpit crew has to perform checks while taxiing. The pilot non-flying has to explicitly report when take-off speed has been reached (he calls out "V one") and when the airplane looses contact to ground (calls out "rotate"). Then he has to take his right hand away from the thrust levers. Procedures then continue with this high degree of prescriptiveness. Rules as explicit as these are, are not to be found in the O.R. although performing surgery on a patient shows similar segmental patterns.

An essential condition for single actions to become joint activities is co-ordination within the team and of the tasks to be performed. In this respect, co-ordination is first of all the joint definition of next tasks while considering the situational factors at a given point in time. The examination of the impact of language and speech may take place on different levels in this context. Language is, on the one hand, a medium of co-ordination and, being such, serves as an instrument for explicit co-ordination and, in rarer cases, also for implicit co-ordination (see Grote, Zala & Grommes, this volume: Chap. 4, for a discussion of this terminology). On the other hand, as has been discussed above, it is necessary to co-ordinate the verbal actions themselves. This makes up two features of team activities, which have not yet been mentioned but are of some importance under conditions of increasing task load, which is the focus of our considerations: co-operativeness and the distribution of governance (see Clark 1996: 31).

Communication is a joint activity in this sense, too. It is goal-defined, e.g. to make a decision, to provide information, or to entertain one another. It has to be carried out co-operatively and comprised of single segments – turns and utterances. Communication may go along with other activities without being related to them, e.g. conversation between a driver of a car and a front seat passenger or within a dinner conversation. It can also be a necessary part of another activity as is the case when the front seat passenger supports navigation: Driver: There will soon be an exit. Passenger: Yes, it's the last one to Brooklyn. This is also the case in the task-related communication between two pilots or the operating surgeons and the O.R. personnel.

3 Coherence in Text and Coherence in Conversation

The spontaneous production of speech or a contribution to conversation is the result of a large number of processes. These are mainly cognitive processes of information processing, but, of course, there are also motor processes such as the control of the articulatory apparatus. One may differentiate between processes that are closely language related or immediate linguistic processes and their subsystems that are further away from language. These differences depend on the kind of information processed in each step of production and in the participating systems. On a more cognitive and less linguistic level, the most important processes within the frame of our analysis, besides monitoring and adaptation to the current state of the discourse, are

- constructing an intention for speaking and
- activating and selecting relevant knowledge with respect to the current conversational situation and the intention from long term memory or the immediate perception of a situation such as a sports' commentator.

Processes that are close to language contain all processes of language related planning. Since talk is linear, all information has to be brought into an order in order for the account of the talk to be made linear. This also includes information that is simultaneously activated, such as something like the memory of a sunny Spring walk in a fragrant lawn.

- Almost all information – visual, acoustic, olfactory, tactile, brief – that must ultimately be linguistically expressed, will be conceptualised by being put through a preparatory concept process.
- The bundled concepts have to be partitioned into units the size of utterances, i.e. segmentation has to take place in order to adapt the conceptual input to the syntactic requirements of language. The mental representation of an utterance, the "message", in terms of psycholinguistics, is comprised of concepts from different cognitve categories. These are temporal and spatial concepts, concepts of persons and objects, a conceptual representation of modality, and, of course, a representation of the mentally recoginized event or state, which has to be expressed.

Cognitively and psychologically, one introduces the structure of a message as a variable of a slot structure:
[m [l,t [p/o [a/e [p/o] ...]]]]

The symbols denote the modality (m), the spatial and temporal information (l,t), the person and object information, respectively, for which the state or event is true at the time (t), and the p/o information about the people and objects. This is, naturally, a very general description. For a detailed description see v. Stutterheim (1997) and Dietrich (2002, Chapter 4.3.2).

Within this vague theoretical framework, one must decide on an initial approximation as to where coherence in talk arises. In one descriptive understanding, coherence is the number of relations among pairs of cognitive categories of referential fillings, namely, those that Stutterheim calls fillings of conceptual domains. Given this, both elements of any given pair are components of two different messages from the same texts. As previously mentioned, this concept of coherence is not new, it is a slightly modified formulation of the coherence concept from the discourse structure model as developed by v. Stutterheim (1997, 62 ff.).

As an illustrative example, we will take a look at a clip from a retelling of the Charlie Chaplin-film "Modern Times":

(1) Charlie gerät in eine Demonstration von Arbeitslosen
(2) wird versehentlich für deren Anführer gehalten

(3)   und kommt ins Gefängnis.
(Charlie gets into a demonstration for the unemployed / is mistaken for their leader / and is put in prison.)

When one analyses the clip in such a way that each message is individually expressed, it is made up of three utterances. The analysis of the referential fillings lends itself to the following description:

	Modality	Place	Time	Person/Object	Event
(1)	factual	–	Zeitpunkt der Filmbetrachtung	Charlie	In eine Demonstration geraten
(2)	factual	–	nach t(1)	Charlie	Für Anführer gehalten werden
(3)	factual	Ins Gefängnis	nach t(2)	Charlie	kommen

From the table, the aforementioned pairs of referential fillings can be directly found: These pairs are

– (faktisch (1), faktisch (2)) (factual (1), factual (2))

– (geraten (1); gehalten werden (2)) (get into (1) to be taken for (2))

– (gehalten werden (2), kommen (3)). (to be taken for (2), to be put in (3))

Interesting relations are also obvious for the description of coherence. The relationship between the fillings (factual (1) and factual (2)) is called maintance. The fillings in the category Person/object are also maintained between (1) and (2) and between (2) and (3). "Geraten" (1) and "gehalten" (2) are connected by the relation "new". The series of fillings of the temporal domain between (1) and (2) and (2) and (3) is a series of shift relations. Admittedly, this concept of coherence has another substantial shortcoming. As it is defined now, it is useless for making a distinction between a coherent and incoherent text since any series of well formed utterances exhibits coherence in the sense that relations can be established between referents even if all of these relations are new. On the other hand, coherence is not automatically inherent in texts that also have relations other than just those of the "new" sort.

Last, but not least, this problem is illustrated by the Josefine-example from Bierwisch (1965):

> „Es gibt niemanden, den ihr Gesang nicht fortreißt. Unsere Sängerin heißt Josefine. Gesang ist ein Wort mit fünf Buchstaben. Sängerinnen machen viele Worte." ("There is no one who is not swept away by her singing. Our singer, Josefine. "Gesang" (singing) is a five letter word. Singers use a lot of words.")

In the text linguistic sense, coherence means more than merely the formal net of the referential fillings. The study by Halliday & Hasan (1976), which looked at cohesion as a local level far beneath a cognitive level, has made clear that reference based cohesion requires finding conditions for the referents that are not solely to be found in phonetic or written material. Approaches such as the Rhetorical Structure Theory (Mann & Thompson 1988) then try to isolate and systematise such superior connections in texts. However, an instrument that prohibits an arbitrary expansion of the quantity of relations, is lacking.

In a well formed text, coherence only exists in so far as the referential relations underlie specific restrictions about the contents of references. In a narrative text, for example, all time references refer to past intervals, and each new time reference that follows will refer to an interval subsequent to the interval referred to by the time reference of the preceding message. A well-formed, coherent text then shows shift relations in the temporal domain, whereas the references in the domain of modality are maintained, that is maintenance of factual references. Therefore, coherence in a text is well formed coherence with regards to restrictions that are considered to be valid for the given text. For this reason, the question about the source of these restrictions arises.

The conception of our discourse structure theory, i.e. v. Stutterhein 1997, Klein & v. Stutterheim (1989), assumes that a text is the expression of a type of answer to a type of question and that the type and content of the question systematically imposes coherence constraints on a text that is well-formed relative to the question. For what is meant here, text question and answer are bad terms. What is meant is not direct linguistic phenomena, but cognitive ones. The text question, which is denoted as "quaestio" in the Klein/Stutterheim-Model is the cognitive representation of an information processing task that the speaker him/herself sets, be it in reaction to an actual question the speaker asked or a self developed communicative purpose.

Similar to quaestio, the answer is also a cognitive phenomenon, namely, the cognitive representation of a linearly ordered and coherent series of messages that are verbally coded in the further production process. This representation is called discourse representation. The basis of the restriction coherence exists in the speaker's ability to systematically recognise the constraints of a prevailing quaestio. The constraints determine how well formed the discourse representation is in relation to the quaestio. The quaestio that is answered with 1) through 3) and what follows, must have been the approximate cognitive task: Recall what happened subsequently in the film "Modern Times". The different coherence conditions are derived from the tasks by the conceptualisation system of a speaker, included are the two mentioned above: "continuous temporal shift over intervals in the past" and "maintenance of factual references in the domain of modality." This may suffice in respect to "coherence within talk".

We will now look at the question of how coherence in conversation is organised by those involved. We will look at an example from the aforementioned data. Here is a clip from the communication between the pilot (PF) and co-pilot (PNF) during the approach for landing of the Lufthansa flight LH 2904 from

Frankfurt/Main to Warsaw in September 1993 (Gröning 1997). The landing approach is difficult. From the ground, the crew has been informed of strong cross winds (windshear) over the taxiway.

(1) PNF: ... Bist leicht überm Glideslope. (you are a little over the glideslope <glideslope= a radar beam instrument scale on which the plane has to remain during landing in order to reach the landing strip correctly.>)
(2) PF: Stimmt (true)
(3) PNF: Ungefähr eine Daumenbreite (roughly a thumb's width)
... <brief discussion between PF and cabin crew>
(4) PF: Sonst schaffe ich das nicht (otherwise I won't make it)
(5) PNF: Gute Idee (good idea)

Signs and symbols:
:   lengthening of sound
.   falling information
(-), (--), (---)   length of pauses (estimated, less than 1.0 sec)
(.)   micropause
< >   comments etc.
...   preceding context
=   latching within words: pronounced as two syllables
?   rising intonation
,   slightly rising intonation
;   slightly falling intonation
-      constant level of intonation
(...)   inaudible stretch of speech, or, if filled: presumed meaning of the stretch
[ ]   overlapping speech
(1.0)   length of pause, if ≥ 1 second
?   unidentified speaker

This segment is made up of five contributions to conversation. Even in borderline cases, as one finds here, in which there is only one utterance, each contribution is a speech or text as an entity in and of itself. With (1) PNF produces a talk and one has to assume a quaestio to which he answers. The message expressed by this answer hints at the fact that the flight path of the plane does not match the standard approach path. The message was directed at the pilot. In the given situation it is very likely that the co-pilot responds to the self appointed communicative task: inform the pilot about whether or not his navigation of the aircraft is proceeding correctly.

What particular explanation is there for (2)? Apparently, in the case of (2), the PF expresses several things. One thing is that can be implicitly extracted from the utterance is that PF has understood the quaestio and the talk from PNF.

The second point is that in (2) PF verbalises that he agrees with the talk (1); the answer that PNF gives to the self initiated quaestio will be confirmed by the PF. More is not needed. There will be no new quaestio initiated and naturally, no answer to a quaestio. The quaestio will be maintained and the communication partner's talk will be verified. Initially, we will call this type of turn quaestio-maintanence with confirmation.

With (3) it is a different situation. PNF shows that he has understood the talk from PF, and he has produced one new piece of talk that answers a new quaestio. It could be the answer to the, again, self initiated quaestio "How big is the deviation of the current flight path from the indicated standard flight path?" In turn (3), not only quaestio (2) and talk (2) are confirmed, but a new quaestio is also initiated that connects (content-wise) to talk (2) and is answered by talk (3). We call this type of turn a quaestio-shift. A shift can also be seen in (4) in relation to (3). With (4) what is to be understood is that PF has understood quaestio and talk in turn (3) and that the answer to the connecting quaestio, "in what way is the deviation to be justified?" is "the deviation is justifiable because any other flight movement of the aircraft rules out the success of the landing".

The connection of turn (5) to turn (4) is done by quaestio-shift as well. PNF confirms quaestio and talk in turn (4) and initiates a quaestio connected, in terms of content, to talk (5), roughly, "How is PF's consideration of the steering action to be answered?" This one is answered by the message, "the consideration is a good idea". To sum up:

– Coherence in talk is the result of cognitive planning. The components of a message show a contextual relation to components of previous messages. The ensemble of these relations does not violate the constraints, which are a rule-based result of the communicative task, the quaestio.

– Coherence in conversation is the result of the understanding and cognitive planning of the person who takes over the turn. S/he performs several cognitive actions that are supportive to communication:

(a) Deciding if the quaestio and talk of the preceding turn has been understood and expressing the result of this consideration.
(b) Deciding if the message expressed in the preceding turn should be confirmed and expressing the result of this decision.
(c) Deciding if a new quaestio should be tied in with the preceding talk, elaborating on this – if necessary – and expressing the result.

Coherence in talk is the result of quaestio-controlled referential movement from message to message. Coherence in conversation is the result of a well formed link of one turn with the previous turn through confirmation of understanding and either talk confirmation/non-confirmation (i.e. quaestio-maintanence) or quaestio-shift and an answer to the new quaestio in a new talk.

A speaker is therefore, apparently, not fully unconfined by taking over a turn in the development of an established quaestio. The new turn is, on the whole, well formed in that it adds to the development of the conversation by bringing the conversation further. Whether or not the contribution to conversation is suited to this purpose, is decided through the quaestio to which it answers. The quaestio does not only have to contextually tie in with the preceding turn, it must also be relevant. It is relevant when it contributes to the achievement of the conversation's goal. With this, a new variable is established in the examination: the conversation goal. Here, it may suffice to say that the conversational goal, as in the previously mentioned cases, can be the successful co-ordination of joint actions. For this reason, it comprises something like a problem definition or a perceived solution. Here we will not further articulate the cognitive nature of a perceived goal. In the present context we will make due with the conclusion that the role that the conversational goal plays in the control of coherence in a conversation is similar to the role that the quaestio plays in the coherence control in monological talk.

4 Cockpit and Operating Room Communication: A Field Experiment

A field experiment is not an experiment, at least not in the sense of restrictive experimental psycho-linguistics. Authentic field data shows a close relationship to the phenomena of interest, but, as the cost of this higher ecological validity they include an unknown level of circumstance, and the influences of this on the data cannot be controlled. On the other hand, results from systematically selected authentic data are directly useful for the development of an explanatory model if this is still the process of its development, as is the case here. Results from field experiments are more meaningful the more the conditions, which are relevant, can be explicated and, therefore, tested for. This seems to be sufficiently possible in this case. For more on this, see the following section.

The logic of analysis is as follows: when it is the case that the coherence in a conversation is dependent on the success of the goal oriented quaestio-movement (maintenance and shift respectively) then it is to be expected that under terms that complicate exactly this performance, the coherence of conversation will also be compromised to the point of communication failure. Whereas the competence of the speaker to plan a coherent contribution to conversation and to express him/herself coherently should not be compromised.

4.1 About the Data

As samples of data, clips from authentic cockpit and operating room conversations will be used. First, transcripts from Cockpit-Voice Recorders will be used, as they are published on the website for the National Transportation Safety Board, NTSB, the national security authority for transportation in the USA. The operating room data is being collected from the records of previous operation in the Robert-Rössle Clinic in Berlin-Buch. Where do they get there eligibility? The processes of speech production, of understanding and co-ordinating the content and the dynamics of a conversation are influenced in their contextual and formal parameters by the discourse frame. Relevant frame

parameters include temporal and spacial terms, and speech verses writing of the channel, see Clark (1996: 4–10). Cockpit and operating room communication take place within a similar frame.
1 Simultaneous spacial presence of the participant
2 Immediate visual contact
3 Immediate acoustic contact
4 Immediacy, i.e. the participants perceive actions without temporal time delay
5 Brevity i.e. the acoustic part of the discourse is rapidly scattered
6 Simultaneity i.e. the participants can directly and simultaneously speak and hear

Beyond the shared face-to-face character, both types of conversation are similar due to the fact that the content of the conversations is highly restricted by the goal of the conversations, which is to contribute to the solution of a primary task, which in itself belongs to the professional tasks of the interlocutors. Briefly, conversation in the cockpit and the O.R are, to the same degree, subject to the discourse frame of non-personal face-to-face conversations. Of course there is a difference in the settings that is also relevant to communication. Other ways of communicating are also to be found in cockpit communication, primarily, the two way radio interaction with air traffic control and, more seldom, with the crew members of other air crafts in the air. Communication in the cockpit is temporally acoustically recorded, whereas in the operating room this is not normally case. In the case of both the given and the observed situation, the known observer paradox cannot be ruled out. It may be the case that in the cockpit, pilots are accustomed to observation and that conversation is, therefore, not affected. In the operating room there is at least anecdotal evidence that supports the idea that the actors of the observation are not continuously aware of the observation, and in this particular case, there is also a familiarizations effect due to the fact that the hospital is a teaching hospital in which there are frequent visitors and observers. In the end, content and form are more strongly prescribed in cockpit communication, in some cases, even literally. Apart from technical terms, the form of the utterances in operating room communication is not at all prescribed, and the interaction is freer – at least in Europe, this is the case. A common trait of both is that the setting permits temporary personal communication, which is different from what is provided by a strict institutional understanding of communication (see Clark 1996: 5).

4.2   Coherence in the Cockpit and Operating Room Communication under low task load

As stated, the assumption proceeds from the fact that the cognitive processes of the organisation of coherence in conversation, in particular the planning of the quaestio shift, can be managed without significant interference as long as there are lower additional demands for the cognitive system.

Phases with lower task load in the cockpit include rolling to the starting position and flying at cruising altitude on a given course with auto-pilot activated. Mid-level task load exists in phases that include many standardised actions such as are found in starting, in climbing to cruising altitude, in approaching the scheduled airport and with landing. High task load develops for the crew through the necessity of managing an unexpected disturbance in a flight. A typical example of cockpit communication under low task load is found in T-1.

(T-1)	Flight FF41, 20 Dec. 1995, New York-Miami, 11:00 am, Boeing 747-136. (NTSB (1996)) Phase: rolling to the starting position at the John F. Kennedy airport In the cockpit: Captain (CPT = Pilot), First Officer (FIO), plane engineer (FE) and a jumpseat passenger (JSP) (Jump Seat=extra seat in the cockpit). The aircraft has been de-iced and has received staring permission. At 11:16 it rolls slowly to the correct starting position and now stands on the taxiway.
(1) CPT	I'm gonna stop and run these engines right here (CPT announces his intention: to stop on the way to the take-off position and to start up the engines <to remove the rest of the ice>).
(2) FIO	O.K.
(3) CPT	Mike, keep your eye outside. If we start to move, let me know.
(4) FIO	... tell ground what we're doing?
(5) CPT	Naw.
(6) FIO	Feels like we're moving.
(7) JSP	It started to move.
(8) ?	Yep.
(9) JSP	Slippery out there.
(10) CPT	It's an ice rink here.

At this moment, the crew's primary task is to test – on the way to the starting position – how slippery the ground is. In order to do this, a stop-and-run-manoeuvre is carried out. The goal is to obtain insights into the condition of the runway. The accompanying communication is task oriented. Each speaker coherently inserts his or her turn in the conversation.

(1)–(2)	Quaestio-maintanance
(2)–(3)	Quaestio-shift; CPT makes it clear that he has registered the confirmation from FIO and produces an answer to the self-initiated quaestio, "How FIO should be involved in the maneouvre?"
(3)–(4)	Quaestio-shift; FIO makes it clear that he has understood the speech (3) and as an answer to the, again, self-initiated, quastio,

	gives the suggestion that the airport's ground control be informed of the maneouvor.
(4)–(5)	Quaestio-shift: refusal of the proposition contained in (4).
(5)–(6)	Quaestio- resumption
	...

In the sequence of events in operation, there are also phases with low, medium, and high task load. Typically, cognitive and psychomotor stresses are not found in the preliminary phase: in a lung operation, for example, the incision to open the thorax and approaching the area from which the tissue is to be removed. Medium task load includes phases in which one is close to the main blood vessels or a tumour to be resected. High task load emerges through difficult operating conditions: the beginning of hemorrhaging and during the removal of the tumourous tissue. Here is a segment from a conversation during the preliminary phase of a lung resection (removal of the tumourous part of the lung).

(T-2)	Situation: Operation. Participants: Operating surgeon (COP), Assistant (AST); Actual task: The opening of the thorax from the position of the sixth rib
(1) cop	a) das hier is die sechste rippe. (this here is the sixth rib) b) und danach gehste rein mit dem (...) ICR Thorax. (and then go in with the ...)
(2) ast	also (.) hier (.) drauf; (then (.) here(.) on that,)
(3) cop	na auf der hier (well, on this here)
(4) ast	o.k. und das hier rein? (okay, and then in this here?)
(5) cop	da rein.(in there)
(6) ast	gut. (.) bitte elektrisch- (good (.) please electrical-(electrical coagulation to cut through the tissue and, at the same time, to close the vessels))
(7) cop	aber das sind schon teufelskerle- (but they are tough ones (she is referring to the previous conversation segment))
(8) ast	(aber mit) da hat er n bisschen brutal ((but, with) there he was a little brutal-(reference as above))
(9) cop	pass auf (.) und jetzt machste[=so=d]ass de n bisschen- (watch out (.) and now you do it so that you . . . a little . .)
(10) ast	[=ja=a=] (yes)
(11) ast	am oberrand mehr oder- (more on the upper edge, or-)
(12) cop	ja=a also gut- wenn de- aber nicht nach unten weitergehen. (yes, then, good. When the--but ... don't go further down)
(13) ast	hm=hm.

(14) cop	eher n stückchen nach oben. ja? (first/rather a little bit up, yes?)
(15) ast	okay.
(16) cop	n millimeter weiter nach oben. aber sons okay (a millimeter more up, but otherwise okay)
(1)–(2)	AST makes it clear that conversation from COP(1) has been registered in and expresses his answer to the (self initiated) quaestio, "Should I make sure that I mean the same point as COP. (Quaestio-shift through precise rendering of the local reference)
(2)–(3)	Quaestio-maintenance (definition of the place of incision) and shift (Precision of the local reference)
(3)–(4)	Maintenance of the quaestio from (3) and adding information about an instrument to be used.
(4)–(5)	Quaestio-maintenance

Except for the references to earlier segments of the conversation in (7) and (8), the communication is almost task oriented. It is coherent. The coherence admittedly is brought about from a somewhat different method than in the cockpit communication. Similar to this, are segments (1) to (5).

In contrast to the segment from cockpit conversation, one can see, at first glance, that there is a higher ratio of deictic place and object references: 'das hier' (1), 'hier drauf' (2), 'der hier' (3), 'hier' (4), 'da' (5). But up to (7) one can trace the steps of the coherence organisation with the linguistic interaction. That changes between (7) and (9). From understanding (7)–(8), one is not able to recognize which quaestio was answered by (9). (9) neither further clarifies that COP has registered (8) nor to what extent the contributions to (9)–(11) answer a quaestio that ties in to (8). The deictic element, "jetzt" (now) in (9) delivers the key. COP watches AST's actions and develops the quaestio, "How should AST proceed now?" from AST's perception of the situation. This is not tied into a contribution to a conversation but rather to a perceived circumstance. The coherence is rendered true because COP assumes that AST perceives the same situation at hand, at the same time, because his attention and, with that, his cognitive processing, is directed at the situation at hand. The analysis of the subsequent samples will show that this is the point at which OR and cockpit communication diverge from one another. Both are face-to-face settings, however, in the operating room, primary tasks involve participants of conversation whose attention is directed towards and maintained on a common field of perception. In the cockpit this is not continuously the case. There, it is – dependent upon the division of labor – rather typical that the pilot and co pilot are busy with separate fields of the current situation. This is also similar with the members of a nuclear power plant control room. (See article from Straeter in this issue.)

4.3 Coherence in Cockpit and Operating Room Communication under Conditions of High Task Load

We will look at the organisation of coherence in both work places under the condition of high task load through the primary task. First a sample from the cockpit data (T-3):

(T-3) Flight ASE 529, 21.8.1995, Atlanta–Gulfport, Time: 12.53 pm. Embraer 120 ER: a turbo propeller machine with two engines (NTSB (1996a))

Phase: Climbing to cruising altitude. In Cockpit: Captain (CPT=Pilot), First Officer (FIO)

Additionally: Air control on the ground (CTR) Situation: in climb flight (16 knots). They lose a blade from one of the propellers of the left engine. The propeller will not remain idling, so the left side of the aircraft decelerates. The aircraft rolls to the left and begins to sink. The cockpit crew has three problems to handle:
(a) to continue to fly the aircraft
(b) to gain control of the technical consequences of the incident: i.e. preventing the inflammation of the damaged engine, switching on help systems, etc.
(c) adjusting the flight plan to the emergency situation

Because of a fixed distribution of tasks, the crew members have their own areas of responsibility and, therefore, they have to constantly inform one another about their planned and performed actions, as well as about their perceptions.

(1) CPT	We got a left engine out. Left power lever. Flight idle. Left condition lever. Left condition lever.
(2) FIO	Yeah.
(3) CPT	Feather.
(4)	(Series of rapid beeps for one second similar to engine fire warning.)
(5) CPT	Yeah, we're feathered. Left condition lever. Fuel shut off.
(6) CPT	I need some help here.
	(Mechanical voice messages for engine control and oil cease. Chimes and auto-pilot warning continues.)
(7) FIO	OK.
(8) CPT	I need some help on this.
(9) ?	You said it's feathered.
(10) CPT	Uh ...
(11) FIO	It did feather.

(12) CPT	It's feathered.
(13) FIO	OK.
(14)	Master warning chimes and voice warning continues.
(15) CPT	What the hell's going on with this thing.
	...
(16) CPT	I can't hold this thing. Help me hold it.
(17) FIO	OK.
(18) CPT	All right comin' on head set.
(19) FIO	Atlanta center. AC 529, declaring an emergency. We had an engine failure ...

Here, FIO takes over the radio communication with flight control. The aircraft is initially called back to the departure airport. Simultaneously, CPT orders that they go through the checklist. Then they go through the checklist together, carry out the prescribed actions and inform one another about the action. At the same time, CPT flies the plane, gives orders, and FIO takes over the radio communication with air traffic control. After the checklist for engine failure has been completed, the CPT orders that they begin to work through the "single engine" checklist.

(20) CPT	All right, single-engine checklist please.
(21) CTR	AC 529, I've lost your transponder. Say altitude.
(22) FIO	We're out of four point five at this time. ...

The interaction takes almost one and a half minutes.

| | ... |
| (23) CPT | Sing, single, single-engine checklist, please! |

Further radio traffic between FIO and CTR.

| (24) CPT | Help me, help me hold it, help me hold, help me hold it. |

The course of communication shows three phases. In the first phase, CPT gives a series of commands in order to improve the machine's flight ability after the engine failure. This includes the instructions for placing the propeller blades in horizontal gliding position (feathered), so that wind resistance is minimized. Nevertheless, steering is obviously difficult (8), and the pilots must, once again, inform one another about the success of this action (9) – (13). Between most turns, the coherence is organised through quaestio-maintenance (1) – (2), (2) – (3), (6) – (7), (11) – (12), (12) – (13), (16) – (17). In the second phase, two strands of communication take place simultaneously: The one between CPT and FIO and the one between FIO and CTR. The first one accompanies the handling of the checklist, the second, the planning of the flight. In this phase, the CPT and FIO succeed in coherently organising their particular communication. In phase three, as time pressure increases, FIO concentrates his attention on the interaction with CTR and is no longer responsive to CPT (20) – (22) or to the urgent appeal from CPT, (23) and (24). The communication between CPT and FIO breaks down and, with that, the team work in the cockpit and the chance of dealing with the primary task – the landing of the aircraft.

In CPT's emergency landing that follows, 8 of 29 people aboard loose their lives, among them, 7 passengers. Therefore one can conclude that when participants in a conversation are working under high task load, organisation of coherence becomes increasingly unsuccessful. The cognitive task load on FIO that comes from the fact that his attention is divided between two areas of activity – flying the aircraft with CPT and the approach to the airport – influences the successful co-ordination of communication with CPT.

This data, together with results from (T-1) allows us to assume that the capacity to organise coherent communication during phases of increasing task load gradually decreases. Under conditions of relatively low task load, as in (T-1), coherence emerges more frequently through quaestio-shift than it does through quaestio-maintenance. Under higher task load, as in phases 1 and 2 from (T-3), nearly no quastio-shift takes place, but quaestio-maintenance still succeeds. The mental capacity to perform quaestio-maintenance is exhausted by increasing cognitive task load, because of the division of attention. FIO seems to no longer be able to acknowledge the speech directed at him by CPT, and even less, to be able to acknowledge the content of the speech. Presumably, he is no longer able to process it at all.

This finding is supported by an observation from Silberstein & Dietrich (in this issue). The results from 14 samples examined by conversation analysis tools, reported that the ability to take in information (receptivity) decreases under increasing task load and, in the end, may break down completely. (See Silberstein & Dietrich, Chap. 6.1.3.) If one applies the assumption that ability to process referential movements is impaired under increasing cognitive task load when a team member increasingly focuses the breadth of his/her attention, then it is to be expected that under the alternative conditions of a largely shared attention field, the disruptive influence on the ability to produce coherent communication will not appear. (T-4) is a segment from operating room communication under high task load.

(T-4) situation: Operation of a large tumour in the region of the left gluteus of the patient. Several circumstances make the operation in the final phase a bit complicated. The tumour is uncommonly large and it had spread in the gluteus of the patient. The surgical task lies in seperating the tumour completely from the surrounding tissue, completely removing the tumour tissue, pinching off the veins that nourish the tumour, and making sure that no blood leaves them. After roughly 90 minutes of operation, the team has succeeded in approaching the tumour. A particularly high task load originates suddenly through haemorrhaging, that follows the surgeon's action. Participants: operating surgeon (COP), assistant (AST) and a doctor in training (AIP)

(1)(a) cop	War nich gu:t. (.) (wasn't good)
(b)	Scheiße. (---) (shit)
(c)	Pinzette. ( ) (tweezers)
...	(1.0) <1 seconds with no verbal communication>
(2) ast	Für mich 'ne feine Klemme. (for me a fine clip)
...	(7.0)
(3) cop	Sche:re. (scissors)
...	(5.0)
(4)	Einspannen. (threading) <An order to thread the instrument>
...	(3.0)
(5) ast	'hm=hm.
(6) ast	Weißt du, welche ich mein? (Do you know which one I mean?)
(7) aip	Ja, ich hab's jetzt hier. (yes, i have it now here)
(8) cop	Kommt das von da:? (does this come from there?)
(9) aip	Das kommt von hi=er = (that comes from here)
(10) cop	=ja=a= (yes)
(11) ast	=lass uns ma da auch diesen stehn. (let's stop this one too) Dann is nämlich ruhe auch. (then it's also quiet)

The communication is markedly reduced, but, at the same time, coherent. In the utterances, important references remain linguistically unexpressed and between the turns there are long pauses – from (1) to (5) around 16 seconds, in which 12 words are said. In a conversation with a normal flow of talk, an average of three words are produced per second. In (1a) COP does not articulate what has happened nor to whom he directs his speech or what is supposed to be done with the tweezers. The fact that their attention is directed on a common part of the situation and that this knowledge is continually supplemented by visual perception explains how it is that the communication is at the same time apparently coherent, that all individuals involved understand which quaestio a talk answers and to which preceding information the quaestio is connected. With this, the balance between linguistically expressed information and information provided by knowledge about the situation may be shifted towards this second area, as happens in (1) – (4). This does not mean that no communication takes place. Each utterance constitutes a complete answer to one of the parts of the understood quaestio that is coherently embedded in the information flow. For example, (2) ties in with (1c), which makes it clear that this is taken to be acknowledged and answers the shifted quaestio "Who should ISR give what next?" Coherence in the communication that follows is also maintained through quaestio-shift. A self explanatory example with explicit confirmation of the talk of the preceding turn is found in the transition from (6) to (7).

It can also be recorded that coherent communication under conditions of high task load can be cognitively organised, provided that the attention fields of those involved adequately overlap. This seems to fundamentally contribute something like "common ground" in the sense of Clark (1996), i.e. to produce a common knowledge basis that is necessary for co-ordinated joint actions. For a discussion of the status of shared mental models, see Grote, Zala & Grommes (in this issue), for terminology, see Lee (2001).

Summary and Discussion

The initial question was, with which cognitive procedures people involved in a conversation connect the contributions to talk across turn changes and, with that, make the conversation coherent. Starting with the theory that coherence in monologues is established through referential relations between utterances, it has been proposed that coherence in dialogues may be planned in an analogous way but on a higher level of discourse processing. It has been assumed that a conversation constitutes a common activity that is guided by the conversational goal for the people involved.

Oriented on the jointly recognized goal, a speaker ties his/her contribution into the preceding turn by acknowledging understanding of that turn and by either acknowledging the previous quaestio and answering with respect to the previous turn or by denying the original quaestio. Thus, his/her turn is coherent by way of quastio-maintenance. The second possibility is to signal understanding of the previous turn by acknowledging its quaestio and developing, from this, a new one that is oriented towards the conversational goal – the answer to which helps to achieve this goal jointly. This outline of an explanatory framework has been tested by means of samples of authentic communication.

The samples, which were otherwise similar, were selected so that, due to situational changes, coping with the planning of coherence is impaired by cognitively increasing task load due to an additional cognitive task (cockpit condition) The results of these field experiments confirm the outline. Increasing task load in the cockpit as a result of the division of labour between pilot and co-pilot leads to a situation in which the focus of attention is taken away from one of the fields of action – in this case, the internal cockpit communication. With this, the capacity to process the contribution of the discourse participants is impaired, and with it, the pre-condition to coherently connect one's own contributions. The communication breaks down. In the operating room setting, with its strongly overlapping realms of attention in dealing with the primary task, communication remains coherent even under higher cognitive task load.

In light of the many miscellaneous differences between the two work places that have been compared, the question that naturally arises, is if other work place specific differences explain the different success in coherence organisation or not. In order to test this, we will, in concluding, look at a segment from cockpit communication under high task load with a largely shared scope of attention for the pilot and co-pilot. When it is supposed that overlapping or non-overlapping areas of the attention of the interlocutors in a certain situation are the relevant factors for successful organisation of coherence, one would expect that (in this case and under such conditions) coherence could be maintained despite the high task load. This segment is, by the way, the final phase of the sample section that has been discussed in section 3 above. Here are the details:

(T-5) flight LH 2904, 14.09.1993, Frankfurt/Main–Warsaw. Time:15.43. Airbus A320-211.

Phase: Approach and landing to the Warsaw airport Okecie. In the cockpit: captain (CPT, also the pilot flying, PF); First Officer (FIO, pilot not flying PNF); Further components: Tower (TWR) and approach control (AAP). The approach takes place in adverse weather conditions: strong cross winds (windshear) over the landing strip, which can lead to breaking problems and ultimately to a dangerous approach to the concrete wall beyond the end of the runway. The air craft is situated four hundred feet above the ground, strong gusts of cross wind.

	ACO	Four hundred <eine automatische Höhenansage>
	...	
	ACO	Two hundred
(1)	FIO	Von rechts kommt jetzt (coming from the right now)
(2)	CPT	Jetzt kommt die **windshear** <Bö> (now the cross wind (windshear) comes)
	ACO	One hundred
(3)	FIO	Dreht, dreht (turns, turns) <the airplane is being slightly turned around its vertical axis by the wind>
	...	
	ACO	Thirty
	ACO	Retard, retard <verlangsamen, verlangsamen>
(4)	CPT	Brems mal mit (break with) Full breaking
(5)	FIO	Reverse auf? (is reverse on?) <Asks if reverse thrust is turned on.>
(6)	CPT ...	Ja's voll (yes, full)
(7) (a) (b) (c)	CPT	Weiter bremsen! (break more) Scheiße (shit) Was machen wir jetzt (what are we doing here?)
(8)	FIO	Tja, du kannst nix mehr machen (yeah, you cant do anything else)

(9)	CPT	Ich möcht' da nicht gegen knallen. (I don't want to crash against there.) <against the wall beyond the end of the runway>
(10)	FIO	Dreh'n weg (turn it away)
(11)	CPT	Was? (what?)
(12)	FIO	Dreh ihn weg (turn it away)

CPT steers the airplane, still at 72 knots, to the right of the runway, it rolls another 90 meters over the field and then touches the wall beyond the end of the runway sideways. One crew member and one passenger are fatally injured.

The situation is typical for situations with higher cognitive task load. The attention of both the pilots is, in this phase, on the same part of the situation: specifically, on the runway, the end of the runway with the wall, and on the movement of the airplane. This looks similar to (T-2) in the use of deictic expressions for references to the whole situation, (7c), and to places ("da" in (9)). The communication is coherent. The transition from (9) to (10) is a prototypical example for quaestio-shift. This data validates the expectation that planning of coherence in the cockpit under high cognitive task load is successful, as long as the attention of the individuals involved in conversation is focused on a common field.

References

Bierwisch, M. (1965): „Poetik und Linguistik". In: Kreutzer, H. & Gunzenhäuser, R. (Eds.): Mathematik und Dichtung. München: Nymphenburger. 49–65.

Clark, H. H. (1996): Using language. Cambridge: Cambridge University Press.

Cushing, S. (1994): Fatal words. Communication clashes and aircraft crashes. Chicago: The University of Chicago Press.

Dietrich, R. (2002): Psycholinguistik. Stuttgart: Metzler.

Garrett, M. F. (1980): "Levels of processing in sentence production". In: Butterworth, B. (Ed.): Language Production: Vol. 1. Speech and talk. New York: Academic Press. 177–220.

Gernsbacher, M. A. & Givón, T. (1995): "Introduction: Coherence as mental entity". In: Gernsbacher, M. A. & Givón, T. (Eds.): Coherence in spontaneous text. Amsterdam/Philadelphia: John Benjamins Publishing Co. vii–x.

Givón, T. (1995): "Coherence in text vs. coherence in mind". In: Gernsbacher, M. A. & Givón, T. (Eds.): Coherence in spontaneous text. Amsterdam/Philadelphia: John Benjamins Publishing Co. 59–115.

Gröning, M. (1997): "Selected appendices from the Airbus A320-211 Warsaw accident report". In: Ladkin, P. B. (Ed.): Abstracts of References and Incidents. (= http://www.rvs.uni-bielefeld.de/publications/Incidents/DOCS/ComAndRep/Warsaw/appendices.html (Part 5 and 6))

Grommes, P. & Dietrich, R. (2002): "Coherence in operating room team and cockpit Communication. A psycholinguistic contribution to applied linguistics". In: Georgetown University Round Table on Languages and Linguistics 2000 – Linguistics, Language, and the professions: Education, Journalism, Law, Medicine, and Technology. Georgetown: Georgetown University Press. 190–219.

Grote, G, Zala-Mezö, E. & Grommes, P. (2003): (this volume)

Halliday, M. A. K. & Hasan, R. (1976): Cohesion in English. Harlow, England: Longman.

Klein, W. & Stutterheim, C. v. (1989): "Referential Movement in Descriptive and Narrative Discourse". In: Dietrich, R. & Graumann, C. F. (Eds.): Language Processing in Social Context. Amsterdam: Elsevier Science Publishing Co. 39–76.

Kohlmann, U. (1996): Objektreferenz in Beschreibungen. Frankfurt am Main: Peter Lang.

Lee, B. P. H. (2001): "Mutual knowledge, background knowledge and shared beliefs: Their roles in establishing common ground". In: Journal of Pragmatics 33. 21–44.

Levelt, W. J. M., Roeloffs, A. & Meyer, A. S. (1999): "A theory of lexical access in speech production". In: Behavioral and Brain Sciences 22. 1–75.

Levinson, S. (1992): "Activity types and language". In: Drew, P. & Heritage, J. (Eds.).: Talk at Work. Cambridge: Cambridge University Press. 66–100.

Mann, W. C. & Thompson, S. (1988): "Rhetorical Structure Theory: Toward a functional theory of text organization". In: Text 8 (3). 243–281.

NTSB (= National Transportation Safety Board) (1996): Aircraft Accident Report: Runway departure during attempted takeoff, Tower Air flight 41, Boeing 747-136, N606FF, JFK International Airport, New York, December 20, 1995 (Report No. NTSB/AAR-96/04). Washington, D.C. (= http://www.ntsb.gov/Publictn/1996/aar9604.pdf)

NTSB (= National Transportation Safety Board) (1996a): Aircraft accident report: In-flight loss of propeller blade, forced landing, and collision with terrain, Atlantic Southeast Airlines, inc., Flight 529, Embraer EMB-120RT, N256AS, Carrollton, Georgia, August 21, 1995 (Report No. NTSB/AAR-96/06). Washington, D.C. (= http://www.ntsb.gov/Publictn/1996/aar9606.pdf)

Schwarz, M. (2000): Indirekte Anaphern in Texten: Studien zur domänengebundenen Referenz und Kohärenz im Deutschen. Tübingen: Niemeyer.

Silberstein, D. & Dietrich, R. (2003): (this volume)

Sträter, O. (2003): (this volume)

Stutterheim, C. v. (1997): Einige Prinzipien des Textaufbaus: Empirische Untersuchungen zur Produktion mündlicher Texte. Tübingen: Niemeyer.

Wiener, E. L., Kanki, B. G & Helmreich, R. L. (Eds.) (1993): Cockpit Resource Management. San Diego: Academic Press.

Berlin   Rainer Dietrich and Patrick Grommes

Humboldt University at Berlin, Institut für Deutsche Sprache und Linguistik, Unter den Linden 6, 10099 Berlin, Rainer.Dietrich@rz.hu-berlin.de; Patrick.Grommes@rz.hu-berlin.de

Effects of Standardization on Coordination and Communication in High Workload Situations

Gudela Grote, Enikö Zala-Mezö, and Patrick Grommes

Abstract

In the following article we outline a research proposal with the main question: how does standardization influence coordination processes. We focus on two high risk systems, aviation and medicine, where work processes in the former are much more standardized than in the latter. We show the theoretical background from both traditional and more recent research perspectives. In our methodology we combine methods from linguistic and from organizational psychology: we analyze the communication processes quantitatively based on observational categories related to information flow and leadership as well as more qualitatively using linguistic categories (Grommes & Dietrich, this issue) and indicators for heedful interrelating (Weick & Roberts 1993). The aim of the study is to identify different types of coordination patterns under conditions of high versus low work load and high versus low standardization.

1 Introduction

Coordination defined as tuning of interdependent work processes to promote concerted action towards a superordinate goal (Kieser & Kubicek 1989) is needed for any activity which cannot be carried out by one person and which cannot be subdivided into independent parts (Hackman & Morris 1975). Coordination is therefore a core activity in any work organization. As Tesluk et al. (1997) formulate: "The essence of organizational action is the coordination, synchronization, and integration of the contributions of all organizational members into a series of collective responses." As a consequence of the degree and type of division of labour and specialization more or less effort will be required for coordination and different kinds of coordination mechanisms will be more or less successful. Crucial in this respect is the type of interdependence created by the chosen division of labour in combination with the general demands of the task and the task environment. Generally, three types of interdependence of work activities are distinguished (e.g. Tesluk et al. 1997; Thompson 1967):

Pooled interdependence is present, when system performance is an additive function of individual performance. The performance of other members of the system can have an effect on the work of the individual members but only indirectly through parallel contributions to a superordinate goal. Coordination in this case is usually achieved via centrally determined work programs which every individual has to follow independently and which assure that subtask serve the superordinate goal.

Sequential interdependence is a unidirectional work flow arrangement, where individual performance depends on the proper fulfilment of prior subtasks. Synchronization is needed here based on centrally determined programs and plans which spell out the exact content and temporal requirements of subtask fulfilment.

Reciprocal interdependence means that information and results of work activities have to be exchanged between team continuously. Coordination is mainly achieved via direct communication, be it in the form of personal directives or multilateral flow of communication between the individuals involved in self-regulated task performance.

In view of special demands created by task performance in high risk situations like flying an airplane or operating on a patient, Tesluk et al. (1997) have added a fourth form of interdependence called intensive work situations where team members work very closely together and work flow is poly-directional, flexible and very intensive, because the team repeatedly faces novel situations with new problems which have to diagnosed and solved within the team.

In the following, the focus will be on such intensive work situations and the specific requirements for coordination in these situations. Studying accident and incident reports one can state that failures occur most often not because of technical or individual insufficiency but because a team fails to coordinate its mutual action (Hackman 1993). Standardization, i.e. coordination via centrally determined and highly formalized programs and plans, as a widely used form of coordination in high risk work systems will be discussed in terms of its advantages and disadvantages for achieving successful performance. A more differentiated approach to coordination via standardization will be suggested and a study design outlined in order to investigate the effects of standardization on team performance. In the study linguistic concepts of coordination (see article by Grommes & Dietrich; see also Kanki & Palmer 1993, for a summary of previous communication research) are incorporated as a means to analyse in more detail how communication in work teams serves coordination and how in turn standardization as prescribed form of coordination influences communication. As Kanki & Palmer (1993) formulate: "Communication variations may be (1) solutions that represent the means by which tasks are carried out verbally; or (2) symptoms representing behavioural styles that distinguish various ways in which crewmembers interact and coordinate their work". Combining categories stemming from organizational as well as from linguistic research on co-ordination is hoped to form a more global and integrated interdisciplinary approach which can lead to a better understanding of the observed phenomena.

2 Standardized coordination in high risk organizations

In order to understand the reasons for and affects of standardized coordination in high risk organizations, it is helpful to conceptualise organizational activities in terms of the management of uncertainty. The kinds of uncertainty an organization has to deal with and how these uncertainties are handled by the organization has been a core issue in organization theory. Prominent authors in this field like Thompson (1967), Perrow (1967) and Susman (1976) have helped to systematize the nature of uncertainties relevant to organizations and the ways organizations deal with them. Two general sources of uncertainties were identified, i.e. the transformation processes an organization has to perform and the environment within which these processes take place. In order to describe the organization's capabilities of handling these different types of uncertainties, characteristics like degree of specialization, types of task interdependence, forms of coordination, degree of standardization and formalization, and degree of centralization are used.

There are two extreme approaches to handling uncertainty. The first one tries to minimize uncertainty or at least the effects of uncertainty in the organization using mainly feedforward control based on high standardization and programming of work flows. Enormous efforts are put into centralized planning and continuous monitoring of the execution of these plans, providing minimal degrees of freedom to the people in charge of carrying out the plans. If the organization's environments become more and more complex – or rather the complexity is more and more acknowledged – then more effort has to be put into reducing the uncertainties connected with the complexity. The other approach having been advertised by organization theorists and work scientists for several decades now is – instead of fighting uncertainties in an attempt to minimize the uncertainties themselves or at least their effect in the organization – to enable each and every member of an organization to handle uncertainties locally and to allow for feedback control. From this perspective, planning is understood primarily as a resource for situated action (Suchman 1987), not as blueprint for centrally determined and monitored action. Local actors need to be given as many degrees of freedom as possible, achieving concerted action mainly through lateral, task-induced coordination. Disturbances are also regarded as opportunities for use and expansion of individual competencies and for organizational innovation and change.

Another way of looking at the two approaches to uncertainty is to describe them in terms of the distribution of autonomy and control in the organization. Differing from the frequent almost synonymous use of the two terms autonomy and control, they are used here to indicate two quite different types of influence (cf. Grote 1997). Autonomy is defined as self-determination regarding goals and the rules to be followed in achieving these goals. Control is defined as the influence on a given situation allowing to reach goals which have been determined either autonomously or by others. When attempting to minimize uncertainty, autonomy stays completely with centrally located decision-makers who also try to maximize their control by prescribing in minute detail how the people implementing their plans have to use their influence in a given situation. Competent coping with uncertainty on the other hand is characterized by maximum local control as well as sufficient local autonomy in order to choose or at least modify goals and rules for goal achievement in view of maximum effectiveness in the exertion of local control.

Standardization can be regarded as the key element in the minimising uncertainty approach, while the competent coping with uncertainty relies much more on personal and lateral coordination mechanisms. There are some critical voices regarding the usefulness of high levels of standardization, mainly pointing to the systems reduced capability to adequately act in the face of requirements stemming from internal and external disturbances of normal operation (e.g. Amalberti 1999; Perrow 1984; Grote 1997). But at the same time, the critics of standardized coordination have not been very well able to give concrete suggestions for what coordination mechanisms to use in order to improve the predictability and controllability of a system while at the same time increasing its flexibility (e.g. Perrow 1984). Following, some newer concepts will be presented that may help in shaping standardization in a way more conducive to safe operation in high-risk systems.

3 New directions for thinking about standardization

In most high risk systems, standardization in the form of standard operating procedures has been developed with ever increasing detail in order to streamline human action and to reduce its influence as a risk factor. Procedures are often a direct consequence of incidents and accidents the analysis of which provides knowledge of unforeseen wrongful courses of action against which new rules are developed as a defence. While generally there is an understanding that rules are useful guides for safe behavior, there is also an increasing concern that too many rules incrementally developed will not make up a good system to help human actors do the right thing especially in states of abnormal operation where they would need strong, but also flexible guidance (e.g. Amalberti 1999). These concerns go back to basic observations on how rules specifying the exact operations to execute can have a detrimental effect on action because they do not allow the performing person to develop an underlying plan of their own, but instead further the atomization of actions and the focus on micro-difficulties (Vermersch 1985). As Hoc writes (1988: 206):

> By giving the impression that they make up a plan, instructions may give users the feeling that no planning activity is necessary on their part for implementation. However, instructions are generally not hierarchized. The action sequence is described, but the goal structure is not explicit and the rationale is never presented. Nonetheless a hierarchical structure linking actions and functions is probably crucial to the development of sufficiently adaptive procedural knowledge. To date there is no clear-cut empirical evidence on this point.

Another basic problem with standardization is that especially in non-routine situations reliance on common standards may turn into an overreliance, impeding switches to more explicit coordination and with that switches to higher levels of common action regulation, i.e. switches from skill-based to rule-based or from rule-based to knowledge-based behavior.[1] This problem can be exacerbated by the fact that standardization is a strong force towards shared understanding of a situation and its demands in a team, because it creates a common framework for team behavior reducing the need for explicit coordination. The expectation of shared goals, plans, perspectives, and knowledge bases created by reference to the same set of standard operating procedures, as helpful as it is under most conditions, does involve the risk of not realizing the need for explicit coordination, e.g. in non-routine situations.

Making a similar distinction between minimizing uncertainties vs. competently coping with uncertainties, as was suggested before in this article, Rasmussen has argued that "rather than striving to control behaviour by fighting deviations from a particular pre-planned path, the focus should be on the control of behaviour by making the boundaries explicit and known and by giving opportunities to develop coping skills at boundaries" (Rasmussen 1997: 191; italics in the original). Rules then would have the function to clarify boundaries and to suggest ways of handling system states close to those boundaries.

In line with this approach to rules, some authors have begun to develop typologies of rules in order to help the design of rule systems directly tailored to the needs for guidance as well as for autonomy and control arising in different stages of action regulation (e.g. Hale & Swuste 1998; LePlat 1998). From an action regulation perspective, rules can concern goals to be achieved, define the way in which decisions about a course of action must be arrived at, or prescribe concrete actions.

Hale & Swuste (1998) also suggest some criteria to help decide at which level of the organization these rules should be defined: Predictability of the system (the higher the predictability the more action rules decided upon at higher levels of the organization); innovation rate in the system (the higher the innovation rate, the more action rules need to be decided upon on operative levels of the organization); interaction requirements (the higher the interaction requirements, the more action rules need to be decided upon at higher levels of the organization); local expertise (the higher local expertise the more action rules should be decided upon on operative levels of the organization). These criteria can be easily related to the general issue of minimising vs. competent handling of uncertainties, where minimising uncertainties through centrally determined action rules is only recommended in systems with a generally low level of uncertainties (high predictability, low innovation rate). Also, these recommendations are linked to the idea of second order autonomy stating that

---

[1] It is to be noted that rule-based behaviour refers to a special kind of action regulation effort, i.e. the selection of behaviour based on choices between fairly prescribed alternative courses of action. Rules in the meaning used above as standard operating procedures can be related to this level of action regulation, but also to the other two levels, depending on the type of rule (LePlat 1998).

people should be involved in decisions restraining their operative autonomy (Grote 1997; LePlat 1998), especially in organizations with high local expertise.

Systematic research into the design and management of safety-related rules has only recently begun, providing tentative classification schemes mainly based on the rules' relevance for individual action regulation (Hale & Swuste 1998; Leplat 1998; Reason, Parker & Lawton 1998). From an organizational perspective, rules should also be discussed as elements of the coordination mechanisms operating within and between parts of an organization.

During the last decade, coordination in high-risk environments has been addressed in an increasing number of studies. Usually, coordination on team level has been analysed with no explicit reference to or systematic variation of organizational coordination mechanisms and the types of rules the teams have to adhere to, however. The vast majority of the studies have been carried out in aviation settings, taking for granted a high level of standardization. Following, the evidence on coordination requirements for successful performance provided by these studies will be critically reviewed.

4 Studies on coordination in work teams in high-risk environments

Given the definition of work teams as "(...) two or more people with different tasks who work together adaptively to achieve specified and shared goals" (Brannick & Prince 1997), coordination is one of the team's main activities. "Individuals must coordinate their decisions and activities by sharing information and resources to attain shared goals" (Dickinson & McIntyre 1997). A core concept in many of the studies on team coordination is the distinction between explicit and implicit coordination in relation to coping with high levels of workload. Explicit coordination is considered necessary when an agreement must be arrived at about how an action should be organised. It occurs typically during new tasks and new situations or when a new group of people make up a team to accomplish a job. People have to devote extra resources (very often communication) to organize the activities. Implicit coordination occurs when every one in a team knows his/her job, the actions harmonise with each other based on some kind of shared understanding (cf. also Clark's 1996, notion of conventions as tool for coordination), and therefore little noticeable effort for coordination is required.

It is assumed that teams can handle high workload situations better when they are able to reduce effort required for coordinating individual team members' activities. It is further assumed that less explicit coordination is needed when teams can rely on shared mental models of the task at hand and of the team itself. These mental models allow team members to predict each other's needs and actions and to act on them without explicit communication (cf. e.g. Entin & Serfaty 1999; Stout & Salas 1993). Finally, it is assumed useful to prepare high workload situations with a phase of explicit coordination where a shared model can be built up to be able to reduce communication and coordination "costs" in the high workload phase (Orasanu 1990; Orasanu & Fisher 1992; cited in Orasanu 1993). Supplying another team member with critical information without being requested to do so is generally considered as one important indicator for implicit coordination (e.g. Stout & Salas 1993).

The set of assumptions just described has been tested in a number of studies, supporting for instance:

- the effectiveness of team training aimed at conscious shifts between explicit and implicit coordination for improving performance in naval air surveillance teams (Entin & Serfaty 1999),
- showing positive relationships between planning, development of shared mental models, providing unsolicited information, and performance in a complex military flight task (Stout, Cannon-Bowers, Salas & Milanovich 1999),
- indicating links between shared mental models, task-appropriate coordination, cooperation and communication patterns, and team performance (Mathieu, Heffner, Goodwin, Salas & Cannon-Bowers 2000), and
- providing evidence for a positive relationship between team performance and captains' communicating goals and plans more than giving specific commands in high workload situations in a full mission flight simulation (Orasanu 1990; Orasanu & Fisher 1992; cited in Orasanu 1993).

Another concept often mentioned in connection with team coordination is that of team situation awareness. Artman (2000: 1113) describes the relationship between shared mental models – considered to be a crucial prerequisite for implicit coordination – and team situation awareness as follows: "Shared mental models include the team members' models of the coordinating routines and knowledge within the team, while SA (situation awareness, G.G.) is the conception of the situation 'out there' (...)". Thus appropriate situation awareness relies on individual and team mental models, which is also stated by Paris, Salas & Cannon-Bowers (2000), who additionally mention characteristics of team communication that can support the building of team situation awareness: "(...) team members must voice communications that promote collective awareness of the surrounding environment, both internal and external to the team, and make timely and accurate reports of deviations from the norm or potential problems. Team leaders can continually update team members during times of stress to keep them abreast of rapidly changing priorities and performance objectives" (Paris et al. 2000: 1067).

Finally, Weick & Roberts (1993) have provided case-study based and more qualitative accounts of similar phenomena of more or less effective team coordination in their analyses of high-reliability organizations mentioned previously. In order to explain effective team coordination, they suggest the concept of "heedful interrelating". A core idea of this concept based on Asch's theory on group interaction is that safety operations in highly complex situations require deliberate efforts by all actors to constantly (re-)consider effects of their own actions in relation to the goals and actions of others, or in Weick and

Roberts' words: "(...) (to) construct their actions (contribute) while envisaging a social system of joint actions (represent), and interrelate that constructed action with the system that is envisaged (subordinate)" (Weick & Roberts 1993: 363; see also Table 1 for tentative indicators of heedful/heedless interrelating). As Artman (2000) states, this concept stresses more the process of the active construction of partly shared and partly distributed situation models as compared to the concept of shared mental models, which is more oriented towards describing mental states.

Indicators for	
heedful interrelating	heedless interrelating
detailed representation of others	less detailed representation of others
contributions shaped by anticipated responses	contributions shaped less by anticipated responses
broad boundaries of envisaged system	narrow boundaries of envisaged system
attention focus on joint situation	attention focus on local situation
good comprehension of the implications of unfolding events	little comprehension of the implications of unfolding events

Table 1: Tentative indicators for heedful vs. heedless interrelating
(adapted from Weick & Roberts 1993)

As was stated already, research on team coordination in high-risk environments usually has not explicitly addressed which organizational coordination mechanisms provide the framework for the observed team behaviors. This is partly due to the frequent use of laboratory settings in which no organizational framework exists, but presumably also an effect of taking a high level of standardization for granted in the studied task environments. Besides this general shortcoming, there are also a number of more specific problems concerning the findings on team coordination, which will be addressed before a proposal for future research is outlined.

Central to the assumption of implicit coordination as the most effective way of handling high workload situations in a team is the reduction in communication requirements which frees resources for dealing with the additional demands in the situation. The indicator most frequently used for this reduction in communication is the amount of unsolicited information provided to other team members and/or an overall reduction in overt communication. There are a number of studies, though, that show an increase in communication or a shift in the nature of the information communicated to be related to good performance in high workload situations (cf. e.g. Mathieu et al. 2000; Orasanu 1993). Wiener (1993) concluded several years ago that there are no clear-cut results on the relationship between amount of communication and team performance and also argued that looking at the quality of crew communication might be more relevant than looking at quantity. Some more qualitative indicators of "good" communication have been suggested in the meantime, e.g. as part of classification systems for the assessment and training of crew resource management (e.g. Avaermaete & Kruisen 1998; Helmreich, Butler, Taggart & Wilhelm 1995). The distinction between explicit and implicit coordination and communication, though having stimulated a lot of interesting research, as such has not proven very helpful in deriving indicators because the terms themselves are not very clearly defined. For instance, "explicit" often seems to be used in the sense of overt or observable communication, but "implicit" is also based on observable communication, e.g. providing unsolicited information. Also, the assumptions about shared mental models as prerequisites for implicit coordination have been criticized. In the epilogue to a journal special issue on shared cognition it has been argued that the concept of creating shared mental models in order to improve coordination and performance is too simple and more knowledge is needed on what knowledge needs to be distributed in what way in a team to further coordinated action (Cannon-Bowers & Salas 2001). A more theoretically guided approach to what coordination is and how different kinds of communication and shared understanding can contribute to fulfilling different demands on coordination is needed in order to develop more systematic indicators of coordinated action.

5 The effect of workload on coordination processes

A more qualitative and systematic approach to team coordination seems also warranted because situational demands can vary drastically within the generally used classification of high vs. low workload, potentially requiring very different communication and coordination strategies. Is high workload, for instance, mainly generated by increasing numbers of routine tasks within a given time, making it necessary to reduce resources spent on each of these tasks, or is high workload created by facing an unknown system failure? Each of these situations will require quantitatively and qualitatively different patterns of communication.

To add to these problems, there is no clear use of the term workload itself. In the following, we will use the term task load, when we describe objective difficulties connected to the properties of a task, e.g. landing on a particularly short runway. We will use the term workload, when referring to how a situation is perceived by the people facing the task. It is quite likely, for instance, that a very experienced pilot perceives less workload compared to an inexperienced one when confronted with the same task. In general, workload for individuals depends on the relationship between the cognitive resources of the individual and the demands of the situation (Norman & Bobrow 1975). Many studies from laboratory and field settings prove that practice enhances resource efficiency, which can be related back to a reduction in workload (for an overview see Bowers, Braun & Morgan 1997: 87–90).

To complicate the issue, when looking at team performance, there should also be some understanding not only about individually perceived workload, but also about team workload.

In an early attempt to study team workload, it was assumed that coordination involved additional task load, which should be kept as small as possible. It was found that performance and communication have a negative relation: if a team has to communicate, performance declines. Due to this fact teams should be designed such that verbal communication is not required (Williges, Johnston & Briggs 1966). In a similar vein (Bowers, Braun & Morgan 1997) compared team and individual workload based on the difference between task workload and team workload. They argue that coordination tasks in teams add extra task load: "Team performance requires team members to engage concurrently in two broad categories of activities; namely, taskwork and teamwork activities. Taskwork refers to a team's interactions with tasks, tools, machines and systems. Teamwork refers to the interpersonal interactions among individuals that are necessary for exchanging information, developing and maintaining communication patterns, coordinating actions, maintaining social order, and so on." To draw attention to this additional task in teams is important for our understanding of how teams operate. However, one should not distinguish different types of workload because coordination and its main tool communication is an inherent part of the team assignments. The real question is how coordination pattern changes when workload increases. Some observations show that there is a clear change in communication patterns due to workload (Orasanu 1990; cited in Kani & Palmer 1993). From the work of Orasanu we know that one possible strategy is to plan before something happens, namely in the low workload phase. There are no systematic results about coordination strategies which help to overcome high workload situations, however.

6 Standardization and coordinated action: A research proposal

As a starting point for developing a more systematic and theory-guided account of team coordination in high-risk and high workload situations, Weick and Roberts's (1993) concept of heedful interrelating appears to be most promising because of its roots both in systemic organization theory and social psychology. Unfortunately, up to now, it has remained sketchy and no attempts have been made to derive measurable indicators for coordinated action from it. Some tentative, still very abstract indicators for heedful vs. heedless interrelating taken from Weick and Roberts' accounts of the concept are presented in Table 1. Also, a first quite promising attempt was made to concretise the indicators on the basis of linguistic categories. According to the approach outlined in Dietrich & Grommes (this volume) heedful interrelating has been supposed to be related to well-formed, i.e. coherent, discourse structures. Coherent discourse emerges when discourse participants coordinate their discourse contribution in line with a joint communicative task – which itself maybe evoked by demands from the task at hands. This task comprises the formulation and comprehension of a quaestio – i.e. the mental representation of an abstract question the speaker is setting out to answer – and the comprehension of the implications of unfolding events in terms of the interplay of shifting, restoring and summing up linguistic references to certain conceptual entities. In Grommes & Grote (2001) it has been demonstrated that indeed there is this relation between speech production according to the so called quaestio-model and heedful interrelating. Patterns of smooth quaestio-movements result in more efficient discourse sequences and can be rated as more cooperative.

Team coordination as measured by indicators for heedful interrelating should then be studied in task environments with different degrees and types of standardization as evidenced by different sets of rules laid out by the organization, using Hale & Swuste's (1998) classification scheme of safety rules as an operational framework (see Table 2 for examples of this taxonomy applied to a flight operations manual).

In order to do this, we have chosen the comparison between cockpit crew coordination and coordination in the emergency room. Both types of teams operate in high risk environments, where they are expected to avoid irreversible failures, which endanger human life. Sundstrom et al. (1990) describe work teams according to:

– team differentiation: how specialised and skilled are the team members,

– external integration: how well integrated are they within the organization they belong to,

– work cycle: how long they work together, and

– typical output: what will be produced in the mutual action.

Our two teams are called "action teams" in this typology, which comprises the following characteristics: (a) The teams are highly differentiated from other teams: exclusive membership of expert specialists. (b) The integration within the organization is high they are closely synchronised with counterparts and with support units. (c) The work cycle is short. (d) They execute brief operations or missions repeatedly under new conditions, which requires extended training and preparation.

Given these task-related similarities between the cockpit crew and emergency room teams, the organizational background, team composition and the strategy to fulfil their tasks is very different in these two work environments, however. Also, the types of uncertainties the teams have to handle differ. While flying an airplane involves mainly uncertainties stemming from the environment, preparing a patient for surgery in the emergency room is characterized by uncertainties stemming from the transformation process, in this case the patient's physiological conditions and processes.

In the field of aviation the attempt to standardize the work processes in order to reduce risk has a long tradition. In medicine so far very few written rules are available. There are rather local and unwritten rules and a quite strong hierarchy which define the task solving strategy. Xiao et al. (1996) describe the conditions under which an emergency medical team has to operate:

- Team members have different professional background,
- they have permanent visual and auditory contact with one another,
- they have to share a relative small work space around the patient,
- the task is often extraordinarily complex: there are concurrent tasks, which brings potential conflicts,
- high uncertainty about the physiological status of the patient,
- they have to change plans, if an alternative is not executable, and
- unlike most of the other medical care teams, they have to work under time pressure, so they often have to compress work procedures.

The suggestion from the authors is: "design of work procedures", which means more standardization, and to train explicit communication, which would lead to a better information distribution within a team. In line with this suggestion, especially concepts developed in aviation have recently been adapted to medical contexts, including the introduction of standard operating procedures. Analysing advantages and disadvantages of different degrees of standardization on team coordination and team performance in these settings should be very beneficial from a theoretical, but given these current developments in medicine, also from a very practical point of view.

To summarize, in our study we are asking the following four questions:
- Are there differences in patterns of coordination behaviors between teams in cockpits and emergency rooms as a result of differences in degrees of standardization?
- Can these differences be linked to team performance under varying degrees of workload?
- Can these differences be described in terms of explicitness vs. implicitness of coordination and in terms of heedful vs. heedless interrelating?

Based on the answers to these three questions, we hope to also find first answers to a fourth question:
Which types of rules in what combination, and derived from that which specific forms of standardization support successful coordination?

7 Method

In Figure 1 the overall design of the study is presented. The effects of varying workload and varying degrees and types of standardization on coordinating behaviors and indirectly on team performance are to be analysed in the two settings cockpit and emergency room.

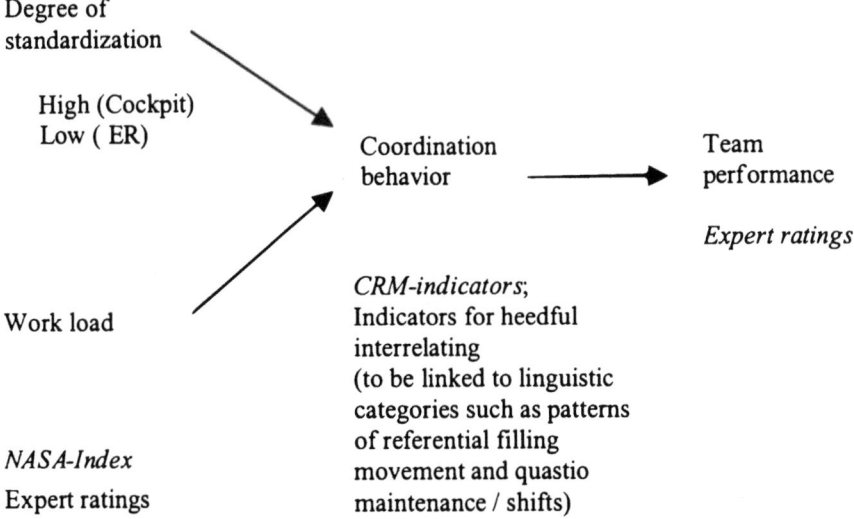

Figure 1: Study design
(ER= Emergency Room; CRM = Crew Resource Management)

While the data from the medical setting are still in the process of being collected, flight data are available already from 80 simulator training sessions, which were taped as part of another project (cf. Naef, Klampfer & Häusler 2001) within the umbrella project "Group Interaction in High Risk Environments" to which our study belongs as well. Of the four scenarios contained in each training session, we chose one scenario, during which an approach and landing has to be performed without flaps and slats. This so-called clean approach entails high landing speed, unusual visual information due to unusual attitude of airplane and the requirement of very good manipulative skills by the pilot flying.

Workload is operationalized by means of the NASA Task Load Index (Hart & Staveland 1988). This is a measure of task requirements perceived by the team members individually regarding mental and physical workload as well as time pressure. An external expert (in the case of cockpit crews the instructor present during the simulator training sessions; in the case of the emergency room teams a surgeon not involved in the actual situation) also rates workload for the team members overall based on the NASA-Index. Standardization was broadly operationalized in terms of the two setting studied, i.e. low standardization in the emergency room and high standardization in the cockpit. A more fine-grained analysis of the types of rules relevant in the two settings will be performed by means of document analysis and expert interviews based on the categories developed by Hale & Swuste (1998) (see also Table 2 for a simple example from a preliminary analysis of the flight operations manual of an airline).

Type of rule	Example
Rules concerning goals to be achieved	"It must be clearly understood that not all combinations of cumulative operational problems (engine failure plus e.g. terrain, weather, availability of aerodromes etc.) can be covered by this policy. In such situations the solution offering the highest degree of safety should be sought."
Rules defining the way in which decisions about a course of action must be arrived at	"In order to complete a replanning, any documented cruise systems and all means available may be used, such as flight management systems and data contained in the respective AOMs (aircraft operating manuals)."
Rules defining concrete actions	"Every evacuation must be carried out as quickly as possible. The passengers must be assisted to leave the aeroplane without their belongings and directed to a point at a safe distance from the aeroplane."

Table 2: Examples for rule types
(taken from the flight operations manual of an airline)

Team performance is rated by the team members themselves and by an external expert (same as for external workload rating) according to technical and social performance.

Coordinating behaviors are analysed based on observational categories. Videotapes of cockpit simulator training sessions and emergency room operations are rated based on these categories, using the ATLASti (Thomas Muhr, Scientific Software Development, Berlin 1997) program. These categories as can be seen below are based on relatively broad characteristics of communication. Non-verbal actions are not included in the categories. This method allow us to obtain a general impression about the whole coordination process and to identify sequences within the process. Thereby particularly relevant sequences can be determined for further analysis with the much more detailed and time-consuming linguistic categories which have not been worked out fully yet, but will follow the lines of the analysis presented by Grommes and Dietrich (see Dietrich & Grommes, this volume). This interdisciplinary approach, combining psychological and linguistic factors and categories, seems especially promising, since there are already some early results that hint on answers to the questions posed in the last paragraph of the previous section. Linguistic behavior, and here specifically speech processing, can be supposed to be affected by standardization, because there seems to be a preset mechanism for dialogue organization, which need not fit to standardized dialogue patterns. There also is a clear relationship between workload and linguistic performance (see Dietrich & Silberstein, this volume; Krifka et al., this volume; Dietrich & Grommes, this volume), and this hints on effects on team performance under high workload, since there is a relationship between heedful interrelating and discourse production (Grommes & Grote 2001). This latter argument also points in direction of an answer to the third question, whether explicit vs. implicit and/or heedful vs. heedless interrelating can account for different communicative outcome under differing workload. The fourth question may receive only an indirect linguistic answer, in that it can be checked if rule formulation and the proposed communicative routines are linguistically well-formed.

7.1 Observational categories

We developed four main groups of categories driven by both theoretical and practical considerations. We used two behavioral marker systems for the evaluation of crew resource management, LOSA (Line Oriented Safety Audit, Helmreich et al. 1999) and NOTECHS (NOn-TECHnical Skill proficiency, Avermate & Kruijsen 1998), as references. While LOSA and NOTECHS have been developed to obtain overall ratings of individual and/or team performance in cockpit crews on a number of quite general characteristics (leadership, decision making, planning, situation awareness etc.), our categories are intended to allow coding of all utterances in the two settings cockpit and emergency room. Therefore we could use the LOSA/NOTECHS-categories as an orientation regarding relevant areas of communication in the cockpit, but had to develop more specific categories within each topic and also develop categories that are applicable to both the flight and medical situation.

The first set of categories concerns the information flow on a general level without much reference to the content of the information. The aim was to create mutually exclusive categories and to be able to code all utterances made during the observed situation. Also, it was attempted to differentiate elements of explicit and implicit coordination as described in the previous sections of this article. The category type Information flow-explicit coordination contains the following categories:

– Provide information

– Request information

– Provide information upon request

– Information containing a summary of a state of affairs or a process

– Reassurance (e.g. feedback about comprehension of a communication)

– Giving order

– Asking for help

– Communication with Air Traffic Control (specific for aviation)

– Discussion

– Standard communication (specific for aviation)

The category type Information flow-implicit coordination contains the following categories:

– Provide unsolicited information

– Offer assistance

– Silence

– Chatting

In the case of silence and chatting it is important to look at the whole situation to decide whether these categories indicate implicit coordination or absence of coordination. An important point regarding the other two categories is the anticipation effect, namely that a team member realizes the needs of other team members and provides the needed information or support without being explicitly requested to do so.

The information flow categories also provide a general quantitative account of the observed communication, concerning e.g. speaker dominance and proportion of standard versus non-standard information exchange. These categories – and clearly also the categories of heedful interrelating below – can and will also be tested linguistically. If their realization by the team members is effective this should find co-evidence in the linguistic structures.

The other two groups of categories are not fully exclusive and don't cover all utterances made. The second group of categories is connected to leadership, which was chosen as a focus due to the strong relationship between type of leadership and coordination and the effects of standardization on this relationship. In general, standards can be regarded as a form of depersonalised leadership, with personal leadership being made redundant in some respects and obtaining a different function as complementing or overriding standards.

The category type leadership contains the following categories:

– Making plans

– Assigning task

– Giving order

– Making decision

– Initiate an action

– Accepting decision or initiated action

– Questioning decision

– Ignoring initiated action

– Autocratic behavior

The third group of categories contains elements of *heedful interrelating*:

- Considering others
- Considering the future
- Considering external conditions
- Initiate an action
- Questioning decision
- Providing unsolicited information
- Offering assistance
- Correcting the behavior of others
- Teaching others
- Giving feedback about performance

These categories for heedful interrelating have then to be integrated into broader qualitative evaluations of the indicators listed in Table 1. In this process it has to be considered that some of the indicators are more directly linked to observable behaviors, while others are cognitive states which can only be inferred via the other indicators. The indicator "Detailed representation of others", for instance, refers to mental models about the team members whose adequacy can only be judged by looking at the indicator "contributions shaped by anticipated responses", assuming that expectations about responses by the other team members are formed based on mental representations of their capabilities, dispositions, and needs. For this later indicator, however, a number of observable categories are available, namely Considering others, Providing unsolicited information, Offering assistance and Giving feedback. Similarly, the indicator "Broad boundaries of envisaged system" is a characteristic of a mental representation of the overall situation which can be inferred partially at least by means of the indicator "attention focus on joint situation", which itself is linked to the observable categories Considering external conditions and Questioning decisions. Also, some of the categories are related to more than one indicator, which is due to overlap between the indicators suggested by Weick & Roberts (1993), but also due to the fact that evaluation of the indicators requires context-sensitive interpretation of communicative behavior. Initiating an action may indicate, depending on the type of action and timing of it, good comprehension of the implications of unfolding events and/or an attention focus on joint situation.

7.2 Illustration of use of observational categories

We tested our observational categories by coding four of the simulator training scenarios.

Figure 2 and Figure 3 shows the results for the categories of information flow for one of those four teams, distinguishing between the actors, not the

single categories, however. For studying communication in the flight scenarios, three segments were defined:
1. Take off: highly standardised, nothing unexpected happens, task load is low.
2. Problem solving: the crew realizes the failure, they have to go through a checklist to find out the specific conditions and operations for landing the airplane.
3. Approach: clean approach, which happens very rarely in the reality and means an unusual, high speed landing. Task load is high.

Those segments are shown with a line on the bar chart in Figure 2 and Figure 3.

We plan to compare team processes in the first and in the third segment where task load is very different. We also plan to compare teams according to their subjectively perceived workload, because of large differences in workload perceptions by the different crews.

The following examples may illustrate the planned procedure for data analysis.

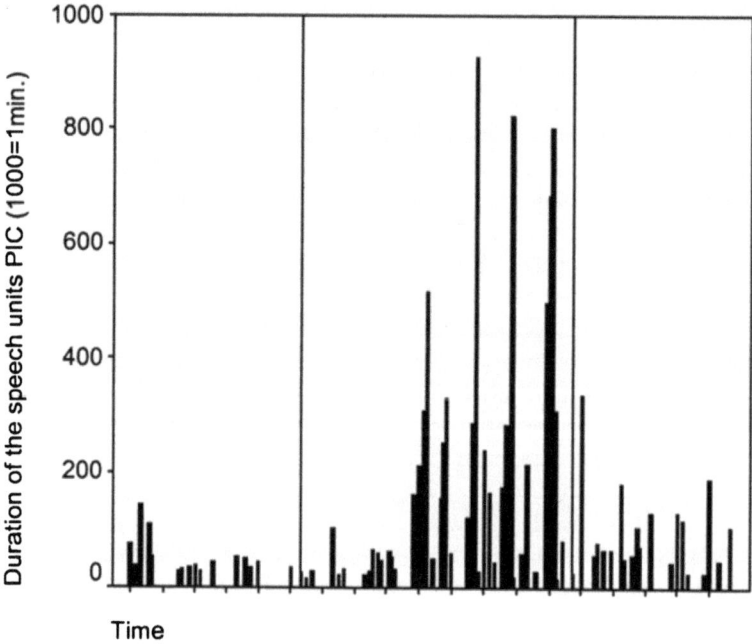

Figure 2: Distribution of the communication performed by the captain (PIC) during the simulator session

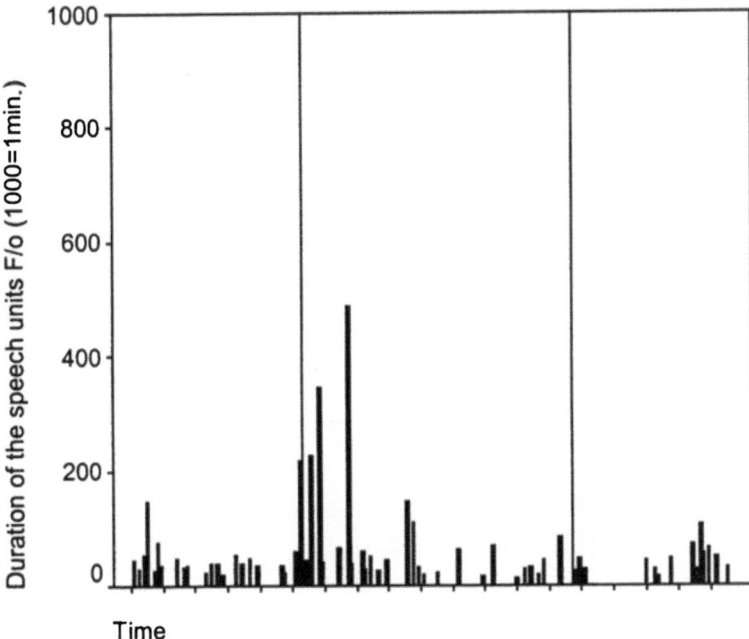

Figure 3: Distribution of the communication performed by the first officer (F/o) during the simulator session

The vertical axis shows the duration of every single speech unit in minutes and the horizontal axis represents the length of the simulator session (37 minutes). The bars follow the chronological order of the speech units. Comparing Figure 2 and Figure 3 one can read that the captain is getting more and more dominant, he speaks more often and longer than the first officer. He does not motivate his colleague to contribute, who says hardly anything at the end. If we suppose that the ideal way is to use all available resources in this situation, we can state, that team performance is not optimal. The other impressive result is that the speech units in the second segment are a lot longer than in the first or third segment. It seems that the task they have to carry out, take off vs. approach vs. problem solving has an influence on the form of coordination.

Because the problem solving phase shows significant differences in the amount of speech, which led us to assume that during this phase there is a higher pressure to a more explicit form of coordination, it seems to be promising to have a closer look at a segment from this phase in order to show how psychological and linguistic analyses might work together. The segment reproduced below as example X. occurs right at the beginning of the problem solving phase, when the pilots recognize the technical failure (described above). At this point they have to determine the kind of failure and its consequences for approach procedure they are about to perform. In the following we will illustrate how to gain insights into the functioning of the team from both the linguistic and the psychological analysis.

Example X. (transcription done by the CLAN-software, cf. MacWhinney (2000), conventions follow those proposed in the GAT framework (Selting et al. (1998)). This example has been extracted from simulation B35, time units 13865–15476. Participants here are the captain (cpt) and the first officer (fio).

According to the next table we can follow in parallel the two coding systems.

line	speaker	utterance	coding according to the behavioral categories	coding according to the linguistic categories: quaestio movement
1	F/o	da machen wir mal flaps one please then we set flaps one please	giving order	new (which next action)
2	PIC	speed s checked (---) flaps:	standard info pause neutral info giving	shift (provide info about next action)
		(3.0)		
3	F/o	da passiert nix, he? there happens nothing?	neutral info giving	shift (how to evaluate outcome of 2)
4	PIC	passiert go:r nix::- happens nothing	reassurance	maint (evaluation as in 3)
5	F/o	jawu:ll:: ö. yes		maintenance
6	PIC	gor nix passiert; nothing happens		maintenance
7	F/o	kchey a:zeige nothing on display	neutral info giving	maintenance
8	PIC	(nei) (no...)	reassurance	(maintenance)
		(6.0)		
9	PIC	lose ich ga nochmal mit de klappe i:nne listen I try the flaps again	initiate an action, neutral info giving	new (propose next action)
10	F/o	ja. tuesch nochmal en rE:cycle machen. yes. perform (2nd Sg.) a re-cycle	reassurance, accepting initiated action	shift (specify next action)

11	PIC	des is below äh max flap speed; that is below maximum flap speed	info discussion (down to 18)	new (new info about attitude of the plane)
12	F/o	jawohl. yes		maintenance
13	PIC	-goa nochmal u:f ei:s-set it once againto one		shift (propose next required action)
14	F/o	ja. yes		maintenance
		(3.0)		
15	PIC	do is gor ni:x ha? there is nothing, right?		shift (which state is expected after next action)
16	F/o	do passiert gor nix= there happens nothing		maintenance
17	PIC	=do hen mir kein kontakt mittem computer= there we do not have contact to the computer		shift (hypothesize about source of the problem)
18	F/o	=ja- yes		maintenance
		(2.0)		
19	PIC	okAY:. mir mün en clEAn approach mache; he? okay. we'll have to perform a clean approach	making decision, neutral info giving	new (next action)
20	F/o	ja. yes	reassurance	maintenance
21	PIC	das de e bisschen ziet hast zum präpariere; that you have some time to prepare	neutral info giving	shift (motivate next action)
22	PIC	sag ich no mal mir wäle zurück uf torino	neutral info giving	shift (spell out next action)

		I'll announce again that we want to go back to torino		
23	F/o	zuruck auf torino; jawohl. back to torino, yes.	reassurance	maintenance

conventions for transcription
:   lengthening of sound
Capitals: remarkably stressed syllable
( )   parentheses: unintelligible speech
(text)   text in parentheses: speech as understood by transcriber, sometimes alternatives are given
=   next turn immediately attached to prior
?/;/-/,/. intonation markers: highly rising/rising/keeping steady/falling/deeply falling
(-) – (---) pauses within turn below one second
(1.0)   pauses between turns in seconds
%   dependent tiers according to CLAN, contain general or analytical comments

From a linguistic point of view one can identify at least three subsegments within the whole. They are marked by the quaestio-label new. This label signals that the speaker elaborates on a new communicative task which – in extended coherent conversations – has to show some ties to former utterances. These ties can be formulated with respect to referential relations between utterances according to the quaestio-model (see above for a brief introduction and see Dietrich & Grommes, this volume). An example can be found in lines 16/17. Here the local adverbial da – realized by the dialectal do – refers to a component of the system needed for the handling of the flaps and slats. In 16 it is confirmed that the component does not react, in 17 the captain refers to the same component but is now no longer talking about its functioning but about possible sources for its malfunction.

    Thus the overall picture is one of a coherent sequence, although there are more than one quaestiones under discussion. Coherence, however, also proves to be a necessary though not sufficient condition for successful task-related conversation. The analysis shows that there are relatively small utterance units related to quaestiones, i.e. the coding of linguistic actions is quite fine-grained. There is, however, no such fine-grained coding possible for the psychological categories. Instead, the psychological categories often embrace several conversational turns, which may be an indication of some redundancy in the interaction, i.e. the linguistic action performed might as well have been done in lesser words. For an exemplification one might have a closer look on lines 11 onwards. These lines have been coded as a discussion of information. This discussion continues until line 19 where finally a consequence from their findings gets acknowledged, a state which could have been arrived at much earlier. As mentioned a few lines above, this sequence is far from being incoherent, but it, too, is not very effective. Now the question is whether there are any indications in the linguistic analysis of this sequence of its inefficiency. And indeed these indications can be found on the level of quaestio-movement. The basic expectation for quaestio-movement in natural conversation is that shift is the dominating relation. In this sequence, however, there is a very high proportion of maintenances, i.e. sequences that do not add new information and that contribute to problem solving, but that simply confirm the level of information up to the respective point. Therefore, although there is quaestio-coherence, the conversations does not proceed effectively. And interestingly, in most cases it is the co-pilot who does simply maintain the quaestio: a further, and at this time a linguistic, argument for the captain's dominant behavior. Thus, although the linguistic coding units and their psychological counterparts are not expected to converge fully in the actual utterances they consist of, an imbalance between linguistic and psychological coding like in this example may be a useful indicator for defective communication.

In Figure 4 the distribution of the other two groups of observational categories can be seen:

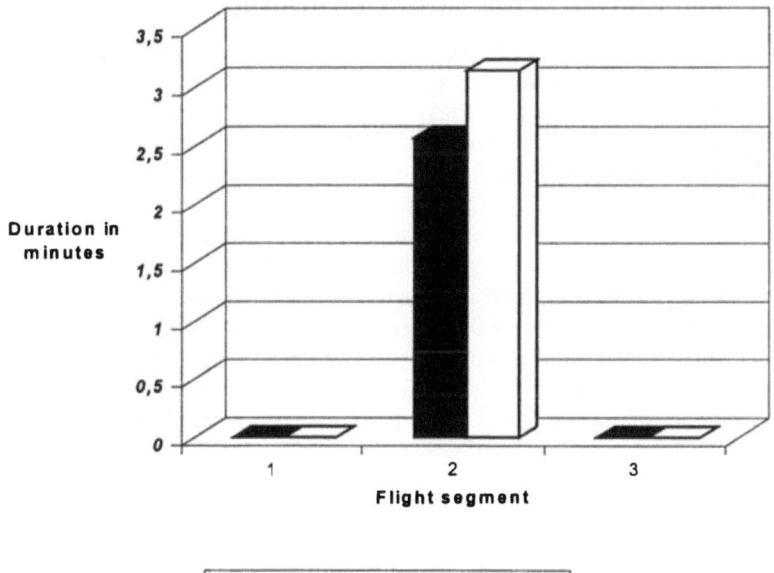

Figure 4: The distribution of the category groups (without information flow) during the different flight segments

The vertical axis shows the total duration of the two groups of behavioral categories and the horizontal axis shows the flight segments. During the first and third flight segment we can hardly observe any other kind of communication than information exchange. It is all right for the first segment where no unexpected situation or problematic task appears. During the landing however, which is a rare and unusual task, a helpful or rather heedful team-mate can be really crucial. Observing the second segment it is not surprising that it was not the case by that team.

The following facts observed in the second segment explain the passivity of the first officer during the difficult landing:

– The captain speaks more and more (nearly 10 minutes while the first officer only 4.5 minutes) the first officer take less and less courage to say anything at all.

– The captain does not involve the first officer in the decision processes, he assigns the tasks and makes the plans.

– What is more he behaves like an expert, explains a lot.

The redundancy mentioned in the linguistic analysis comes more and more into view. The time they needed from the end of take off until the beginning of landing is about 20 minutes, which is for some teams enough time to manage the whole simulator exercise

Thus, we have been able to show, that psychological and linguistic factors are interrelated in coordination behavior. The linguistic analysis informs about the general wellformedness of sequences of conversation. Noticeable findings from this structural analysis may provide evidence and hints about the qualitative properties of conversations for the observational analysis, based on psychological concepts, which tries to draw an overall picture about the coordinated team behavior during a task situation.

So far, analyses have only served the testing of the categories, therefore no results regarding the research questions can be provided yet. While within the two professional fields aviation and medicine, quantitative comparisons between scenario segments and teams will be performed along the lines illustrated above, the comparison between the two fields will be done mainly based on qualitative evaluations taking into account the fundamental differences between the two organizational settings and also the difference between simulated and real work situations.

8 Outlook

In this article, a research proposal and some specifics about the methods to be used have been outlined. Regarding the theoretical benefits of the proposed research, its main contribution is seen in filling the void concerning detailed knowledge on the effects of different forms of standardization on team behavior.

From research on implicit team coordination, for instance, one could derive the assumption that a high degree of standardization reduces the need for explicit, i.e. conscious and overt, coordination due to the reliance on a shared set of rules and derived from that also the expectation of shared goals, plans, perspectives on the situation, knowledge activated in the situation etc. summarized under the heading of shared mental models of the task and the team. This assumption is also quite obvious, given the fact that in organization theory standardization is defined as a form of depersonalised coordination. Some authors seem to assume, however, that higher levels of standardization could also further an increase in communication and explicit coordination, as for instance seen necessary in highly automated cockpits (e.g. Wiener 1993). Which of these assumptions turns out to be correct, depends strongly on the specific nature of standards chosen of course, e.g. standards requiring certain ways of carrying out an operational task vs. standards requiring certain ways of communicating about carrying out operational tasks. So more specifically, it is to be asked which degree of standardization based on which types of rules can support teams in developing and maintaining flexible and situation-adaptive patterns of coordination. This as of now is a completely unanswered question.

Research aiming at answering this question will allow the development of a framework for rule design and management which would guide flexible human action instead of constraining it to a degree rendering it difficult or impossible for humans to assume a role as a safety factor in the system. One finding might be that instead of mainly employing rules that describe very specific courses of action – as is the case in many industries now – it would be more beneficial to draw up rules that provide heuristics for finding appropriate courses of actions in different contexts. Such rules would guide behavior while at the same time leaving the actor with sufficient autonomy and control over the situation needed for flexible action. Also, it should be considered systematically whether a rule applies to individual or collective action requirements and how it affects individual and collective autonomy and the relationship between the two. For instance, a rule could specify that several actors have to decide together whether to follow a particular course of action or that one person is in charge of deciding for others.

On the most general level, it is hoped that the research outlined here will support a shift from minimizing uncertainties to competently handling uncertainties even in high-risk organizations, achieving a more balanced approach which will avoid both over reliance on rules as well as inappropriate deviation from rules.

Acknowledgements

We gratefully acknowledge the financial support for this project by the Daimler-Benz-Stiftung as well as the stimulating discussions in the umbrella project "Group interaction in high risk environments (GIHRE)" to which our project belongs. Also, we are very grateful for the enormous support by the GIHRE aviation project through making their raw data available to us.

References

Amalberti, R. (1999): Risk management by regulation. Paper presented at the 19th Myron B. Laver International Postgraduate Course "Risk Management", Dept. of Anaesthesia, University of Basel, Switzerland, March 26–27, 1999.

Artman, H. (2000): "Team situation assessment and information distribution". In: Ergonomics, 43. 1111–1128.

Avermate, J. A. G. van & Kruijsen, E. A. C. (Eds.) (1998): NOTECHS. The evaluation of non-technical skills of multipilot aircrew in relation to the JAR-FCL requirements (Final report), Research for the European Commission, DG VII, NLR-CR-98443.

Bowers, C. A., Braun, C. & Morgan B. B., Jr. (1997): "Team Workload: Its Meaning and Measurement. Team Performance Assessment and Measurement. Theory, Methods and Applications". In: Brannick, M. T., Salas, E. & Prince, C. (Eds.): Team Performance Assessment and Meassurement. Mahwah, NJ: Lawrence Erlbaum. 85–108.

Brannick, M. T. & Prince, C. (1997): "An Overview of Team Performance Measurement. Team Performance Assessment and Measurement. Theory, Methods and Applications". In: Brannick, M. T., Salas, E. & Prince, C. (Eds.): Team Performance Assessment and Meassurement. Mahwah, NJ: Lawrence Erlbaum. 3–16.

Cannon-Bowers, J. A. & Salas, E. (2001): "Reflections on shared cognition". In: Journal of Organizational Behavior, 22. 195–202.

Clark, H. H. (1996): Using language. Cambridge: University Press.

Dickinson, T., L. & McIntyre, R. M. (1997): "A Conceptual Framework for Teamwork Measurement. Team Performance Assessment and Measurement. Theory, Methods and Applications". In: Brannick, M. T., Salas, E. & Prince, C. (Eds.): Team Performance Assessment and Meassurement. Mahwah, NJ: Lawrence Erlbaum. 19–43.

Entin, E. E. & Serfaty, D. (1999): "Adaptive team coordination". Human Factors, 41. 312–325.

Grommes, P. & Grote G. (2001): "Coordination in action. Comparing two work situations with high vs. low degrees of formalization". In: Kühnlein, P., Newlands, A. & Rieser H. (Eds.): Proceedings of the Workshop Coordination and Action at ESSLLI 2001, Helsinki. 27–39.

Grote, G. (1997): Autonomie und Kontrolle – Zur Gestaltung automatisierter und risikoreicher Systeme (Automomy and Control – On the Design of Automated and High-Risk Systems). Zürich: vdf Hochschulverlag.

Hackman, J. R. & Morris, C. G. (1975): "Group tasks, group interaction process, and group performance effectiveness: A review and proposed integration". In: Berkowitz, L. (Ed.): Advances in experimental social psychology. New York: Academic Press 8. 45–99.

Hackman, J. R. (1987): "The design of work teams". In: Lorsch, J. (Ed.): Handbook of organizational behavior. New York: Prentice-Hall. 315–342.

Hackman, J. R. (Ed.) (1990): Groups that work (and those that don't). Creating conditions for effective teamwork. San Francisco: Jossey-Bass.

Hackman, J. R. (1993): "Teams, Leaders and Organizations: New Directions for Crew-oriented Flight Training". In: Wiener, E. L., Kanki, B. G. & Helmreich R. L. (Eds.): Cockpit Resource Management. San Diego: Academic Press.

Hale, A. R. & Swuste, P. (1998): "Safety rules: procedural freedom or action constraint?" In: Safety Science, 29. 16–177.

Hart, S. G. & Staveland, L. E. (1988): "Development of NASA-TLX (Task Load IndeX): Results of empirical and theoretical research". In: Hancock, P. A. & Meshkati, N. (Eds.): Human Mental Workload. Amsterdam: Elsevier.

Helmreich, R. L. (1991): The long and short term impact of crew resource management training. AIAA/NASA/FAA/HFS conference on challenges in aviation human factors: The national plan, Vienna, VA.

Helmreich, R. L., Wilhelm, J. A., Klinect, J. R. & Merritt, A. C. (1999): "Culture, Error and Crew Resource Management". In: Salas, E., Bowers, C. A. & Edens, E. (Eds.): Applying resource management in organizations: A guide for professionals. Hillsdale, NJ: Erlbaum.

Helmreich. R. L., Butler, R. E., Taggart, W. R. & Wilhelm, J. A. (1995): "Behavioral markers in accidents and incidents: Reference list". NASA/UT/FAA Technical Report 95-1. Austin, TX: The University of Texas.

Hoc, J.-M. (1988): Cognitive psychology of planning. London: Academic Press.

Kieser, A. & Kubicek, H. (1992): Organisation. Berlin: de Gruyter.

Leplat, J. (1998): "About implementation of safety rules". In: Safety Science, 29. 189-204.

MacWhinney, B. (2000): The CHILDES project: Tools for analyzing talk. Third Edition. Mahwah, NJ: Lawrence Erlbaum Associates.

Mathieu, J. E., Heffner, T. S., Goodwin, G. F., Salas, E. & Cannon-Bowers, J. A. (2000): "The influence of shared mental models on team process and performance". In: Journal of Applied Psychology, 85. 273-283.

Naef, W., Klampfer, B. & Häusler, R. (2001): "Aviation". In: Group Interaction in High Risk Environments (GIHRE), Project extension proposal submitted to the Gottlieb Daimler- and Karl Benz-Foundation, Ladenburg.

Norman, D. A. & Bobrow, D. G. (1975): "On Data-limited and Ressource-limited Processes". In: Cognitive Psychology 7. 44-64.

Orasanu, J. M. (1993): "Decision-making in the Cockpit". In: Wiener, E. L., Kanki, B. & Helmreich, R. L. (Eds.): Cockpit Resource Management. San Diego: Academic Press. 137-172.

Paris, C. R., Salas, E. & Cannon-Bowers, J. A. (2000): "Teamwork in multi-person systems: A review and analysis". In: Ergonomics, 43. 1052-1075.

Perrow, C. (1967): "A framework for the comparative analysis of organizations". In: American Sociological Review, 32. 194-208.

Perrow, C. (1984): Normal accidents. Living with high-risk technologies. New York: Basic Books.

Rasmussen, J.(1997): "Risk management in a dynamic society: A modelling problem". In: Safety Science, 27. 183-213.

Reason, J., Parker, D. & Lawton, R. (1998): "Organizational controls and safety: The varieties of rule-related behavior". In: Journal of Occupational and Organizational Psychology, 71. 289-304.

Selting, M., Auer, P. & Barden, B. et al. (1998): „Gesprächsanalytisches Transkriptionssystem (GAT)". In: Linguistische Berichte 173. 91-122.

Stout, R. & Salas, E. (1993): "The role of planning in coordinated team decision making; Implications for training". In: Proceedings of the Human Factors and Ergonomics Society 37th Annual Meeting. 1238-1242.

Stout, R. J., Cannon-Bowers, J. A., Salas, E. & Milanovich, D. M. (1999): "Planning, shared mentals models, and coordinated performance: An empirical link is established". In: Human Factors, 41. 61-71.

Suchman, L. A. (1987): Plans and Situated Actions: The Problem of Human-Machine Communication. Cambridge: Cambridge University Press.

Sundstrom, E. K., De Meuse, P. et al. (1990): "Work Teams. Applications and Effectiveness". In: American Psychologist, 45 (2). 120-133.

Susman, G. I. (1976): Autonomy at Work. A Sociotechnical Analysis of Participative Management. New York: Praeger.
Tesluk, P. E., Mathieu, J. E. et al. (1997): "Task and Aggregation Issues in the Analysis and Assesment of Team Performance". In: Brannick, M., Salas, T., E. & Prince, C. (Eds.): Team Performance Assessment and Measurement. Theory, Methods, and Applications. Mahwah, New Jersey, LEA: 197–226.
Thompson, J. D. (1967): Organizations in Action. New York: McGraw-Hill.
Vermersch, P. (1985): "Donées d'observation sur l'utilisation d'une consigne écrite: L'atomisation de l'action". In: Le Travail Humain, 48. 161–172.
Weick, K. E. & Roberts, K. H. (1993): "Collective mind in organizations Heedful interrelating on flight decks". In: Administrative Science Quarterly 38. 357–381.
Wiener, E. L. (1993): "Crew coordination and training in the advanced-technology cockpit". In: Wiener, E. L., Kanki, B. G. & Helmreich R. L. (Eds.): Cockpit Resource Management. San Diego: Academic Press. 199–229.
Williges, R. C., Johnston, W. A. & Briggs, G. E. (1966): "Role of verbal communication in teamwork". In: Journal of Applied Psychology 50. 473–478.
Xiao, Y., Hunter, W. A., et al. (1996): "Task Complexity in Emergency Medical Care and Its Implication for Team Coordination". In: Human Factors 38 (4). 636–645.

Zürich/Berlin   Gudela Grote, Enikö Zala-Mezö, and Patrick Grommes

Swiss Federal Institute of Technology, Zurich (ETH), Institute of Work Psychology, NEL D 13, CH-8092 Zürich, grote@ifap.bepr.ethz.ch

Swiss Federal Institute of Technology, Zurich (ETH), Institute of Work Psychology, NEL C 14, ETH Zentrum, CH-8092 Zürich, zala@ifap.bepr.ethz.ch

Humboldt University at Berlin, Institut für Deutsche Sprache und Linguistik, Philosophische Fakultät II, Unter den Linden 6, 10099 Berlin, Patrick.Grommes@rz.hu-berlin.de

Investigation of Communication Errors in Nuclear Power Plants

Oliver Sträter

Summary

Communication is a major aspect for assuring safety of a Nuclear Power Plant (NPP). However, it's impacts is also one of the most difficult things to investigate, since communication means verbal and non-verbal exchange of information between several operators in several locations inside and outside of the plant. In order to approach this complex issue, a "top-down" investigation procedures was set-up. It starts with an investigation of operational events regarding possible communication problems. In a sequel of this work, a detailed experimental setting is investigating the interrelation between communication and cognition.

The investigation of 232 events showed that factors like workload and situational pressure influence the communication process and communication failures also have an impact on the operational side (they lead, for instance, to more initiators of technical failures than procedural driven actions). This observation suggests that errors in communication and errors on the operational side cannot be treated independently from each other.

Communication problems were further investigated regarding their underlying causes. In the investigation it was observed that they can be traced back to cognitive compensation strategies like reduction of problem spaces or reduction of the set of goals. Their common appearance with operational errors is reflecting a common problem in cognitive processing of operators.

However, operational experience also shows that good communication can be observed in high workload conditions. Detailed analysis of the events is showing that this contradiction can be resolved if the communication task is related to the operational task that has to be performed at the technical system. Communication problems are explainable if the cognitive load caused by the operational task of the operators is considered as either in distraction or in consonance with the communication task.

The aim of the second phase of the project is to investigate the nature of these limitations of communication due to cognitive processing in more detail.

This work has been funded by the Daimler Benz foundation in the framework of the multidisciplinary project GIHRE (Group Interaction in High Risk Environments) and was performed at GRS (Gesellschaft für Reaktorsicherheit) in Germany. The work described in this paper does not necessarily reflect the opinion of GRS or EUROCONTROL.

1 Overview about communication in NPPs

Operating a NPP means coordination of several people either working in the control room or on the spot. The number of people involved at different places heavily differs depending on the plant state. During full power operation the plant is driven by one shift while usually two shifts work in parallel to run the plant during low-power and shut down states. The number of shift personnel working in one shift in the control room during full power – for instance – ranges usually from 5 to 8 depending on the plant's policy. Besides there is always ongoing work in the plant performed by maintenance personnel during operation as well as during shut-down states. The number of persons involved in plant operation outside the control room may easily rise up to about 300 persons.

It is obvious that communication in such environments is difficult to be investigated. In safety of NPPs usually two general types of communication are distinguished as follows:

Procedural based communication: This includes every interaction where paper based material is used (e.g., procedures, ad hoc procedures, check-lists, work permission forms etc.).

Verbal communication: This is defined by all direct communication activities (like face to face communication, phone calls).

In the following the term "communication" basically stands for verbal communication. If procedural based communication is concerned this is explicitly mentioned.

Basic approach to investigate the communication aspects is the sender-receiver model (e.g., Shannon & Weaver 1949), because this has the advantage to be compatible with other models for the analysis of working environments (see Sträter 1997). A simple work system with a hierarchical organization that is often encountered in NPPs is depicted in Figure 1.

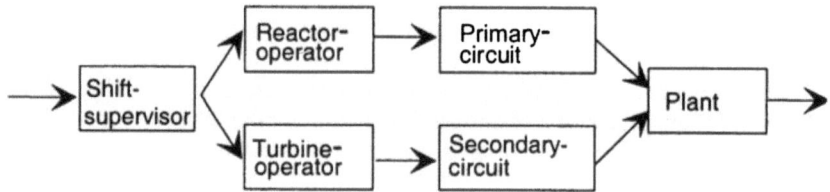

Figure 1: A typical work system in a NPP consisting of the shift-supervisor, reactor operator and turbine operator

1.1 Problem spaces of communication in NPP

Whereas only a few human interventions are necessary to run a highly automated nuclear plant while the automatic systems are running, "Good

Communication" is one of the major aspects of safety in Nuclear Power Plants, if automatic systems do not work appropriately or if they have to be taken out of order for maintenance reasons (i.e. in so-called low-power and shutdown states). In such system states, the humans take over the control of the process and naturally these interventions have to be planned and coordinated by several people in the control room as well as on the spot.

Other investigations do show that the problem of communication is expected to be of much higher relevance if the control system is changed from a conventional control room into a computerized control room (as in the Figure 2 below), because the control system is a common one in the former ones whereas every operator is working in a more separated cockpit and more on his own in the latter ones.

Figure 2: Computerized control room

Such control systems are already usual in many technical control systems like coal fired power plants, chemical plants, plane-cockpits or air traffic control, or are planned (e.g. in tele-operating in medicine).

2 Procedure for evaluating events regarding communication aspects

2.1 Data used for the investigation

Within the German framework for nuclear safety, one task of GRS is to evaluate plant experience in German nuclear power plants regarding the safety impact of the events happened (Figure 3). To facilitate this regulatory task, GRS is collecting special events (i.e., events beyond a certain safety criteria) since about 1969. The database includes now about 5000 event descriptions. Several related institutions and companies provided additional input for the investigation presented here project. Besides GRS, some German Utilities, the IAEA (International Atomic Energy Agency), and the OECD Working Group Risk were involved in the discussion of the study.

Reporting System for Abnormal Events in Nuclear Power Plants

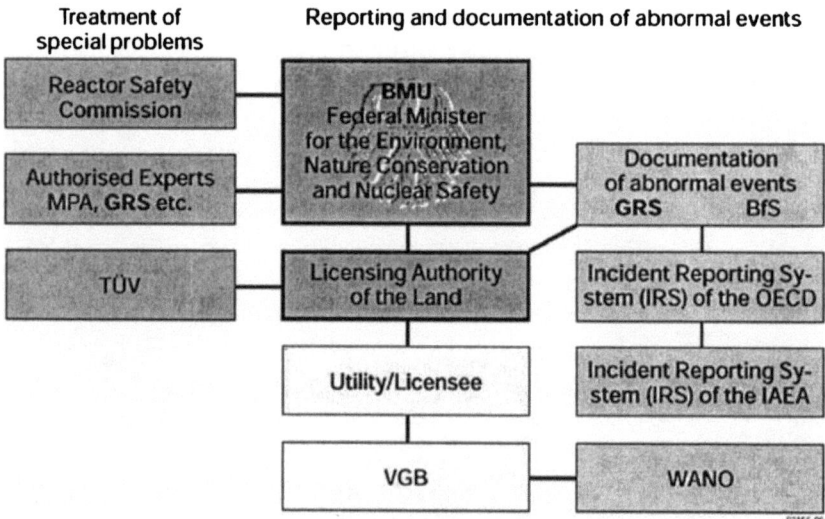

Figure 3: Overview about the event reporting of abnormal events in nuclear power plants in Germany

The GRS database includes events with technical malfunctions as well as events with human failures. Of main interest for the GIHRE-project is the evaluation of events regarding human failures, especially due to inappropriate communication.

2.2 Method for event evaluation

The sub-project of GRS concentrates on the investigation of events available at GRS concerning human failures in connection with communication aspects and cognitive aspects. For this purpose, the method CAHR was used. The method enables to combine event analysis and assessment and therefore to base human reliability assessment on past experience (Sträter & Bubb 1998). Several applications in the past showed the value of the method especially in the field of cognitive error investigation. CAHR was developed at GRS in the years 1992 to 1997.

2.2.1 CAHR Overview

CAHR means "Connectionism Assessment of Human Reliability". The term "connectionism" was coined by modeling human cognition on the basis of artificial intelligence models. Connectionism is a term describing methods that represent complex interrelations of various parameters (known for pattern recognition, expert-systems, modeling of cognition). By using the connectionism idea, the CAHR-method attempts to consider that human performance is rather affected by the interrelation of multiple conditions and factors (of internal as well as of external nature) than by singular factors that may be treated and predicted isolated. By this, it enables to represent and evaluate dependencies of influencing factors and context of situational aspects on the qualitative side. It further suggests a quantitative prediction method that considers the Human Error Probability (HEP) always as driven by human abilities and the difficulty of situation. Currently, the method is under further development for analyzing events (see IAEA 2001) and for applying it to other fields of Human Factors (Linsenmaier 2000; VDI 1999).

The basic idea of the approach for event evaluation and data collection is a detailed analysis of the information flows that were important in an event. Figure 4 provides a general overview about the event analysis procedure. Besides ergonomical and organizational aspects, the framework also allows to investigate the communication aspect.

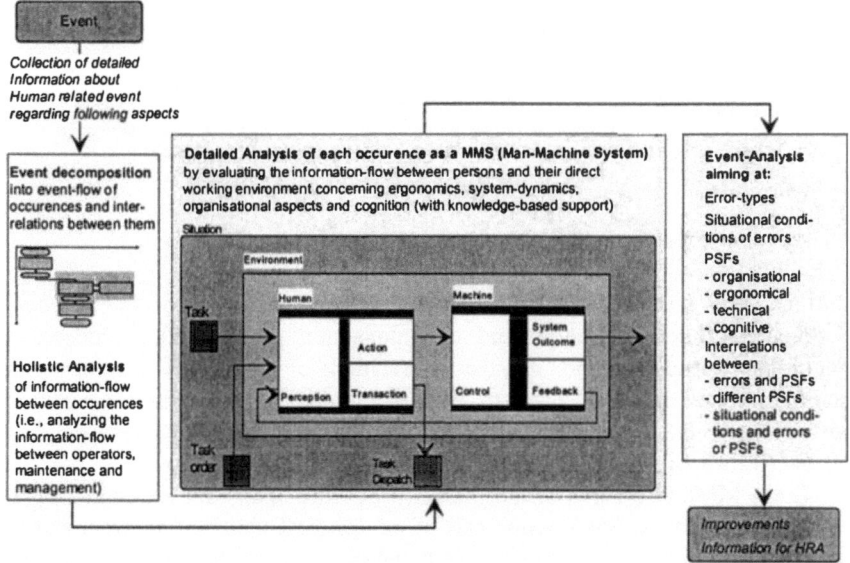

Figure 4: Overview about the CAHR-Method

The communication of several persons is modeled by the two MMS components: task order (receiving of information from another person) and task dispatch (providing information for another person). They represent the basic elements of the sender receiver model within the MMS. If one now looks at the individual sub-paths of figure 1 as individual MMS, then the CAHR approach would represent the working system outlined there as illustrated in Figure 5.

As the figure clearly shows, a complex work system can be described by saying that individual MMS are used in order to sub-divide the overall complex of the occurrence into various sub-systems. On the whole, we thus get a network of different sub-systems that are connected to each other via the elements "task order" and "task dispatch" of the MMS.

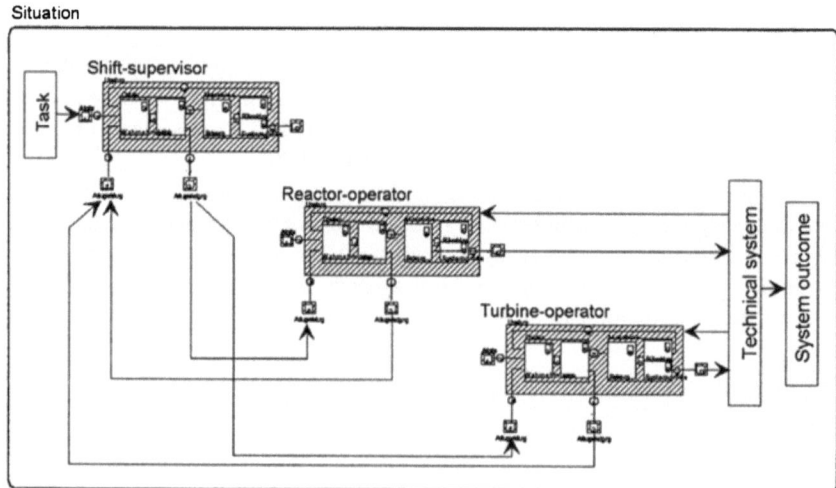

Figure 5: Description of complex events in the work system

2.2.2 Semantic description of event information

In the CAHR method, communication is understood as one aspect of the whole working situation. To understand communication problems, it's embedding within the working situation and the interrelations of situational conditions with communication behavior have to be understood. To describe this working environment, the concept of the MMS (Man Machine System) was used and extended by communication aspects, i.e. a context related approach.

In the MMS an error is defined as a consequence of any deficiency in a stage or in an information transmission part of the MMS. To analyze an event and to find the important information about errors and influencing factors, the following questions must be asked for each aspect within the MMS: (1) What was the object of interest, e.g. "valve"? (2) What was the performed action, e.g. "open"? (3) What was the error, e.g. "omitting" or "too much"? (4) What was the influencing factor, e.g. "bad labeling"? By these questions the factual aspects of each MMS-aspect may be described (the object, the action, the errors, and the influencing factors). A fifth factual aspect called 'element' was added in order to be able to describe the event in more detail and to make comments on the previous columns. This distinction is of importance because each step means a deeper insight into reasons for the error within the observation. According to epistemology, in (Keller, 1990) these steps were consequently called phenomenological view (assignment of an error, step 3), causal view (relationship of step 1 and 2 to step 3) and actional view (step 4).

Answering all these questions (description of all factual aspects for every stage of every MMS that were identified within an event) leads to information about the context of an event. Context is defined here at least as the task-order and tasks, the information from the system to perform the tasks (feedback), and the characteristics of the situation (e.g., time constraints) or of the technical system (e.g., dynamics) as well as the interrelationship of various MMSs (the operators, the management or organizational staff). All these aspects together build the error situation or error context. In total, one finds plenty of specific questions that may be of relevance to describe the context. The derived answers concerning the MMS-aspects and the description-aspects may be compiled in a table as outlined in Table 1.

Line	Component	Sentence	Object	Action (verbal)	Indication (error)	Property (PSF)	Element (Subgeneric term)
0	:		-				
1	Task	Sentence 1	Valve				Type X
2	,,	,,	,,	Open	Omit	Time Pressure	High
3	Person	Sentence 2	Control station personnel				
4	Activity	Sentence 3	Valve				
5	,,	,,	,,	Opened	Too much		
6	,,	,,				Labeling	Legibility
7	,,	,,	,,			Labeling	Insufficient
8	,,	,,	,,			Legibility	Poor
9	:						
10	Feedback	Sentence 4	Message				Position-indication
11	,,	,,	Position-indication	recognize			
12	,,	Sentence 5	Display				Pressure gauge
13	,,	,,	Pressure gauge	Read off			
14	:						

Table 1: Illustration of possibilities of error description on the basis of a hypothetical example

2.2.3 Semantic processing of event information

The descriptions of events according to the scheme outlined in table 1 lea(
event descriptions similar to the flexibility of describing events in a free
form but is systematic enough to be elaborated commonly. Sentence 1 of tal
for instance means "the task to open the valve of type x was omitted to open
to time pressure".

The connectionism approach of CAHR facilitates qualitative and qu
tative analyses of the data collected. As a result, it becomes possible to dep
in a uniform database, both information for the evaluation of human reliat
and for the optimization of the technical system. It also makes it possibl
interrogate interrelationships of random concepts within the data structure
example, relationships of errors and PSF; see Figure 6).

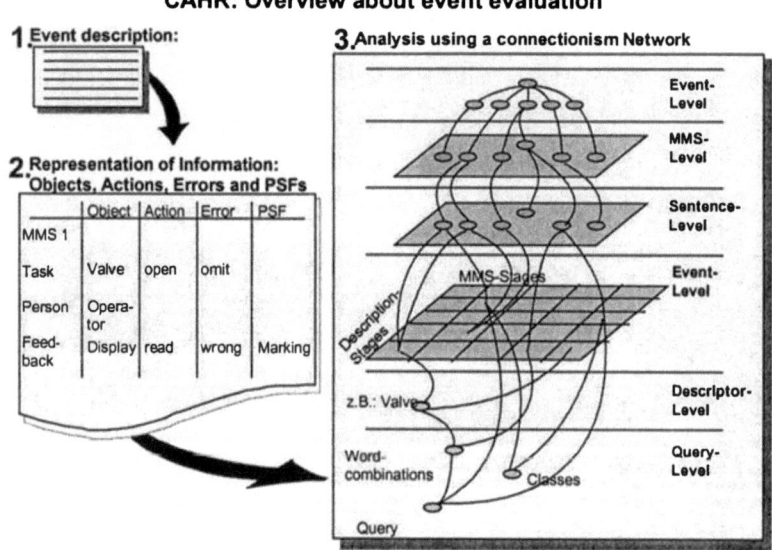

Figure 6: Overview about the semantic processing of the event information

The connectionism approach represents some kind of language retention
production system. It contains language elements and represents diffe
semantic elements on various syntactic layers. The procedure is therefo1
language processing approach:

In grammar for instance, we usually make a subdivision of language
ments into phonemes (sound symbols), morphemes (significance bea
symbols), words and sentences (see Dorsch et al. 1994). To model langu
processing, speech events are considered as a process – in psycho linguis
building on speech elements – in which the elements for instance cooperate
a probability process (a Markov Process). McClelland & Rummelhart (19

showed with the help of their word recognition model that language modeling is basically also possible with connectionism networks.

The problem in language processing is to achieve a suitable structuring of the language elements; for instance, one uses hierarchical graphs as form or organization (for instance, Chomsky 1965), then the problem is represented by the fact that the complexity of language cannot be illustrated without a combinatory explosion of the modeling apparatus and this basically is the same problem that prevails in the analysis of practical operational experience.

If one looks at the CAHR model from this linguistic angle, it basically represents a language recognition system in which each language element is implemented as one level within the network. The network here permits any connections between the levels so that linguistic interconnections materialize by virtue of the frequency with which certain relations are used. The correct reproduction of learned knowledge is then ensured by the propagation and back propagation through the network. The network designed here, however, starts only at the word level (although theoretically it could also be expanded to the level of phonemes and morphemes) and ends on a higher level than the sentence level because a MMS can grammatically speaking be viewed as a section and an event can be seen as a chapter. This means that the model presented here overall constitutes a contribution to language retention and processing.

3 Application results regarding communication aspects

The database of GRS with a total of approximately 5000 events of German Nuclear Power Plants was taken as input source for the investigation. 232 of them have been selected for the detailed analysis. During the GIHRE project, these 232 events were investigated in depth with the CAHR method regarding the relationship of situational conditions and communication failures and the interrelation of communication and cognition. The 232 events could have been further cut down to 439 sub-events (i.e. each event contains 1,89 sub-events on average).

3.1 Overview of Findings

The study is showing that about 10% of all human failure events are due to communication failures. Table 2 gives an overview about this aspect together with other results regarding the nonverbal aspects of communication and the cognitive aspects investigated.

| | event frequency & percentage ||
	related to 436 sub-events	related to all 232 events
verbal communication aspects (without procedures)	34 14,7 %	21 4,8 %
nonverbal communication aspects (with procedures)	64 27,6 %	57 13,0 %
communication aspects in total (nonverbal and verbal)	98 42,2 %	76 17,3 %
cognitive aspects in total (regarding all 232 analyzed events)	98 42,2 %	86 19,6 %

Table 2: Summary of descriptive results of the evaluated events

This general value stating that about 10% of all Human Factor related events are due to communication failures is also supported by publications of German utilities (Bassing 1999). According to the results of the VGB/HF-System for event evaluation, communication problems are about 11% of all Human Factor problems in plants (Eisgruber & Janssen 1999).

The detailed evaluation of the events showed no significant difference between Pressurized Water Reactors (PWRs), Boiling Water Reactors (BWRs), or other plant-types.

The table also includes the number of events and the percentage of occurrence of communication aspects in total (nonverbal and verbal). These events (n=76) are to a great extend an additive result of the nonverbal communication aspects (with procedures, n=57) and verbal communication aspects (without procedures, n=21). Only 3 events contain procedure-based as well as verbal communication problems. Therefore both aspects seems to be independent from each other to a great extend.

The difference of verbal communication aspects related to the 232 events in comparison to the 436 sub-events is due to the fact that communication problems described in sender sub-events usually also implies a description of problems in the receiver sub-events.

3.2 Qualitative Results regarding situational aspects of communication problems

In the assessment of safety aspects, several implicit assumptions are made about where communication problems are more critical and where not. The event analysis performed may first of all provide insights for the following issues of importance (c.f. paragraphs 3.2.1–3.2.4)

- Is communication during Control Room tasks less critical than communication on the spot, because the operators are closer together in the control room and have additional information about the communication partner (e.g., whether he is distracted from the communication process)?
- Is communication less critical in regular tasks than in irregular tasks, because regular tasks are well trained and used to the operators?
- Is communication less critical during shift than during shift handover, because the amount of communicational tasks is higher during shift handover?
- Is communication less critical in usual plant situations (e.g., full-power) than during some unusual plant states (e.g., start-up, shut-down), because each plant state has a specific amount of communicational tasks implied?

These questions were answered based on the consideration of the 439 identified sub-events. In order to prove these statements, some measure of importance of an aspect regarding communication problems has to be derived.

The CAHR method provides frequencies for the descriptors used in the event description. For the further evaluation of the events, the absolute number of these words is of less importance. Much more relevant is the relative importance of a given descriptor. This relative importance will be defined as

$$\text{Importance for communication} = \frac{Frequency\ of\ Item\ /\ communication\ was\ inappropriate}{Frequency\ of\ Item\ in\ all\ Events}$$

If – for instance – 107 sub-events were observed in the control room and 10 of them were observed with inappropriate verbal communication, the importance for verbal communication under the condition of a control room activity is $10/107 = 9,3\ \%$.

This measure assures that the statements are not biased by the absolute number of observations but are seen in their relative importance (cf. Straeter & Bubb 1998).

3.2.1 Control room / on the spot

Is communication during Control Room tasks less critical than communication on the spot, because the operators are closer together in the control room and have additional information about the communication partner (e.g., whether he is distracted from the communication process)?

The result regarding communication problems in control rooms is shown in the following figure 7 in comparison with the results on the spot. This comparison shows the interesting fact that communication in not related to the working place itself. Though the number of observed events is reflecting that there are more communication problems on the spot, the importance for verbal com-munication is quite the same in the control room as well as on the spot. It has to be concluded that the location in the plant is not a distinctive characteristic for communication problems.

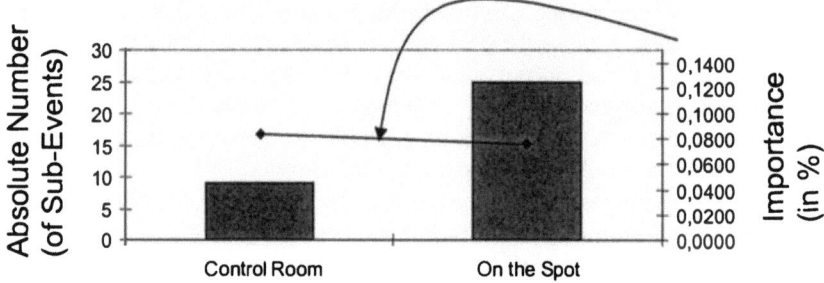

Figure 7: Comparison of communication problems in control-room and outside control room

3.2.2 Shift/Shift handover

Is communication less critical during shift than during shift handover, because the amount of communicational tasks is higher during shift handover?

The result regarding the comparison of shift vs. shift handover is shown in Figure 8. The number of observed events is reflecting that there are more communication problems during shift, but the importance for verbal communication is higher during shift handover. However, since the number of observed events during shift handover is small, it is concluded here that the importance is equal during shift operation and shift handover. It has to be concluded that shift-mode is also not a distinctive characteristic for communication problems.

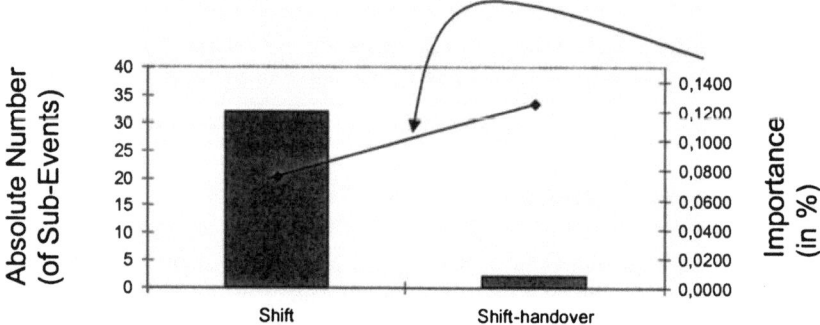

Figure 8: Comparison of communication problems during shift and shift handover

3.2.3 Regular tasks/irregular tasks

Is communication less critical in regular tasks than in irregular tasks, because regular tasks are well trained and used to the operators?

Investigation of Communication Errors in Nuclear Power Plants   167

The result regarding the comparison of regular and irregular tasks is shown in figure 9. This comparison also shows that the importance for verbal communication is quite the same during regular and irregular tasks.

The figure also indicates the interesting or unexpected result that the importance is slightly higher in regular tasks than in irregular ones. However, irregular tasks usually are combined with higher individual workload since they imply higher mental effort to resolve the irregularities.

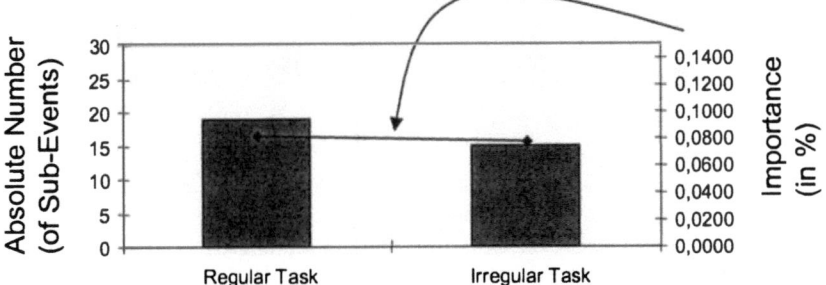

Figure 9: Comparison of communication problems during regular and irregular tasks

Therefore this result implies that higher workload not necessarily leads to more inappropriate communication. This is an observation that is confirmed also by detailed analysis of events. During the Davis Besse event for instance, communication went extraordinary good, though the workload and stress were considerable high during the event. The crew was close to loose the entire plant in a very short time period but successfully coped with the plant due to good crew performance (Reer et al. 1999). Such events (with less safety significance) were also observed in this study. Very efficient communication was observed even in quite unusual and high workload situations with very low available time.

3.2.4 Usual plant / unusual plant situation

Is communication less critical in usual plant situations (e.g., full-power) than during some unusual plant states (e.g., start-up, shut-down), because each plant state has a specific amount of communicational tasks implied?

Figure 10 shows the distribution of communication aspects regarding the different plant states. Most important is communication during shut-down and revision/fuel exchange states followed by start-up phases. This observation is in accordance to the low-power and shut-down study of GRS (Müller-Ecker et al. 1998). The figure also indicates a different importance of start-up and shut-down. It indicates that shut down states are far more prone to communication problems than start-up situations. The reason for this difference is not clear and needs further analysis.

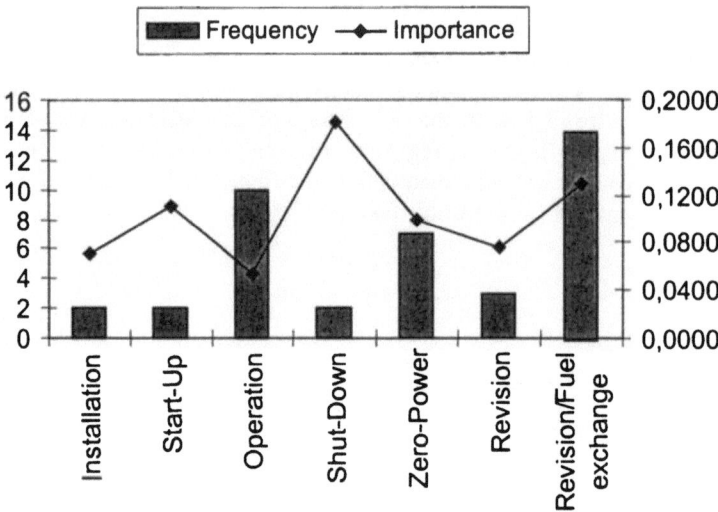

Figure 10: Comparison of communication problems during regular and irregular tasks

3.3 Observed types of system failures and communication

The evaluation of events shows sub-events with different impact on the technical system. The different impact is usually classified into types of system failures. These types are defined as (based on IAEA 1995 and Sträter 1997):

Type A0: This type is characterized by human interactions, where personnel have performed the work as planned. Therefore, in these actions there was no error in the action itself but the action was a necessary condition for an error that occurred at the same time or later in the event sequence (e.g. the "error-free" part of two interfering maintenance actions). Type A: All actions before the initiating event leading to latent failures. Type Ba: This type describes actions performed as intended but resulting in an initiating event due to previous errors of Type A actions (i.e. the outcome of a latent failure). Type B: Initiating event actions. Type C: Successful or unsuccessful recovery actions.

According to the figure 11, there are three aspects to be highlighted: Interference of maintenance actions (Type A and Type A0), errors in recovery from initiating events (Type C) and the role of communication for initiating events (Type B).

Interference of maintenance actions: Maintenance tasks are usually well designed beforehand according to the optimal flow of a whole plant state (e.g. a revision). The common view on the Type A and Type A0 category implies that communication is of quite high importance during such maintenance tasks. A detailed look on the events shows that the importance of communication is growing if two maintenance tasks were not seen as worthwhile to be designed beforehand as coordinated tasks but should be designed this way.

Errors in recovery from initiating events: The result regarding Type C failures underlines the statement of above since it here by definition the task is to cope with a not beforehand designed situation.

Role of communication for initiating events: In relation to other types of system failures, initiating events are superior regarding the importance for communication. This is one of the most important aspects from the safety point of view since initiating events reveal problems in existing measures or means for safety.

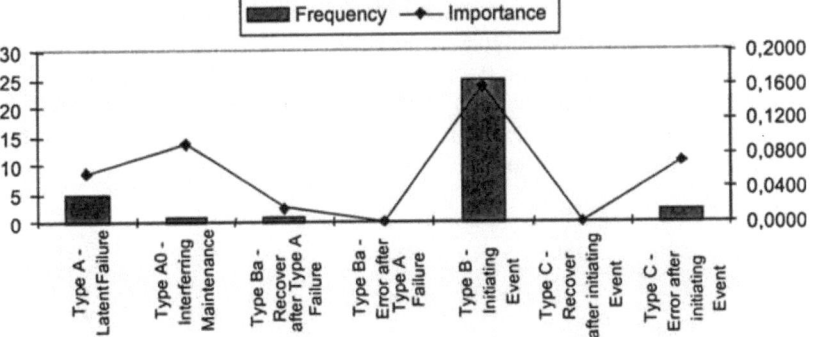

Figure 11: Comparison of communication problems during observed types of system failures

3.4 Procedural vs. verbal Communication

In NPP safety, the defense in-depth approach covers the main safety relevant human interactions in procedures. Consequently, it is interesting and important to compare verbal (i.e., non-procedural) based communication with procedural based communication in order to find important aspects of situations in which procedures fail in administrative measures and safety only relies on verbal administrative performance. Therefore verbal communication is important to be reflected against nonverbal communication.

In order to gain information about different error mechanisms in different contexts, the CAHR method allows to derive profiles about the circumstances of interest and then to derive systematic relationships to causes and conditions relevant for the circumstances of interest. Based on such profiles, finally specific error mechanisms can be identified as shown for the aspect of communication in the following.

First of all, it is interesting to find out whether procedural or verbal communication has a different impact on the technical system. To investigate this, the following Figure 12 shows the relative importance of communication for the aspects.

Compared to procedure based communication, verbal communication is especially a problem in production phases whereas procedural based communication is connected more to maintenance and work control processes. It appears that verbal communication is more prone to problems in situations where operators are busy with certain tasks at the system (closed loop) instead of already being open for information from outside (like during checking or work-control processes).

We also observe that irregular tasks are related more to verbal communication, whereas procedure based communication plays a greater role in regular tasks. Most interesting to mention is that verbal communication is more important in understanding initiating events. This underlines the fact that was already stated in Figure 12. Since initiators based on human behavior are in principal difficult to handle, the importance of this aspect may also be elaborated further in connection with the second generation HRA methods. The third aspect worthwhile to mention is the observation that communication is essential for short-term anticipation of a situation (at the same time, immediately afterwards, closely in time).

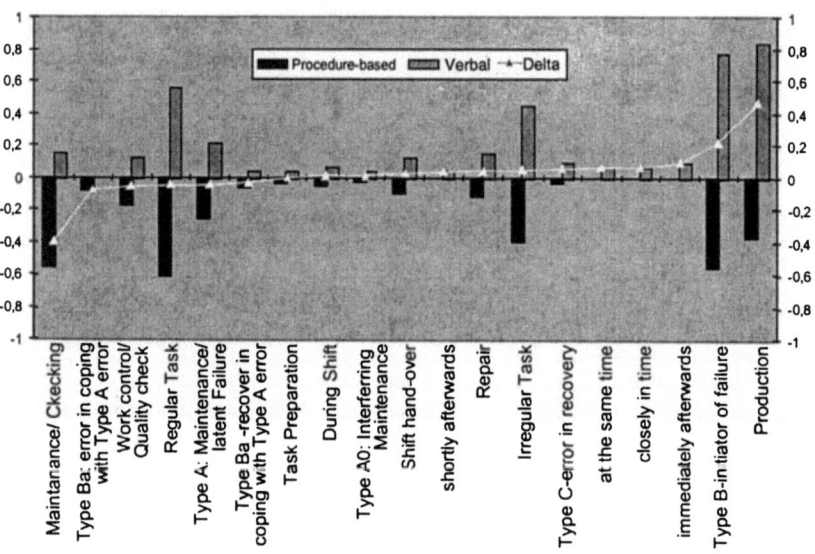

Figure 12: Profile of situational aspects combined with communication failures

To go one step deeper into understanding communication failures, figure 13 shows the relative importance of PSFs (Performance Shaping Factors) for verbal and procedural communication. The figure clearly indicates that verbal communication is always problematic if the communication partners are exposed to a certain degree of pressure (time-pressure or situational pressure, task-demands, task organization or preparation). On the other hand, procedural communication tends to fail more often due to ergonomic problems, like completeness of information in procedures, labeling or others (see Sträter 1997 for the definition of the PSFs).

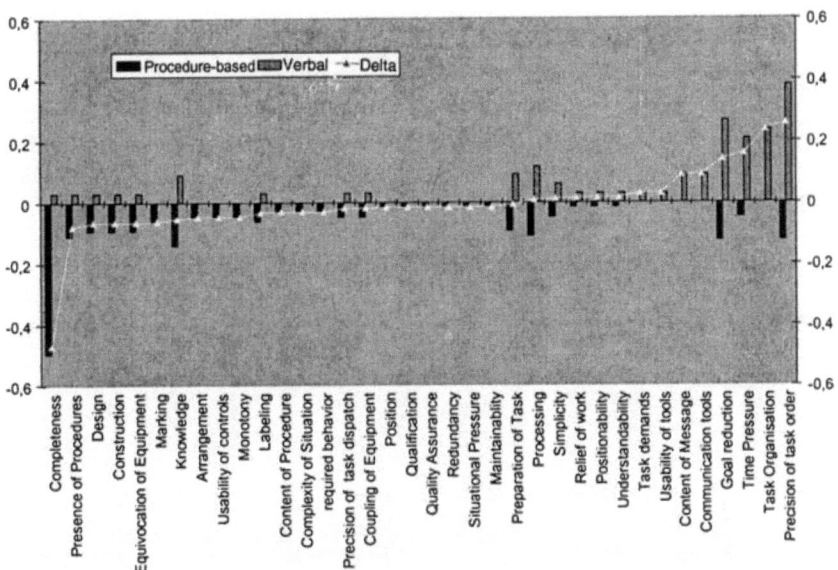

Figure 13: Profile of influences on procedural vs. verbal communication

Hence, verbal communication is clearly linked to a much greater extend to the mental capacity and mechanisms to cope with situations than procedural based communication.

4 Cognitive Aspects of Communication Behavior

The link between cognitive aspects of communication behavior is known from many basic psychological research activities. Verbalization of knowledge (Eberleh et al. 1989) and investigations, e.g. in the Halden Reactor Project (Braarud et al. 1997) show similar effects like the ones observed in this study: Communication gets more difficult the higher the demands of the situation are and the more difficult the coping is for the operator.

In addition, the events investigated also indicated that not only perceptual aspects (like precision of task or clearness of order), but also attitudes like willingness to send or openness to receive information in the current situation are important factors for communication (goal reduction, processing of information).

The evaluation of the events regarding the cognitive activities during communication errors as outlined in Figure 14 shows the observed interrelations of communication and cognition. The Figure shows that the cognitive activities are a distinctive characteristic for communication problems.

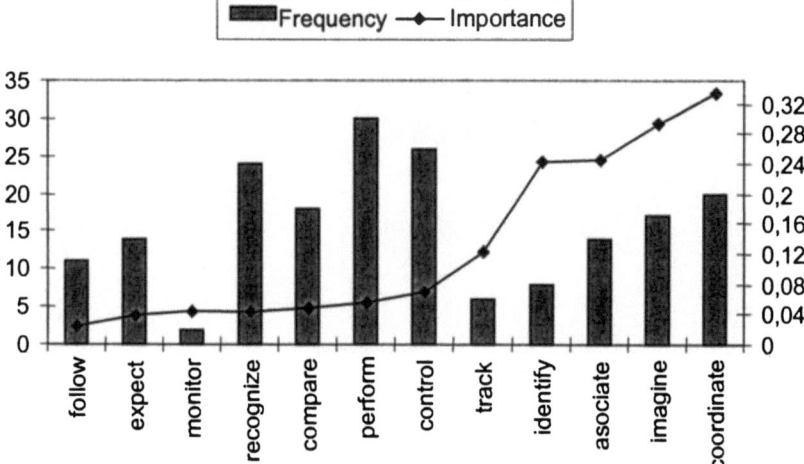

Figure 14: Importance of communication for cognitive activities

The importance of communication raises in different cognitive activities from "follow" to "coordinate". The different cognitive activities can be distinguished into the following groups and are to be understood as follows (see Sträter & Bubb 1998):
- Follow and monitor: Activities of perceiving external information in a more topographic cognitive behavior according to Rasmussen (1986).
- Expect, recognize and compare: activities of perceiving external information in a more symptomatic cognitive behavior according to Rasmussen (1986).
- Perform and control: more open loop active inputs of operators into the system.
- Track: more closed loop active inputs of operators into the system.
- Identify and associate: combining external information with internal representations.
- Imagine and coordinate: run internal representations in the mind.

The analysis of the cognitive activities leads to the following conclusion: In open loop situations where the operators are usually also receptive for information from outside their internal world, communication problems are much less compared with closed loop situations where the operators are busy with applicating their own thinking on a situation. The more items are to be considered during closed loop operation, the more difficult it is to get information from outside into the cognitive loop. In cognitive states where operators are faced with several tasks and several cognitive aspects that have to be matched (i.e., in states where the people had to associate, imagine or coordinate), communication problems are superior.

What can be concluded from here for the link between communication and cognition?

4.1 Approach for the Communication Model

The well founded psychological metaphor of the cognitive mill implicates that human errors are a result of a mismatch between situational circumstances and internal representation of the world (well known as cognitive dissonance, compatibility problem, situation awareness). The following mechanisms can be observed in a relatively stable manner (cf. also Linsenmaier & Sträter 2000; Sträter 1997; Mosneron-Dupin 1998):

- A mismatch may not be observed as critical by the person (selective or focussed attention, fixation). In such cases the difference between external available information and the internal representation of the world concerning the aspect of interest in not recognized. Example: Driving by car to the office as usual day by day task making us ignoring the surrounding we are driving through.
- A mismatch may secondly be perceived and cognitive behavior lies in not perceiving the appropriate information (bounded or uncompleted search, eager-ness to act). In such cases the external available information implies more opportunities than the operator(s) currently want(s) to cope with. Example: Driving by car to the office and the usual way is blocked; we then usually take a known alternate way without diagnosing whether it is better to stay in the jam because it is very short.
- A mismatch may thirdly be perceived and cognitive behavior lies in not elaborating well enough the hypotheses in the diagnosis process (well known as frequency gambling, bounded rationality, routine reaction). In such cases the internal representation of the world concerning the aspect of interest is providing more opportunities then are currently indeed given by the external available information. Example: Car-Light failure is more likely assumed as a broken lamp, not as a fuse-failure.
- A mismatch may finally be perceived and cognitive behavior lies in both, not perceiving the appropriate information and not elaborating well enough the hypotheses in the diagnosis process (i.e. a mixture of case 2 and 3). Example: Car is broken and one has to decide between the two alternatives that have pros and cons (buying new one, repair of old one).

Table 3 summarizes this approach based on the above considerations. It was first revealed in the work of the EARTH- group (Mosneron-Dupin et al. 1998).

cognitive dissonance / situational complexity	no dissonance (operator does not care about situation)	dissonance (operator cares about situation)
apparently simple	a omission (e.g., no action) b marking, labeling c fixation Example: Driving by car to the office as usual day by day task making us ignoring the surrounding we are driving through	a omission (e.g., no action) or commission (e.g., wrong action) b reliability and equivocation of equipment c frequency oriented reasoning Example: Car-Light failure is assumed as a broken lamp, not as fuse-failure
obviously complex	a quantitative commissions (e.g., too much/less) b precision and design of procedures c eagerness to act Example: Driving by car to the office and the usual way is blocked. We then usually take a known alternate way quickly.	a delay (e.g., too late) b arrangement of equipment, reliability c reluctance to act Example: Car is broken and one has to decide between the two alternatives that have pros and cons (buying new one, repair of old one)

Table 3: Relation of cognitive dissonance and situational complexity
principal error types (a), samples for typical PSFs (b) and cognitive behavior (c)

Meanwhile the approach of cognitive tendencies was successfully applied on the evaluation of events in German Nuclear Power Plants (Sträter, 1997 a, b) and adapted by many other methods for human error assessment (OECD, 2001). This approach suggest to systematically combine certain situational conditions and certain cognitive aspects by considering certain coping-strategies an operator may choose. This concept may be seen as a combination of the usual concept of assuming certain processing stages (like perception, decision and action) and processing phases (skill-, rule-, knowledge-based).

Having found a set of cognitive tendencies and a first structuring of them by using the mismatch approach, a further question is how these tendencies may play a role in communication.

4.2 Communication and Cognition Model

The four cases of mismatch we observed as general human mechanisms in plant experience for modeling of communication issues also hold for communication. This is possible since the cognitive mill represents some central mechanism that impacts both, motoric behavior as well as communicational behavior. One can find the following tendencies in failures of communication:

- Carelessness about information on the side of the receiver (fixation on task performance of receiver leading to information ignorance of sender) which leads to lack of communication mainly due to wrong identification of the information by the receiver.

Focusing on performing the task within the technical system and/or complexity and situational efforts may lead to a break-down of communication due to prioritizing the technical task instead of the communicative task on the receiver side. In this case the receiver is no more able to identify the meaning connected with a certain information sent to him.

- Wrong assumption about information received on the side of the receiver (frequency oriented reasoning of receiver on what is meant by sender) which leads to a wrong association of the receiver about the system meant by sender (like taking the whole for part for instance)

In cases of an overlap in tasks in combination with lack of experience, the receiver of information may understand the information sent in a wrong way (what leads to wrong decisions) if the sender gives an abstract input (assuming that the receiver may know what he means).

- Communication avoidance on the side of the sender (fixation on task performance of sender leading to communication avoidance) which leads to lack of communication.

Due to reluctance of the information sender and/or due to wrong imagination of receiver needs, the sender is not considering the needs of a potential receiver or lacks in cognitive sensitivity that a receiver may need information. This leads to misinformation of the receiver.

- Communication breakdown, no provision of information on the side of the sender (reluctance to communicate due to being busy with other tasks, e.g. problem solving).

If several of the above mentioned communication problems appear in common, communication breakdown is the probable result. Break-down of communication is a hint for lack in coordination between receiver and sender needs.

5 Conclusions

The defense in depth concept for the safety of Nuclear Power Plants relies heavily on technical safety measures and administrative rules. Both concepts can only provide a corridor for the work on the operational level wherein verbal communication of operators is an important safety issue as well. The events investigated in this project revealed hints relevant to the so-called "defense in depth concept":

- Communication is one aspect of plant safety that is observable in about 10% of all human failure events.
- Procedural and verbal communication can be distinguished in terms of types of errors and underlying reasons of failure: Time- and situational pressure is more important for verbal communication than for procedural communication.
- Verbal communication has a higher potential for initiating events and hence should be considered in the further development of human error assessment methods, especially since they seem to have a higher potential for initiating events.
- The impact of workload on the cognitive behavior of the sender as well as on receiver is ambigue and should be investigated in more detail. Different types of workload (situational constrains vs. ergonomical constraints) may – for instance lead to lack of communication due to focusing on performing the task. On the other hand also very good and efficient communication was observed during some event sequences.
- Verbal communication problems were observed as having a strong link to cognitive errors. Cognitive aspects are essential to understand problems in communication especially because there was not seen a unidimensional relationship of communication quality and workload but also good communication under high workload.

Other results worthwhile to mention regarding the methodological approach chosen for this research project are:

- Analysis of communication errors and related cognitive mechanisms is possible even with events differing in detail.
- The approach of cognitive tendencies that is meanwhile accommodated in most of the so-called second generation HRA methods was seen also valid for understanding and modeling communication aspects.

Good communication is also detectable quite often during high workload situations even in very short times like a few seconds for instance. Note that such a quick anticipation of a situation is usually not assumed in Methods for Human Reliability Assessment (HRA-methods).

The second part of the projects tries to resolve this contradiction (good as well as bad communication in high workload conditions) by performing an experiment. The experiment seeks to find out in detail how specific effects observed as important do influence the quality of communication. The main reasoning behind the hypothesis, which is based on the event investigation, is:

- Communication is always an added task that is to be performed in addition to the operational task at the plant (e.g. resetting a system one is responsible for); this means that there are always two sub-tasks for an operator in an operating/communicating situation: One operational and one communicative.
- Communication is a disturbing additional task for the receiving operator if the information he obtains disturbs the sub-task currently at hand (or vice versa, a disturbing additional task for the information sender if the information-need of the other is not seen as part of the own task).
- Communication is a compatible additional sub-task for the receiving operator if he needs the information for his current sub-task (or vice versa, a compatible additional sub-task for the information sender if the information need of the other is seen as part of his own or of a common task).

The experiment will be performed in the NPP simulator of GRS that is similar to a fully computerized control rooms. Eye-Tracking behavior will be used to trace the current status of the operators cognitive processing regarding the operational task, communication quality will be measured depending on different types of transients (system failures). The underlying hypothesis of this investigation is: If the communicative task fits (in terms of timing and content) to the needs of the operational task of an operator, no communication problems, perhaps even good performance, will be observed. If the communicative task does not fit the needs of the operational task of an operator, communication problems will be observed with causes similar to the ones observed during the event investigation.

Literature

Bassing, G. (1999): „Zur Praxis des betreibereinheitlichen VGB-Human Factors Systems im Kernkraftwerk Phillipsburg". Jahrestagung Kerntechnik des Deutschen Atomforums, Karlsruhe. Deutsches Atomforum. Bonn.

Braarud, P. O., Droivoldssmo, A. & Hollnagel, E. (1997): Human Error Analysis Project (HEAP) – The fourth Pilot Study: Verbal Data for Analysis of Operator Performance. Halden Reactor Project. Halden/Norway.

Bubb, H. (1993): „Systemergonomie". In: Schmidtke, H. (Hrsg.): Ergonomie. München: Hanser.

Chomsky, N. (1965): Aspects of the theory of syntax. Cambridge, MA: MIT Press.

Dörner, D. (1997): Die Logik des Mißlingens, Strategisches Denken in komplexen Situationen. Hamburg: Rowohlt.

Dörner, D. (1999): Bauplan für eine Seele. Hamburg: Rowohlt.

Dorsch, F., Häcker, H. & Stapf, K. H. (Hrsg.) (1994): Dorsch – Psychologisches Wörterbuch. Bern: Hans Huber.

Eberleh, E., Neugebauer, C. & Sträter, O. (1989): „Modelle des Wissens und Methoden der Wissensakquisition: Eine Übersicht". RWTH Aachen: Arbeitsbericht Nr. 1–55. Institut für Psychologie.

Eisgruber, H. & Janssen, G. (1999): "VGB Human Factors System: HF-Maßnahmen der Kernkraftwerksbetreiber zur Optimierung der Mensch-Machine Schnittstelle". BFS KT-22/99. BFS. Salzgitter.

Elzer, P., Kluwe, R. & Boussoffara, B. (Eds.) (2000): Human Error and System Design and Management. Berlin, Heidelberg, New York: Springer.

Hollnagel, E. (1998): Cognitive Reliability and Error Analysis Method – CREAM. New York, Amsterdam: Elsevier.

IAEA (1995): "Human Reliability Analysis in Probabilistic Safety Assessment for Nuclear Power Plants". Safety Series No. 50 P 10. IAEA. Vienna.

IAEA (2001): Guidelines for describing of Human Factors in the IRS (Human actions and related causal factors and root causes). IAEA. Vienna.

Keller, A. (1990): Allgemeine Erkenntnistheorie. Stuttgart: Kohlhammer.

Linsenmaier, B. & Sträter, O. (2000): Recording and Evaluation of Human Factor Events with a View To System Awareness and Ergonomic Weak Points within the System at the Example of Commercial Aeronautics. San Diego: IEA 2000.

McClelland, J. & Rummelhart, D. (1981): "An interactive Activation Model of Context Effects in Letter Perception". Psychological Review 88 (4). 375–405.

Mosneron-Dupin, F., Reer, B., Heslinga, G., Sträter, O., Gerdes, V., Saliou, G. & Ullwer, W. (1998): "For more Human-Centered Models in Human Reliability Analysis: Some Trends Based on Case Studies". Reliability Engineering and System Safety 58 (3). Amsterdam: Elsevier. 249–273.

Müller-Ecker, D., Mayer, G. & Sträter, O. (1998): "Probabilistic Safety Assessment for Non-Full-Power States of NPPs in Germany". International Conference on Probabilistic Safety Assessment and Management (PSAM). London: Springer Verlag.

Neisser, U. (1976): Cognition and Reality. San Francisco: W. H. Freeman.

Newell, A. (1990): Unified theories of cognition. Cambridge, MA: MIT Press.

OECD-NEA (2000): Errors of Commission in Probabilistic Safety Assessment. NEA/CSNI/R(2000)17. OECD/NEA. Paris.

OECD-NEA (2001): Errors of Commission in Probabilistic Safety Assessment. Workshop of the OECD/NEA. NRC. Washington.

Rasmussen, J. (1986): Information processing and human-machine interaction. New York: North-Holland.

Reer, B., Sträter, O., Dang, V. & Hirschberg, S. (1999): A Comparative Evaluation of Emerging Methods for Errors of Commission Based on Applications to the Davis-Besse (1985) Event,. PSI. Schweiz. Nr. 99–11.

Santinelli, A., Fiche, C. Jehee, J., Touati, J., Beraha, D., Sträter, O., Welbourne, D., Roth-Seefrid, H. & DeVlaminck, M. (1995): Methods and Systems for Operator Support in Accident Management. FISA-95 Symposium – EU Research on Severe Accidents. 20.–22.11.1995. Luxembourg.

Shanon, C. & Weaver, W. (1949): The mathematical theory of communication. Urbana: University of Illinois Press.

Shastri, L. (1988): "A Connectionist Approach to Knowledge Representation and Limited Inference". Cognitive Science 12. 331–392.

Stolze, P. & Sträter, O. (2000): "Human Performance and Interface-Design – Some Remarks based on Experiments". In: Elzer, P., Kluwe, R. & Boussoffara, B. (Eds.): Human Error and System Design and Management. Berlin, Heidelberg, New York: Springer.

Stolze, P. (1999): Konzeptsammlung und systematische Auswertung theoretischer und empirischer Befunde zu Störfällen in Kernkraftwerken. MeMoVis - T - ISTec - 09. ISTec, Garching.

Sträter, O. & Bubb, H. (1998): Assessment of Human Reliability based on Evaluation of Plant Experience: Requirements and their Implementation. In: Reliability Engineering and System Safety 63 (2). 199–219.

Sträter, O. & Reer, B. (1999): "A Comparison of the Application of the CAHR method to the evaluation of PWR- and BWR-events and some implications for the methodological development of HRA". In: Modarres, M. (Ed).: PSA'99 – Risk-Informed Performance-Based Regulation. American Nuclear Society. LaGrange Park, Illinois, USA.

Sträter, O. (1994): "An Expert Knowledge Oriented Approach For The Evaluation Of The Man-Machine Interface". In: Ruokonen, T. (Ed.): Fault Detection, Supervision and Safety for Technical Processes. SAFEPROCESS '94. Vol. 2. Helsinki: Finnish Society of Automation. 673f.

Sträter, O. (1994): The Role of Plant Experience to Consider the Human Factor in Living PSA. 4th Workshop of the TÜV Nord on Living PSA Application in Hamburg, May 2/3.1994.

Sträter, O. (1996): "A Method for Human Reliability Data Collection and Assessment". In: Cacciabue, P. C. & Papazoglou, I. A. (Eds.): Probabilistic Safety Assessment and Management. Proceedings of ESREL '96 / PSAM-III. Crete, Greece, June 24.–25., 1996. 1179.

Sträter, O. (1997): Beurteilung der menschlichen Zuverlässigkeit auf der Basis von Betriebserfahrung. GRS-138. GRS. Köln.

Sträter, O. (1997): "Investigations on the Influence of Situational Conditions on Human Reliability in Technical Systems". In: Seppälä, P., et al. (Eds.): 13th Triennial Conference of the IEA. June 1997. Tampere. Vol. 3. 76ff.

Sträter, O. (1998): Problems of Cognitive Error Quantification and Approaches for Solution. International Conference on Probabilistic Safety Assessment and Management (PSAM). London: Springer Verlag.

Sträter, O. (2000): Analysis and Assessment of Errors of Commission in Nuclear Power Plant Settings. IEA 2000, San Diego, Human Factors and Ergonomics Society. Santa Monica CA. South Jefferson, St. Lois, MO: Mira Digital Publishing.

Sträter, O. (2000): Using the CAHR-method to derive cognitive error mechanisms. Osaka. PSAM 5 Conference.

Swain, A. D. & Guttmann, H. E. (1983): Handbook of Human Reliability Analysis with emphasis on nuclear power plant applications. Washington DC. Sandia National Laboratories, NUREG/CR-1278.

VDI 4006 (1999): Menschliche Zuverlässigkeit – Teil 1: Ergonomische Forderungen und Methoden der Bewertung – Teil 2: Methoden zur quantitativen Bewertung menschlicher Zuverlässigkeit. Berlin: Beuth-Verlag.

Brussels						Oliver Sträter

Eurocontrol, Rue de la Fusee 96, B-1130 Brussels, oliver.straeter@eurocontrol.int